Whi
NOIR

The Iowa Whitman Series

Ed Folsom, series editor

Whitman NOIR

BLACK AMERICA AND
THE GOOD GRAY POET

EDITED BY IVY G. WILSON

University of Iowa Press, Iowa City

University of Iowa Press, Iowa City 52242
Copyright © 2014 by the University of Iowa Press
www.uiowapress.org
Printed in the United States of America
Design by Richard Hendel

The University of Iowa Press is a member of Green Press Initiative
and is committed to preserving natural resources.

Printed on acid-free paper
ISSN: 1556-5610

ISBN: 978-1-60938-236-0, 1-60938-236-6 (pbk)
ISBN: 978-1-60938-262-9, 1-60938-262-5 (ebk)
LCCN: 2013953640

CONTENTS

LOOKING WITH A QUEER SMILE

Walt Whitman's Gaze and Black America

IVY G. WILSON

In the summer of 1901 after they had returned to the South, James Weldon Johnson and his brother, Rosamond, hosted the most esteemed African American poet of the day—Paul Laurence Dunbar—in their hometown of Jacksonville, Florida. Dunbar had achieved acclaim for his 1896 *Oak and Ivy* after William Dean Howells praised the volume, lavishing particular praise on Dunbar's dialect poems. Johnson was growing weary over how the style threatened to restrict not only his own poetry but the wider field of black cultural production because it was so intimately tied to minstrelsy. Dunbar himself had been equally suspicious, even if he could not find a way to distance himself from the style enough to practice other modes more often. In his introduction to *The Book of American Negro Poetry* (1922), Johnson sees in Dunbar's example the price of the ticket for all African American cultural producers whose aesthetic is too circumscribed by predetermined conventions. Johnson notes that, while Dunbar "carried his art to the highest point of perfection," many of the contemporary poets of the New Negro movement had discarded dialect, both its style and its subject matter, as a suitable aesthetic. Johnson concludes that "colored poets in the United States" need a "form that is freer and larger than dialect, but which will still hold the racial flavor; a form expressing the imagery, the idioms, the peculiar turns of thought, and the distinctive humor and pathos, too, of the Negro . . . and allow of the widest range of subjects and the widest scope of treatment."[1]

Johnson's reassessment of dialect had begun much earlier, around the turn of the century, prompted, importantly, by his encountering Walt Whitman's *Leaves of Grass*. In his autobiography, Johnson describes how he was still writing in the style of Dunbar until he was "engulfed and submerged" by a reading of

Leaves of Grass that sent him "floundering."[2] Although Johnson's censure in *The Book of American Negro Poetry* was primarily directed toward the type of trading in gross stereotypes that was embedded in much of dialect writing, his engagement with Whitman emboldened his experimentation with the form of poetry: "In my muddled state of mind I tried to gain orientation through a number of attempts in the formless forms of Whitman."[3] During the six weeks that Dunbar visited Jacksonville, he and Johnson discussed poetry continually, and in the course of one of these conversations, Johnson took the liberty of showing Dunbar some of the writing he had done under the "sudden influence" of Whitman: "He [Dunbar] read them through and, looking at me with a queer smile, said, 'I don't like them, and I don't see what you're driving at.' He may have been justified, but I was taken aback. I got out my copy of *Leaves of Grass* and read him some of the things I admired most. There was, at least, some personal consolation in the fact that his verdict was the same on Whitman himself."[4]

If we can only speculate which poems Johnson recited, it is not altogether difficult to see why Dunbar did not appreciate them. The prosody of most of Dunbar's poetry was very controlled, not only to musically intone rhythm and sound but perhaps precisely as a way for him to illustrate a certain mastery over the architectonics of his versification when its aural dimensions alone could have easily been misunderstood to constitute the meaning of the poetry itself, independent of form or content. The "formless forms" of Whitman that attracted Johnson would not have the same effect on Dunbar. Ironically, as a musician, Johnson in his Broadway compositions was veering ever closer toward the creation of what Whitman had imagined as a "native grand opera in America" shaped by the contours of African American vernacular.[5] The Johnson-Dunbar episode recalls aspects of Whitman's own experience meeting Ralph Waldo Emerson in 1860 before the publication of the third edition of *Leaves of Grass*, when the Sage of Concord cautioned the younger poet about some of the indelicate aspects of his volume, expressing concern about the poem "Enfans d'Adam" in particular. While it is not altogether evident how *Leaves of Grass* shaped Johnson's next volume of poetry, *O Black and Unknown Bards* (1908), in

IVY G. WILSON

the wake of Whitman's "sudden influence," the Johnson-Dunbar episode nonetheless exposes the spectral presence of Whitman in African American literary production, a presence that has assumed different configurations and materialities throughout the twentieth century to the present moment.

Whitman Noir: Black America and the Good Gray Poet seeks to explore the meaning of blacks and blackness in Whitman's imagination and, equally significant, to also illuminate the aura of Whitman in African American letters from James Weldon Johnson to June Jordan, Margaret Walker to Yusef Komunyakaa. As alluring and proleptic as containing the multitudes might prove to be, African American writers have been vexed by the vicissitudes of being black in America—afflicted with and empowered by what W. E. B. Du Bois termed "double-consciousness"—and, consequently, attracted to Whitman's acknowledgment of the contradictions of the United States. Rather than taking call-and-response as the governing formula for understanding Whitman and black America, these essays examine the relationship between aesthetics and politics by accentuating the metonymic condition of African Americans in relation to the larger promise of America.

Whitman's famous maxim about containing multitudes has often been understood as a metaphor for the democratizing impulses of the nation, but the presence of African Americans—suspended between the material and the apparitional, as it were—within the poetic space of his verse and other writings complicates any understanding of how the US cultural and literary imagination seeks to contain or otherwise demarcate its subject-citizens. This volume attempts to reveal the mutual engagement with a matrix of shared ideas, contradictions, and languages to expose how Whitman influenced African American literary production as well as how African American studies brings to bear new questions and concerns in evaluations of Whitman. By underscoring the centrality (if often phantom-like quality) of African America to Whitman's imagination and of Whitman's importance to African American literature, these essays address important theoretical questions about literary history, the textual interplay between author and narrator, and the translatability of race in writing the nation. Such an approach will put the nineteenth century in conversation with the twentieth and twenty-first centuries, white with black, American literary studies with African American studies, and it will more broadly examine the relationship between culture and social formation.

In the episode described above between Dunbar and Johnson, we can see the shifting interpretations of Whitman in the African American imagination that will continue through the twentieth century and beyond. In the era of racial uplift (not to mention racial terror), where the politics of respectability informed much of how the black intelligentsia and literati fashioned themselves, Whitman may have seemed too unconventional, too unorthodox, too uncouth.[6] This was most likely the opinion of Du Bois, who would remain the most influential black public intellectual for some fifty years. According to Shamoon Zamir, Du Bois had read Whitman and considered him somewhat important; in a discussion of the final paper that Du Bois produced for William James, Zamir quotes Du Bois as writing, "What are the Ends? Shall I be St. Paul, Jeremy Bentham, or Walt Whitman?"[7] Emulating Whitman alone could never appeal to the Harvard-trained aesthete and radical intellectual, but we can see in his magisterial *The Souls of Black Folk* (1903) the alchemy of the fields that these three figures, among others, represented: the spirituality, if not the religion, of Saint Paul; the philosophy of pragmatism of Jeremy Bentham; and the poetics, if not the poetry, of Whitman's writings.

If Du Bois's and Dunbar's evaluations of Whitman at the turn of the century were less than sanguine, then Langston Hughes's views offered a new appreciation for the nineteenth-century poet. This new appreciation had begun with Johnson, who, like Du Bois, was also one of the central figures of the Harlem Renaissance; the latter, however, was already assuming more of the status of an elder statesman to the younger artists of the movement. In his biography of Hughes, Arnold Rampersad recovers a sentence from the original opening section of Hughes's autobiography, *The Big Sea* (1940), where, detailing his trip to Africa and Europe, he recounts throwing overboard all his books from his days as a student at Columbia University except Whitman's *Leaves of Grass*.[8] Whitman may have also been an important figure to Hughes personally for the manner in which he addressed same-sex love in the "Calamus" section of *Leaves of Grass*, perhaps at times affording the poet laureate of Harlem a kind of "queer smile" different from the one that came across Dunbar's face from a generation earlier.[9] Whitman's literary importance to Hughes can be easily seen in his poem "I, Too" (1925), his brief essay "The Ceaseless Rings of Walt Whitman" (1946), and a pair of editorials he published about Whitman in 1953, among other pieces, as several critics have explored.[10]

Less explored, however, has been the importance of Whitman to someone like Margaret Walker, whose poem "For My People" (1937) shares with Whitman the use of themes of the everyday (even if the quotidian for Walker's subjects was more disquietingly sober than Whitman's characteristically exhilarating enthusiasm for his) as well as the deployment of poetic devices like anaphora.

> For my people everywhere singing their slave songs
>   repeatedly: their dirges and their ditties and their blues
>   and jubilees, praying their prayers nightly to an
>   unknown god, bending their knees humbly to an
>   unseen power;
>
> For my people lending their strength to the years, to the
>   gone years and the now years and the maybe years,
>   washing ironing cooking scrubbing sewing mending
>   hoeing plowing digging planting pruning patching
>   dragging along never gaining never reaping never
>   knowing and never understanding;
>
> . . . .
> For my people thronging 47th Street in Chicago and Lenox
>   Avenue in New York and Rampart Street in New
>   Orleans, lost disinherited dispossessed and happy
>   people filling the cabarets and taverns and other
>   people's pockets and needing bread and shoes and milk and
>   land and money and something—something all our own.[11]

Here one encounters a variation of Whitman's all-encompassing ocular perspective, with Walker's narrator able to take sight of wide landscapes, from rural Alabama to the concrete streets of Chicago, but engendered by palpable degrees of intimacy, not just identification, with the subjects of her poem. Here one can hear in Walker's litanies and tallies reminiscences of the Whitman poem that would come to be known as "A Song for Occupations" (1881).[12] And here one can feel the vibrant sensations of the metropolis, similar to Whitman's "Once I Pass'd through a Populous City" (1860). In these stanzas, one can see a number of Whitman traces, even while Walker herself is transforming the good gray poet, figuratively rejuvenating and remixing him for the African American context.

Whitman's influence, but not his presence per se, falls to more muted registers after the Harlem Renaissance in the era that comprises postwar and civil rights America. He emerges, however, in the works of two of the most important twentieth-century black intellectuals: C. L. R. James and Ralph Ellison. For the radical Trinidadian, who analyzes a number of poems—among them "Song of the Open Road" (1856), "Crossing Brooklyn Ferry" (1856), "Once I Pass'd through a Populous City," and "Song of the Exposition" (1876)—Whitman prefigured much of the crisis of modern world-systems where polities were trying to negotiate the relationship between individualism and collectivism, or what Whitman called "en-masse." The genteel Ellison invokes Whitman in a crucial chapter of his epic novel *Invisible Man* (1952) to expose the false pleasures of social integration without black political equality. Elsewhere in his nonfiction prose, Ellison underscores Whitman's experiments with language as an attempt to craft a distinct American vernacular style. In the same decade of the 1950s when James and Ellison wrote about Whitman, so too did Hughes and Allen Ginsberg. Published within two years of each other, Hughes's "Old Walt" (1954) and Ginsberg's "A Supermarket in California" (1956) both present a Whitman perambulating, discovering new sensations with each step, but ultimately left pondering if a new America was on the immediate horizon.

While Whitman's presence wanes somewhat in the third quarter of the twentieth century, which was marked by the Black Arts movement, he reemerges again in the last two decades to the present moment. An important, if not crucial, aspect of Whitman's reemergence in African American letters directly corresponds to the proliferation of new voices by women and other ethnic writers who were looking for early sympathetic voices.

IVY G. WILSON

The poet June Jordan, for example, interpreted Whitman as a white literary father who shared "the systematic disadvantages of his heterogeneous offspring."[13] If the novelist Gloria Naylor uses Dante's *Inferno* as a master narrative in *Linden Hills* (1985), her story about the descent of two young African American male poets in a community obsessed with upward social mobility is punctuated by a key scene when one of the male characters paraphrases Whitman to express his latent homoerotic desire for another man.[14] More recently, Whitman makes an appearance in Yusef Komunyakaa's poem "Kosmos" (1992). These efforts at reimagining Whitman are part and parcel of a larger cultural dynamic engaging the past to engender a new sociality of belonging, evidenced in other works such as Maxine Hong Kingston's novel *Tripmaster Monkey* (1989) and visual artist Glenn Ligon's oil painting *Walt Whitman #1* (1991).

With its accent on Whitman's twentieth- and early twenty-first-century black interlocutors, *Whitman Noir* offers an important assessment of the relationship between the great poet of the American Renaissance and African American culture, extending the exemplary scholarship in monographs like Martin Klammer's *Whitman, Slavery, and the Emergence of "Leaves of Grass"* (1995) and Luke Mancuso's *The Strange Sad War Revolving: Walt Whitman, Reconstruction, and the Emergence of Black Citizenship, 1865–1876* (1997). The volume includes new pieces by such critics as Ed Folsom and George B. Hutchinson, who have written eloquently in the past on Whitman and blacks, as well as a host of new scholars trained in a moment of American studies after Eric J. Sundquist's *To Wake the Nations* (1993) and Toni Morrison's *Playing in the Dark* (1992), among others, that underlined how the study of much of American literature is impossible without confronting the specters of blackness.

Subdivided into two parts, the first half of *Whitman Noir* is comprised of literary criticism ranging from issues of textuality in the manuscripts for *Leaves of Grass* to *créolité* in Whitman's only novel; the second half features reflections primarily by contemporary African American poets ruminating on the significance of Whitman for their own writing and the craft of poetry more broadly. In these creative critical essays by contemporary writers, I have allowed their uncited quotations of Whitman and others to stand, since they are offered more for their sweep and tenor rather than a pure academic charge.

The first section, and the volume as a whole, begins with Ed Folsom's essay "Erasing Race: The Lost Black Presence in Whitman's Manuscripts." Folsom focuses on the "ghost black" in Whitman's writings—the ethereal presence of blacks who are more often found in his manuscripts than his published work—to illustrate a more nuanced understanding of what now appears to be Whitman's sustained thinking about blacks. Folsom concludes by suggesting that perhaps Whitman was imagining "a stunning new vision of a racially healed nation" but has to leave unanswered the neoconservative politics of such a vision premised and underwritten by the very exclusion of African Americans. Turning to Whitman's single work where the racialized presence of blacks is pronounced, *Franklin Evans, or The Inebriate* (1842), Amina Gautier situates Whitman's only novel in the context of national debates about intemperance. Noting that advocates of moderation and restraint frequently associated intemperance as a kind of slavery, Gautier accentuates the "Creole" episode of the story, where race is put into high relief in the scenes where Evans meets, marries, and disavows the beautiful "mulatta" slave Margaret. As his most sustained treatment on "blackness," *Franklin Evans* offers an image of Whitman's early views about race to set in contradistinction to those found in his later writings, including *Leaves of Grass* and the notebooks. In his highly suggestive piece, Matt Sandler recovers the Creole presence of Whitman's time in New Orleans. Debates persist on the importance of Whitman's time in New Orleans as a site for exploring his sexuality, but, as Sandler argues, Creole New Orleans presented Whitman with a version, if not a vision, of hybridity and mixture that might be thought of as a model for his poetics of "merging." Sandler's essay, then, takes the largely unresolved theme of *métissage*, which Gautier does not explore in her essay, and uses it as a theory for Whitman's poetics.

The next two essays in the first section take up Whitman's understanding of racial violence and language by way of James Weldon Johnson and Ralph Ellison, respectively. For Christopher Freeburg, the irony of Whitman circumventing the ribald face of racial violence is in fact constitutive of the larger social practices of how the nation narrativizes progress. While Whitman addresses black-white racial conflict mercurially throughout his works, perhaps most pronounced in the "Lucifer" manuscript passages, such violence is at the center of Johnson's *Autobiography of an Ex-Coloured Man* (1912), and Freeburg uses the specter of lynching to illuminate the two different strategies that Whitman and Johnson deploy to arrive at an "idealistic fulfillment of U.S. democracy." In his essay "Postwar America, Again," Ivy G. Wilson traces Ellison's readings of Whitman and language in relation to Ellison's position as a postwar fiction writer and critic. As Wilson notes, Ellison was attracted to Whitman for the poet's early recognition of the (future) black contribution to the creation of a distinctly American culture; if this recognition remained only latent for Whitman, it was fundamental to Ellison's belief in the promise of America. Wilson is followed by Jacob Wilkenfeld, whose essay on Whitman and the poet Yusef Komunyakaa is meant as much as a conclusion to the first half of the book as it is a precursor to the second half. Wilkenfeld's critical perspective shies away from one of filial genealogy as a means of analyzing the relationship between Whitman and Komunyakaa and turns instead to one of interlocution. The force of Wilkenfeld's argument centralizes in his analysis of Komunyakaa's "Kosmos" (1992), where he sees Komunyakaa "talking back" to Whitman as a form of both communication and revision.

June Jordan's 1980 essay is the lead piece in part 2, which features reflections on Whitman by contemporary African American poets, including both previously published essays and new ones specifically authored for this volume. Jordan, known for her political commitments to a broad canvas of civil rights—ranging from racial to LGBT equality, indigenous to feminist causes— identifies herself as one of Whitman's "traceable descendants" in "For the Sake of People's Poetry: Walt Whitman and the Rest of Us." Jordan lauds Whitman's poetry as much for its content as for its form. Quoting poetry from Pablo Neruda (whom she also identifies as one of Whitman's descendants), she extols both poets' "decision to write in a manner readily comprehensible to the masses" of their compatriots. Importantly, Jordan situates Whitman as a New World poet by associating him with poets from the hemisphere of the Américas like Neruda and Gabriela

Mistral as well as from the black diaspora like Aghostino Neto, Margaret Walker, and Langston Hughes.

Jordan's essay is followed by Natasha Trethewey's "On Whitman, Civil War Memory, and My South." Trethewey locates in Whitman's writings the larger complicated history of how the nation has tried to reconcile its black population into the body politic, and for Trethewey no single ideograph illustrated this complicated history better than the black body in uniform. Commissioned originally for the sesquicentennial of *Leaves of Grass* for the *Virginia Quarterly Review*, Trethewey's essay extends one of Whitman's most well-known thoughts about the Civil War—that the real war would not get into the history books—by turning to the black soldiers whom Whitman himself bypassed to implicitly ask her readers, How would Whitman's impressions have come together had he taken the South as his default region? How would his understanding of the war among brothers have unfolded had he given more consideration to African Americans, signaled and perhaps demanded by the image of the black soldier? Trethewey's essay is followed by that of Rowan Ricardo Phillips, and both essays engage Whitman's lyric, "Reconciliation," thus entering into a conversation with Folsom's essay, as they all put into high relief the "intimate confrontation" of southern history, camaraderie, and death. Indeed, the differing interpretations of "Reconciliation" at play here might best be thought of as the uneasy reconcilability of Whitman to black cultural expression, and, in the broadest sense, they shadow the divergent assessments between the volume's two sections as well as within them.

When Phillips turns to Federico García Lorca's poem "Ode to Walt Whitman," we reencounter an international Whitman. Lorca and others, including José Martí, Rubén Darío, and Jorge Luis Borges, were as much enamored with such Whitman poems as "Salut au Monde" as they were with ones like "Song of Myself," and one can see in this attraction a way to read America from the outside in (and, more specifically, from South America to North America). But we also see in Phillips's reflection a different Whitman, one viewed from a poet not of the first half of the twentieth century (as were Lorca, Darío, and Borges) but of the contemporary moment (as is Phillips), one whose image of Brooklyn is significantly different from that of Whitman in the wake of the Windrush generation of immigrants from the Caribbean. And, as Phillips illuminates in his essay, the function of the East River as the locus classicus in Whitman's poetry would bear special meaning to his development as a young child growing up in New York City, transforming later into a poet, critic, and translator.

Finally, the book closes with a reflection piece by the literary critic George B. Hutchinson, who describes his visit to Whitman's grave and his encounter with Eleanor Ray, the African American caretaker of Whitman's home, in 1987. The inclusion of Hutchinson's piece seems fitting not only because there has probably been no single critic who has done as much work on the relationship between black America and Whitman as Hutchinson but also because Hutchinson's essay is in keeping with the sentiment of Hughes's own visionary impulse when he and Arna Bontemps included Whitman in their 1956 anthology, *The Poetry of the Negro*.

Perhaps no work better illustrates the traces, latent or pronounced, between black America and Whitman while itself constituting another rationale for this volume as a whole than Elizabeth Alexander's "Praise Song for the New Day" (2009).[15] Initially delivered at the first inauguration of Barack Obama as president of the United States, the poem is composed in tercets but approximates the feeling of free verse unhampered by meter; it abandons the sense of aural anticipation engendered by Whitman's characteristic use of anaphora but nonetheless produces a moment of incantation by the repetitive lull of the phrase "praise song"; and it encompasses without delimiting a social belonging that exceeds the nation in ways that Whitman sometimes had difficulty in doing, viewing, as he did, democracy as intimately tied to America. Alexander fulfills Whitman, insofar as Whitman fulfilled Emerson's plea in "The Poet" (1844), but only after "Praise Song for the New Day" is filtered through Ginsberg, through Walker, and through Hughes, such that, looking back at Whitman, he can no longer be seen as white but has to be understood as Whitman noir.

NOTES

1. James Weldon Johnson, *The Book of American Negro Poetry* (New York: Harcourt, Brace and Company, 1922), xxxiii–xxxix, xli.

2. James Weldon Johnson, *Along This Way* (New York: Viking Penguin, 1933), 158.

3. Ibid., 159.

4. Ibid., 161.

5. Walt Whitman, *An American Primer*, ed. Horace Traubel (Boston: Small, Maynard and Company, 1904), 24.

6. For more on the politics of respectability and African Americans at the fin de siècle, see Kevin K. Gaines, *Uplifting the Race: Black Leadership, Politics and Culture in the Twentieth Century* (Chapel Hill: University of North Carolina Press, 1996).

7. Shamoon Zamir, *Dark Voices: W. E. B. Du Bois and American Thought, 1888–1903* (Chicago: University of Chicago Press, 1995), 60–61, 236n70. I am grateful to Amy Nestor for our discussions about this important moment in Du Bois's intellectual development.

8. See Arnold Rampersad, *The Life of Langston Hughes, Vol. 1: 1902–1941* (New York: Oxford University Press, 1986), 377; and George B. Hutchinson, "Whitman and the Black Poet: Kelly Miller's Speech to the Walt Whitman Fellowship," *American Literature* 61, no. 1 (March 1989): 55.

9. For more on Hughes, race, and queer politics, see Paul Outka, "Whitman and Race ('He's Queer, He's Unclear, Get Used to It')," *Journal of American Studies* 36 (August 2002): 293–318.

10. Beyond Hughes's own statements about Whitman through his poetry, editorials, and introduction to a volume of Whitman's poetry, the correlation between Hughes and Whitman has been thoroughly established in the academic literature about them by such scholars as Donald B. Gibson, George B. Hutchison, and Ed Folsom. See Gibson, "The Good Black Poet and the Good Gray Poet: The Poetry of Hughes and Whitman," in *Langston Hughes, Black Genius*, ed. Therman B. O'Daniel (New York: Morrow, 1971), 65–80; Hutchinson, "Langston Hughes and the 'Other' Whitman," in *The Continuing Presence of Walt Whitman*, ed. Robert K. Martin (Iowa City: University of Iowa Press, 1992), 16–27; and Folsom, "So Long, So Long! Walt Whitman, Langston Hughes, and the Art of Longing," in *Walt Whitman, Where the Future Becomes Present*, ed. David Haven Blake and Michael Robertson (Iowa City: University of Iowa Press, 2008), 127–43.

11. Margaret Walker, *For My People* (New Haven, CT: Yale University Press, 1942), 9.

12. Alan Trachtenberg, "The Politics of Labor and the Poet's Work: A Reading of 'A Song for Occupations,'" in *Walt Whitman: The Centennial Essays*, ed. Ed Folsom (Iowa City: University of Iowa Press, 1994), 124.

13. June Jordan, "For the Sake of People's Poetry: Walt Whitman and the Rest of Us" (1980), in *Some of Us Did Not Die: New and Selected Essays of June Jordan* (New York: Basic/Civitas, 2002), 243.

IVY G. WILSON

14. For more on this scene and Whitman and Naylor in general, see Christine G. Berg, "'giving sound to the bruised places in their hearts': Gloria Naylor and Walt Whitman," in *The Critical Response to Gloria Naylor*, ed. Sharon Felton and Michelle C. Loris (Westport, CT: Greenwood, 1997), 98–111; and Kenneth M. Price, *To Walt Whitman, America* (Chapel Hill: University of North Carolina Press, 2004), 98–102.

15. Elizabeth Alexander, *Praise Song for the Day* (St. Paul, MN: Graywolf Press, 2009).

Part One

Erasing Race

The Lost Black Presence in Whitman's Manuscripts

ED FOLSOM

A spectral black presence both haunts and energizes Walt Whitman's work. Black presences that once *were* there or *should be* there finally *aren't*. So much of what we can now say about Whitman and race comes not from what he published but from what he didn't—from what we might call his "discarded writings" instead of his "collected writings": the reported comments that Whitman made in conversations, the odd jottings on nineteenth-century racialist scientific theory that Whitman never used in a published work, the newspaper articles about blacks that he never reprinted, the wealth of unedited poetry manuscripts that frequently contain Whitman's lost race writings.[1] As we unearth more manuscripts, as we keep discovering more reported conversations, as more of his journalism comes to light, we become increasingly aware of the ghost black in Whitman's work, because we see more and more places where we can determine that African Americans were on his mind when he wrote, only to fail to be included when he published. Whitman, it seems, systematically erased race from his published writings.

"Erasing race" is a phrase that has been thrown around a lot in recent years. It is often used in relation to legislative and judicial steps that have been taken in an attempt to overthrow affirmative action guidelines, supposedly making admissions and hiring decisions "race-blind." The phrase has also been used in relation to cyberspace, where Internet users experience an odd anonymity as they interact with strangers in a virtual world where race—which would be immediately obvious if two people in an online chat

{3}

were facing each other across a real table—presumably becomes invisible.² I am using the phrase here in a different, somewhat more literal sense: Whitman, in moving his poetry and prose from manuscript notes to the printed page, often erased the African Americans who were a key to the very inception of his ideas and images. Kenneth M. Price has noted how Whitman "was more daring on racial issues in his manuscripts than in more polished work," and I want to build upon Price's insight to suggest how those lifelong erasures often served as the now-hidden source of the radical energy of Whitman's poetry and prose.³

Let's start with one of Whitman's most powerful images, a passage from "Song of Myself" that was cited frequently in the days and weeks following 9/11, when New York firemen became the new national heroes for their selfless work and sacrifice in the collapsing World Trade Center buildings. David Remnick in the *New Yorker*, for example, evoked Whitman's passage:

> Walt Whitman remains the singular, articulated soul of this city, and in "Song of Myself" he seems to have projected himself forward a century and a half into our present woe, our grief for the thousands lost at the southern end of Manhattan, and for the hundreds of rescuers among them, who walked into the boiling flame and groaning steel:
>
> I am the mash'd fireman with breast-bone broken,
> Tumbling walls buried me in their debris,
> Heat and smoke I inspired, I heard the yelling shouts of my
>   comrades,
> I heard the distant click of their picks and shovels,
> They have clear'd the beams away, they tenderly lift me forth.
>
> Largeness of empathy was Whitman's emotional gift and legacy. It is indecent to look for the good in an act of mass murder, and yet one would have to be possessed of a heart of ice not to have felt in recent weeks the signs of Whitman's legacy: a civic and national spirit of resolve, improvisation, and kindness when panic and meanness might also have been expected.⁴

But Remnick's quote stops just short of the really puzzling part of Whitman's passage, where the poet's persona, his "I," continues speaking its transport into the "mash'd fireman":

I lie in the night air in my red shirt, the pervading hush is for
    my sake,
Painless after all I lie exhausted but not so unhappy,
White and beautiful are the faces around me, the heads are
    bared of their fire-caps,
The kneeling crowd fades with the light of the torches.[5]

Here Whitman channels the first impressions of the injured fire-man as he is pulled from the debris, sensing the "hush" around him, stunned to feel no pain, bathed in the light of the crowd's torches, looking up at the "white and beautiful" faces. The "*white and beautiful*" faces?

The speaker's identification of the color of faces surrounding him is something most white readers, over the years, have read right by. But when we find in one of Whitman's early notebooks his notes that form the earliest draft of this passage, we are immediately struck by just who this "mash'd fireman" is: "Years ago I formed one of a great crowd that rapidly gathered where a building had fallen in and buried a man alive.—Down somewhere in those ruins the poor fellow lurked, deprived of his liberty, perhaps dead or in danger of death.—How every body worked! How the shovels flew! And all for black Caesar—for the buried man wasn't any body else."[6] Edward F. Grier, who edited Whitman's early notebooks, dates this notebook before 1855 and makes the odd claim that the entries in this notebook "bear no direct relationship to the poetry of 1855–1856." Commenting on this particular passage, Grier proposes that "the jocularly racist reference to 'Black Caesar,' the comic victim, is in strong contrast to the treatment of blacks in the poetry."[7] "Black Caesar" was indeed a common epithet for African Americans in mid-nineteenth-century America, a name often assigned to black servants.[8]

Andrew C. Higgins has analyzed this notebook passage in relation to the final poem and argues that "Whitman revises the race of the trapped figure from black, in the notebook, to white in 'Song of Myself.'"[9] But what if the speaker in Whitman's poem has shifted, at this moment, into Black Caesar himself, stunned to find himself saved from the collapsed building by the feverish efforts of the white crowd, who, having dug him out, are themselves stunned into silence by their discovery that their heroic efforts were dedicated to freeing a black man? Higgins argues that "Whitman makes no reference that would lead the reader to read [the fireman] as black; whether or not Whitman secretly saw the fireman as black, he had to know his readers would assume he was white."[10]

But if the fireman in "Song of Myself" is silently black (with his blackness erased from explicit mention) and is in fact a free black fireman, then Whitman here offers us another version of the now-much-discussed "Lucifer" section of "The Sleepers," where he gives voice to the slave (also of course erasing or burying the "blackness" there, too, which was much more evident in the manuscript versions than in the final printed version). In the "mash'd fireman" section, the race of the speaker is apparently a hidden reference—the reader would not know that the figure of the fireman now speaking originated in a black person, but *Whitman* would know, and he would know that, by giving over his "I" to this person, he had on some level humanized poor Black Caesar. But the clue is actually there in the text and may be more obvious to African American readers than to white readers: a white fireman would have taken the white faces for granted and not have specified their color, but a black fireman in the 1850s would at the moment of rescue be struck by the circle of white rescuers around him; it is the only way that the specification of color at this moment makes sense. The reference to the "white and beautiful" faces then becomes even more poignant: of *course* a black man in the 1850s saved by whites would note the color of the faces that have rescued him. And Whitman's ghost-black fireman seems to continue to exert his perspective beyond the "mash'd fireman" passage, as, for example, a few sections farther on in "Song," when firemen reappear: "Lads ahold of fire-engines and hook-and-ladder ropes . . . / Their brawny limbs passing safe over charr'd laths, their *white* foreheads whole and unhurt out of the flames" (my emphasis). Here again, the persona still finds himself specifying the whiteness of the faces he observes. The white that is—to whites—normally transparent becomes instead opaque, worth mentioning, *there.*

This (black) fireman, his race erased yet still operative in the interstices of Whitman's poem, is perhaps part of the racial debris that is scattered throughout the 1855 *Leaves of Grass,* as Martin

Klammer so effectively demonstrated in his groundbreaking 1995 *Whitman, Slavery, and the Emergence of "Leaves of Grass."* Klammer tracks Whitman's evolving attitudes toward race from his early temperance novel *Franklin Evans* through his Free Soil journalism, his growing disdain for slavery, and the emergence of his antislavery beliefs in the 1855 *Leaves*. As Klammer demonstrates, one of Whitman's first key race erasures occurs when we examine the notebook in which we see the original stirrings of *Leaves of Grass*, the so-called "Talbot Wilson" notebook, probably written in the early 1850s.[11] Here, Whitman hesitatingly inscribes a whole new kind of speaking, and, breaking—for one of the first times—into the kinds of free-verse lines in which he would cast *Leaves*, he offers a wild attempt to voice the full range of selves in his contradictory nation:

> I am the poet of slaves and of the masters of slaves
> I am the poet of the body
> And I am
>
> I am the poet of the body
> And I am the poet of the soul
> I go with the slaves of the earth equally with the masters
> And I will stand between the masters and the slaves,
> Entering into both so that both shall understand me alike.[12]

This originating moment of *Leaves of Grass* has sparked a great deal of commentary. If nothing else, the passage reveals that at its inception *Leaves* was not an "abolitionist" work, at least not in the conventional sense of that term, for in abolitionist works the slave is pitted against the demonized slave master, and the irresolvable dichotomies of the nation are intensified. Whitman instead probes for a voice that reconciles the dichotomies, one inclusive enough to speak for slave and slave master—or that negotiates the distance between the two. This is the beginning of Whitman's attempt to become that impossible representative American voice—the *fully* representative voice—that speaks not for parties or factions but for everyone in the nation, a voice fluid enough to inhabit the subjectivities of all individuals in the culture. So Whitman in these early notes identifies the poles of human possibility—the spectrum his capacious poetic voice would have to cover—as it appeared to him at mid-nineteenth century: from slave to master of slaves. His dawning insight had to do with a belief that each and every democratic self was vast and contradictory, as variegated as the nation itself, and so the poet had to awaken the nation, to bring Americans out of their lethargy of discrimination and hierarchy to understand that, within themselves, they potentially contained—in fact potentially *were*—everyone else. The end of slavery would come, Whitman believed, when the slave owner and the slave could both be represented by the same voice, could both hear themselves present in the "I" and the "you" of the democratic poet, when the slave master could experience the potential slave within himself, and the slave could know the slave master within himself, at which moment of illumination slavery would end. It was a kind of spiritual and ontological abolition, a desperate attempt to speak with a unifying instead of a divisive voice, and by the time Whitman put this voice into print in 1855, the nation was only five years away from discovering how fully the forces of division and violence would overpower the fading hopes of unity and absorption of difference.

To accomplish this voice, Whitman imagines himself in a politically and sexually charged space—between the slave and the slave master. Politically, this space defined the gap between citizen and property, between those in power and those powerless. Sexually, this space was the charged and usually unacknowledged space that produced a mixed-race America—the hushed legacy of the peculiar institution as it produced interracial children who became at once the slave master's property and the slave's sons and daughters, as slave owners raped and impregnated their female slaves, creating sons unrecognized by their white fathers and creating additional wealth for the slave owner/father in the form of mixed-race progeny defined as "black." Karen Sánchez-Eppler reads the passage this way: "Claiming to reconcile racially distinct bodies, Whitman locates the poet in a sexually charged middle space between masters and slaves" where he can enact what Sánchez-Eppler calls "Whitman's poetics of merger and embodiment."[13] Whitman's incendiary passage thus flirts with entering the great taboo subject of the nineteenth-century South—the widespread propagation of new slaves by white slave owners impregnating black women they owned. It is this sexual violence—

ED FOLSOM

perpetrated by many white slave owners on many slave women—that created a national fear that black male slaves, if emancipated, would wreak revenge by raping white women, a fear that generated, among other things, a seventy-five-year legacy of lynching.

Occupying that culturally treacherous space "between the masters and the slaves," Whitman, in a stunning move, goes beyond simply mediating and uses instead the image of penetration to gain access to both: "And I e Entering into both and so that both shall understand me alike."[14] Kenneth Price, in his analysis of the passage, notes that "Whitman occupies and transforms the cultural space of violation," seeking to "remake penetration as a vehicle for purification."[15] It is significant that Whitman in his inceptive moment insists on becoming the voice of both master and slave, in effect taking on a mulatto persona, the only persona who could contain the blood of the master and the blood of the slave and therefore speak as both. It is as if he momentarily and impossibly occupies the space of conception and, disappearing, is born as its speaking product, a new melded being with a new existence: "And I am."

It is a powerful passage, but what is perhaps most striking about it is that Whitman cancels it out, drawing a diagonal line through it, and the only lines from the passage that finally make their way into *Leaves of Grass* are "I am the poet of the body / And I am the poet of the soul."[16] Whitman's radical evocation of a penetration of both slave and slave master is erased, though it appears to be the very source of the key statement of the poem that he would eventually name "Song of Myself." It is as if claiming the power to voice the extreme subject positions of American society—the slave and slave owner, black and white—somehow opened for him the way to speak both the body and the soul in a single unifying voice. Whitman originally learned to absorb dichotomies by confronting and speaking for America's most troubling bifurcation: black *and* white. America's tortured racial history, then, stands at the very conception of *Leaves* and, though erased, is evident in the scatter of racial moments throughout his book, including moments like that of the "mash'd fireman," black in conception even if his blackness has been invisible to most readers.

Klammer has effectively traced how race plays itself out in the

1855 *Leaves*, where "the representation of African Americans . . . is unlike anything Whitman—or anyone, for that matter—had ever written." Whitman, Klammer argues, "portrays African Americans as equal partners with whites in a democratic future and as beautiful and dignified people, the paradigms of a fully realized humanity." And, Klammer points out, "African Americans play a crucial role in the major themes and turning points of what are generally considered the three most important poems of the 1855 edition—poems that were later titled, 'Song of Myself,' 'I Sing the Body Electric,' and 'The Sleepers.'"[17] Klammer is eloquent about the ways Whitman *inscribes* African Americans into the first edition of *Leaves*, and, more recently, he has offered an acute analysis of how it is possible to track Whitman's gradual and partial erasure of African American presence in *Leaves of Grass* as the proportion of poems dealing with or mentioning blacks diminishes from three-quarters in 1855 to one-third in 1856 to one-fourteenth in 1860, only to approach the vanishing point after the Civil War, as the powerful "Lucifer" section is literally erased from the final version of "The Sleepers."[18] And it is worth noting, as I have investigated at length elsewhere, that Whitman's erasures in the "Lucifer" section began even before the poem saw print: the manuscripts of the "Lucifer" passage show clearly that Whitman's original conception was much more explicitly about a black slave, a powerful identification that he had already partially obscured by the time he published the poem in 1855.[19]

Now widely recognized as one of the most powerful passages dealing with slavery in all of Whitman's poetry, the "Lucifer" section was seldom mentioned in Whitman criticism until the 1960s. In fact, it was seldom read by Whitman's readers, because until Malcolm Cowley issued his mass-market reprint of the 1855 edition of *Leaves of Grass* in the late 1950s, virtually all copies of *Leaves* published in the late nineteenth century and the first half of the twentieth century were some version of Whitman's final 1881 edition of the book, the edition he authorized as the one he wanted to be published after his death.[20] In the late 1870s, Whitman revised his book for the new edition that would be the final printing of his poems, and he made a stunning decision. He deleted the "Lucifer" section of "The Sleepers," crossing it out on his working copy of his 1870–71 edition and marking two *d*'s

ED FOLSOM

(one in pencil and one emphatically in dark ink) to indicate to the printer to omit the section, thereby erasing one of the greatest passages in American poetry about a black slave gaining a voice and silencing that voice for over seventy-five years, until readers began once again reading earlier versions of the poem.

It is important to recall what makes the "Lucifer" section so radical. Unlike the other portrayals of African Americans in *Leaves*, Whitman does not *describe* Lucifer from the position of a white poet but rather speaks *as* Lucifer, as the black slave himself:

> Now Lucifer was not dead . . . . or if he was I am his sorrowful terrible heir;
> I have been wronged . . . . I am oppressed . . . I hate him that oppresses me,
> I will either destroy him, or he shall release me.
>
> Damn him! How he does defile me,
> How he informs against my brother and sister and takes pay for their blood,
> How he laughs when I look down the bend after the steamboat that carries away my woman.[21]

Keith Wilhite has investigated the ways that "the early drafts that would lead to 'The Sleepers' reveal the poet's struggle to empty out his poetic persona in an effort to create an absent space for the Lucifer figure to occupy." Wilhite uses an enigmatic note in one of Whitman's notebooks—"his mind was full of absences"—to open up the most radical acts of writing that Whitman undertakes, acts that require him to empty his subjective "I" until it is taken over by and speaks as a radically "other," in this case a white poet speaking *as*—not to or about—a black slave.[22] In one early draft, Whitman spells out the challenge he has set for himself: "I am a curse: a negro thinks me / You cannot speak yourself, negro / I dart like a snake from your mouth."[23] In the heavily revised manuscripts, where he has named his figure "Black Lucifer," Whitman works feverishly to turn his poem over to the consciousness and the sensibility of a black slave, allowing himself to be *thought* by "a negro" (instead of thinking *about* a negro) and then letting his voice emerge from the black slave's mouth. As Wilhite explains, "Whitman allows himself to be possessed by the cognitive mechanisms of an imagined black subjectivity."[24] Whitman's attempt is not to speak *for* the black slave but to speak *as* the black slave, an act that of course hovers precariously between subjugation of the black (who seems to be able to speak only when the white poet imagines himself speaking as a black slave) and full recognition of his subjectivity (the poet imagines himself inhabited by another, in fact *inhabiting* another). Whether the poem enacts Whitman's domination of the slave or the slave's domination of Whitman—or some endless, tensed identity transfer, shifting the slave into the master, the master into the slave—it remains one of the most powerful and evocative passages about slavery in American literature. By the time Whitman settles on the language for the published version of the passage, he has obliterated his own "I" and given the poem's "I" over to Black Lucifer. The slave becomes *subject* instead of object here.

In other passages about blacks in the 1855 *Leaves*, as in the familiar "hounded slave" passage in "Song of Myself," Whitman occasionally moves gradually from describing the slave from the white poet's viewpoint ("The hounded slave that flags in the race, leans by the fence") to claiming an identity ("All these I feel or am") to transferring the "I" from poet to slave ("I am the hounded slave, I wince at the bite of the dogs"), but the experience of the reader in these sections is not that the familiar persona has been *replaced* or *usurped* by another subjectivity but rather that the persona has claimed an empathetic identity with that other subjectivity.[25] In contrast, in the "Lucifer" section, the voice does not gradually shift but abruptly alters, as if the narrative of the poem has been hijacked by an intruding temporary persona. When such an abrupt transference of subjectivity occurs, all the usual surrounding and contextualizing description vanishes, leaving us to wonder just who or what this alien narrator is, leaving us—as was the case with the black fireman interruption—no way (short of seeing Whitman's unpublished manuscripts) of knowing for sure whether or not the narrator is black. Whitman's radical emptying out of the self and turning the "I" over to a radically different "other" may, in other words, be *so* radical that the published versions simply do not leave enough traces of the origin of the new voice, and so we can mistakenly hear the multiple voices

ED FOLSOM

as one overarching "Whitmanian I." What we sense as a particularly powerful and mysterious moment in the poetry may, then, be drawing its energy from Whitman's crossing of the racial line even as the results erase that crossing for most readers.[26]

Many of the early readings of the "Lucifer" section did not even see it as about a slave but rather as about the fallen archangel. In an earlier draft, Whitman had his new speaker give more contextualizing details ("Iron necklace and red sores of the shoulders I do not mind / Hopple at the ankle will not detain me"), but the more Whitman approached giving his poem over to the subjectivity of the slave, the less need there was for that subjectivity to speak the details that would already have been so obvious to him. That is, the more the narrative "I" speaks from within the slave's subjectivity, the less the external markers of the speaker's slavery need to be articulated.

After the Civil War, when slavery ceased to be the burning issue in the United States and was replaced by the question of civil rights for the newly freed blacks, Whitman's racial attitudes are often painful to encounter. The role of blacks in a reconstructed America was an issue with which Whitman, like most white Americans of the time, was uncomfortable and unsure. I have written about this period in Whitman's life and his increasing ambivalence and silence about whether or not African Americans should become full and equal citizens.[27] These were the years in which Whitman stopped adding representations of blacks to his poetry, with the exception of Ethiopia, the hundred-year-old slave woman in "Ethiopia Saluting the Colors," who expresses her wonderment at being freed by white troops as she curtsies to the American flag while wearing a turban in Ethiopian colors and speaks in an odd syntax that allows her to represent herself only as an object ("me") and never a subject ("I").[28] This passive and confused old black woman—seen in Whitman's poem from the perspective of an equally confused young white Union soldier—takes her place retroactively in Whitman's Civil War cluster of poems, "Drum-Taps," in the 1881 edition of *Leaves*, precisely at the moment that Lucifer, the angry and articulate young black slave, vanishes from the book. We never get a representation of Lucifer as a black citizen of the United States. I do not want to go over this particular territory again; instead, I want to focus on some further powerful racial moments in Whitman's poetry near the end of the Civil War, before Whitman goes mute about the issue. This period was the last one in which erased race still played a surprising and productive role for the poet.

Let's look first, though, at one of Whitman's best-known prose passages, first appearing in his 1875 *Memoranda during the War* and then gathered into *Specimen Days* in 1882, a passage in which he describes in detail the scene of Abraham Lincoln's second inauguration. Whitman captures the president's appearance that March day in 1865, when Lincoln "look'd very much worn and tired; the lines, indeed, of vast responsibilities, intricate questions, and demands of life and death, cut deeper than ever upon his dark brown face; yet all the old goodness, tenderness, sadness, and canny shrewdness, underneath the furrows."[29] Whitman wonders about portents as he notes how "the heavens, the elements, all the meteorological influences, had run riot for weeks past" and ruminates about "the weather—does it sympathize with these times?"[30] What an amazing moment it would have been if Whitman had included in his *Memoranda* the following description of the inaugural crowd on Pennsylvania Avenue that fateful March day, a description that in fact Whitman wrote at the same time as the *Memoranda* passages just quoted, and a description that he did indeed include with those passages when he originally published the article in the *New York Times* on 12 March 1865:

> As the day advanced, of course Pennsylvania avenue absorbed it all. The show here was to me worth all the rest. The effect was heterogeneous, novel, and quite inspiriting. It will perhaps be got at, by making a list in the following manner, to wit: Mud, (and such mud!) amid and upon the streaming crowds of citizens; lots of blue-dressed soldiers; any quantity of male and female Africans, (especially female;) horrid perpetual entanglements at the crossings, sometimes a dead lock; more mud, the wide street black, and several inches deep with it; clattering groups of cavalrymen out there on a gallop, (and occasionally a single horseman might have been seen, &c;) processions of firemen, with their engines, evidently from the north; a regiment of blacks, in full uniform, with guns on their

shoulders; the splendor overhead; the oceanic crowd, equal almost to Broadway; the wide Avenue, its vista very fine, down at one end closed by the capitol, with milky bulging dome, and the Maternal Figure over all, (with the sword by her side and the sun glittering on her helmeted head;) at the other, the western end, the pillared front of the Treasury building, looking south; altogether quite a refreshing spot and hour, and plenty of architectural show with life and magnetism also. Among other times, our heavenly neighbor Hesperus, the star of the West, was quite plain just after midday; it was right over head. I occasionally stopped with the crowd and looked up at it. Every corner had its little squad, thus engaged; often soldiers, often black, with raised faces, well worth looking at themselves, as new styles of physiognomical pictures.[31]

Whitman collected his various Civil War newspaper articles and reprinted them in *Memoranda* and *Specimen Days*, but he excised this astonishing passage, leaving it buried in the archives of the *Times*, where it was not found until the 1980s. The passage would have changed everything about how we perceived that somber inauguration just five weeks before Lincoln's assassination. Here, in this erased passage, unlike anywhere else in Whitman's writings, we have an America that has suddenly begun to become a multiracial democracy, where the "streaming crowds of citizens" include for the first time "any quantity of male and female Africans," all struggling together through the equalizing mud that is "amid and upon" them, coloring everyone "black" as it brings the crowds to a stop, where the soldiers marching past include "a regiment of blacks, in full uniform, with guns on their shoulders," marching with their white comrades toward the now-nurturing "milky bulging dome" of the Capitol, with its towering "Maternal Figure" a kind of beckoning erect nipple on the just-completed dome-breast, drawing its tired citizens and battle-weary soldiers to a new national birth and first nourishment.[32] "Pennsylvania avenue," Whitman reminds us, using one of his favorite democratic tropes, "absorbed it all." And the "star of the West," America's own star of Bethlehem, stops now "right over head" as the president takes his oath of office and a new united nation is born. That star—which Whitman would evoke a few months later, after Lincoln's assassination, in "When Lilacs Last in the Dooryard Bloom'd"—brings everyone together as they look up at it as one, including the "soldiers, often black, with raised faces, well worth looking at themselves, as new styles of physiognomical pictures." Everyone else is looking at the Western Star, but Whitman's gaze drifts to and fixes on the upraised faces of the black soldiers as he admires this "new style" of American physiognomy. Never before and never again would Whitman achieve such a powerful vision of a newly integrating America, as messy as the mud-drenched streets, yet somehow serene and hopeful. (The whole scene is portrayed as a kind of birth scene, with all the messiness and hope and wonder of a new identity coming into the world.) The description, had he included it in *Memoranda* and *Specimen Days*, would have provided a telling context for his striking description of Lincoln's "dark brown face," suggesting how the racial darkening of the nation was part of what was now inscribed so deeply in the president's own physiognomy. But as Whitman gathered his Civil War newspaper articles to create *Memoranda*, he simply deleted this passage. After readers of the *Times* read it that March day, it vanished with yesterday's newspapers, not to reappear for 120 years.

Kenneth Price has examined another of Whitman's descriptions of African Americans negotiating a muddy Washington day. An unpublished and heavily revised manuscript clearly intended as a newspaper piece (perhaps its published version is still waiting in some archive to be discovered), this one was written two years earlier than the *Times* article, just months after Lincoln issued the Emancipation Proclamation. Whitman had walked out of his boardinghouse that April morning in 1863 and recorded a "Washington Sight":

> Over the muddy crossing, (half past 8, morning of April 1st, '63) at 14th and L street, a stout young wench wheeling a wheelbarrow—the wench perhaps 15 years old, black and jolly and strong as a horse;—in the wheelbarrow, cuddled up, a child-wench, of six or seven years, equally black, shiny black and jolly with an old quilt around her, sitting plump back, riding backwards, partially holding on, a little fearful and trying to hold in her arms a full-grown young lap-dog, curly, beautiful

white as silver, with sparkling peering, round black eyes—the child-wench bareheaded;—and, all, the dog, the stout-armed negress, firmly holding the handles, and pushing on through the mud—the heads of the pretty silver dog, and the pictorial black round and young & with alert eyes, as she turned half way around, twisting her neck anxious to see what prospect, (having probably been overturned in the mud on some previous occasion)—the gait of the big girl, so sturdy and so graceful with her short petticoats her legs stepping, plashing steadily along through obstructions—the shiny-curled dog, standing up in the hold of the little one,—she huddled in the barrow, riding backwards with the patch-work quilt around her, sitting down, her feet visible poling straight out in front—made a passing group which as I stopt to look at it, you may if you choose stop and imagine.[33]

Price offers a detailed and keen analysis of this passage, noting how Whitman's description seems to "teem with possibilities—this is early in the day and in the month and in the season of renewal; it is early in the lives of the young 'negresses' and the 'young lap-dog'; and it is early in the history of black freedom." He notes how the date—April Fools' Day—"carries with it a carnivalesque tradition of an overturned social order and new possibilities for the underclass, all of which is implied in Whitman's description of these newly freed, half-amusing, half-threatening young women."[34] And he investigates the uneasy tensions inherent in Whitman's use of the word "wench," a term often used for black servants but also for prostitutes, and a term he employed only to refer to African American women. But what is striking about this passage in relation to the *Times* passage just discussed is Whitman's utter fascination with this woman and girl; as with the black soldiers looking up at Venus, he can't take his eyes off them. And his fascination with the young woman is particularly striking: through the racialist stereotyping ("black and jolly," "pictorial black") we can still hear his sincere admiration for the evocative determination he is witnessing as the young woman "firmly hold[s] the handles, and push[es] on through the mud," "so sturdy and so graceful . . . , plashing steadily along through obstructions." She recalls the powerful and determined "negro"

Whitman portrays in "Song of Myself," a portrait that, except for skin color, seems to match the frontispiece engraving of Whitman himself in the 1855 *Leaves of Grass*, as if he wanted to assume the identity of this determined, strong figure:

> The negro holds firmly the reins of his four horses . . . . the
>   block swags underneath on its tied-over chain,
> The negro that drives the huge dray of the stoneyard
>   . . . . steady and tall he stands poised on one leg on the
>   stringpiece,
> His blue shirt exposes his ample neck and breast and loosens
>   over his hipband,
> His glance is calm and commanding . . . . he tosses the slouch
>   of his hat away from his forehead,
> The sun falls on his crispy hair and moustache . . . . falls on
>   the black of his polish'd and perfect limbs.[35]

But unlike this memorable figure from "Song of Myself," the "stout young wench" who might have served as a symbol of emerging black citizenship disappeared into Whitman's unpublished notes, erased from his published works.

I have discussed these two passages not just as additional examples of Whitman's erasing race but because they provide a window onto how Whitman, in the final two, post–Emancipation Proclamation years of the war, was contemplating the racial changes that postwar America was ushering in, and they demonstrate how he was struggling at that time to articulate a new absorptive vision. At the time he published his *New York Times* piece, he was putting his book of Civil War poems, *Drum-Taps*, into print, a book filled with poems based on stories that soldiers had told him while he visited them in the hospitals that dotted the nation's capital. We need to remember that the soldiers he visited included black soldiers as well as white: "Among the black soldiers, wounded or sick, and in the contraband camps, I also took my way whenever in their neighborhood, and did what I could for them."[36] He met with Dr. Alexander Augusta, one of only eight African American physicians commissioned in the war and the first director of Washington's Freedman's Hospital. He kept track of the changing demographics, noting in May 1863 that there "are now 10,000 contrabands in Washington—Alexandria 3,000 . . .

1500 have died."[37] Among his notebooks and newspaper clippings from the war, he saved many stories about the bravery of black troops, about the all-black first regiment Louisiana engineers, for example, or about the first Kansas Colored Volunteers or the Iowa Negro Regiment or the "5,000 colored men in the navy."[38] He jotted a note to himself: "Blacks—Mrs. Hannah Moses anecdotes the fact that several of the best pilots in the U S ships in the attack on Charleston were blacks."[39] He added notes to these articles and highlighted the most positive statements about black soldiers' bravery, courage, and loyalty. He kept articles about how black and white troops were fighting together and articles about how Lincoln's decision to allow freed slaves to enlist in the army and navy gave them a chance, as one article put it, "to demonstrate to the world that a black man is not only qualified for citizenship in a free government in time of peace, but that he can defend the laws and the Government of his country against all foes in the hour of battle. . . . It will be the forerunner of great things, the breaker down of prejudice, and the carrier of good tidings to the poor and oppressed."[40] Whitman's careful collection of these articles suggests he might have been preparing to write something about the emerging new America in which blacks and whites would live together. Two of the last soldiers he visited in the Civil War hospitals, Joseph Winder and Thomas King, were black.[41] He was picking up a lot about and *from* African American soldiers, but these notes and saved articles did not get transformed into poems in the way that so many of his notes of conversations with white soldiers and newspaper articles about white troops did. Or have we missed something?

We saw earlier how the "mash'd fireman's" insistence on the "white faces" around him can be read as an indicator that the speaker is black; only a black speaker would bother to specify "white" faces, because to a white speaker the whiteness of white faces is invisible or transparent. Yet critics have often assumed that Whitman's odd specification of "white faces" in "Song of Myself" and elsewhere, or even of "white skeletons" in "When Lilacs Last in the Dooryard Bloom'd," betrays his racism, his almost unconscious need to identify fully and explicitly with his white comrades and thus to exclude blacks. But if we consider the frequent race crossing evident in his manuscripts, his thrill in violating the taboo of crossing race and of imagining himself fully into the subjectivity of a black, absorbing the energy of the forbidden moment only to erase or diminish the explicit racial component in the final version, we can then see that these references to "white" may in fact be traces of what had originally been inspiring moments of race crossing.

Let's take the "white skeletons" in "Lilacs." Late in that poem, Whitman's persona, for the first time, opens his eyes fully to the vastness of the death wreaked by the war and sees "battle-corpses, myriads of them, / And the white skeletons of young men, I saw them, / I saw the debris and debris of all the slain soldiers of the war."[42] Vivian Pollak observes that "when color is introduced into this scene in the phrase 'white skeletons,' we tend to experience it as a cliché, but the effect is to reinforce, albeit covertly, the racial status quo. Though it could be argued that whiteness is the universalized color of death, that the human body, deprived of its particularizing fleshly hues, is in fact bleached of its living colors, one effect of Whitman's language in this context is to suppress the contribution of black soldiers and civilians to the war effort." Pollak goes on to note how two hundred thousand black soldiers took part in the war effort, a contribution regularly erased in Civil War histories, and she concludes that, "as a war poet, Whitman was reluctant to turn his attention to racial matters."[43]

Yet a not insignificant part of the duties of many of those black soldiers in the war was the gruesome task of gathering up the "battle-corpses" after battles and burying the "white skeletons." That duty did not end with the completion of the war. Indeed, the final Grand Review of the Union troops in May 1865—a month after Lincoln's assassination, when Whitman would have begun working on "Lilacs"—featured (as Whitman described it in a letter to his mother) "great battalions of blacks, with axes & shovels & pick axes, (real southern darkies, black as tar)"; these were the troops armed for the task of burial duty.[44] As Whitman, who visited soldiers from the US Colored Troops, well knew, these black soldiers became instrumental in the massive reburial effort in 1866, led by another Whitman (Edmund B. Whitman, chief quartermaster of the Military Division of the District of Tennessee), who was charged with locating the scattered and often makeshift graves of Union soldiers throughout the South. Locating as many

ED FOLSOM

as forty thousand bodies between Vicksburg and Natchez, he put the black soldiers to work: "Three hundred black soldiers at the Stones River National Cemetery continued to collect and rebury Union bodies from the wide surrounding area at the rate of fifty to a hundred a day," according to Drew Gilpin Faust, who sees this effort as representing "the critical role that African Americans had come to play in honoring the Union dead. Almost invariably units of US Colored Troops were assigned the disagreeable work of burial and reburial."[45] No one experienced the "debris and debris" of the "slain soldiers" like black troops did. And as we know from the erased inauguration prose passage about the black soldiers on Pennsylvania Avenue and from the cache of newspaper articles Whitman collected about black soldiers, Whitman was fascinated with these men. Among the many newspaper clippings he saved and carefully pasted on sheets of paper were a number of articles about these black soldiers burying white corpses.[46]

If we hear the shifting persona of "Lilacs" as another figure engendered at various moments by Whitman's race-crossed imaginings, then the "white skeletons" become not an indicator of racial solidarity so much as a recognition—from the perspective of those black soldiers who were gathering these skeletons—of the ironic mutability of color and the evanescence of skin. These black soldiers were gathering the skeletons of both white and black soldiers, and by the time the soldiers carted them to their graves, the skeletons were stripped of racial markers. The mass death of the Civil War created multiple deep ironies. Just as black soldiers' corpses eventually became white skeletons, so did white soldiers' corpses quickly become black before ending up as white skeletons. Numerous white soldiers commented on what seemed to them to be death's cruel racial joke; one Gettysburg veteran noted that "the faces of the dead, as a general rule, had turned black—not a purplish discoloration, such as I had imagined in reading of the 'blackened corpse' so often mentioned in descriptions of battle-grounds, but a deep bluish *black*, giving to a corpse with black hair the appearance of a negro."[47] Whitman, in his Civil War notebooks, in lines he never published, was haunted by the same phenomenon: "Some of the dead, how soon they turn black in the face and swollen!," and again, "they turn very black & discolored."[48] Death had a way of reversing race, even double-reversing it, and negating its importance. Whitman's narrator's observation of the "white skeletons," then, carries a more ironic tone than Pollak and others have sensed, and the passage could well have emerged from Whitman's conversations with some of the black soldiers who had been doing the actual burying of the "myriads" of "battle-corpses," who had experienced firsthand the workings of death on the body, the way death casually altered white to black and black to white.

The possibilities become even more intriguing when we look at a poem like "Reconciliation," Whitman's powerful lyric of re-turning peace. Twice in the poem, a "white face" appears, and the insistence seems odd:

> Word over all, beautiful as the sky,
> Beautiful that war and all its deeds of carnage must in time
>   be utterly lost,
> That the hands of the sisters Death and Night incessantly
>   softly wash again, and ever again, this soil'd world;
> For my enemy is dead, a man divine as myself is dead,
> I look where he lies white-faced and still in the coffin—
>   I draw near,
> Bend down and touch lightly with my lips the white face
>   in the coffin.[49]

Many readers will read through the whiteness here, finding nothing remarkable in the description and perhaps hearing it only as a reference to the pallid complexion of the corpse. But the double reference in the final two lines draws attention to itself, and it is difficult not to hear some racial edge to the description. Again, some might hear the insistence as the sign of Whitman's affirming a racial bond with his white Southern enemies, the ex-plicit reference to "white" becoming an exclusionary statement, as racial solidarity finally trumps sectional enmity. David Blight, for example, sees the poem as underscoring Whitman's "virtual kinship" with "all the 'white-faced' dead brothers," thus enacting "the ultimate betrayal of the dark-faced folk whom the dead had shared in liberating."[50] Similarly, Natasha Trethewey hears Whit-man's emphasis on the "white face" in this poem as an indication that he "leaves out the reality of so many dead soldiers whose faces were not white."[51]

The opposite may be the case, however: if, as was the case with the "mash'd fireman" section of "Song of Myself," the persona was originally conceived of by Whitman as black—here, as a black soldier—and the "I" of this poem is heard as another of Whitman's excursions into black subjectivity, then the peculiar insistence on the white face makes sense, for this reconciliation promises now to transcend race, to bring black and white together, as the war produces (if only temporarily) a previously unimaginable reconciliation between the races. "Reconciliation" is, after all, an outdoor poem, taking place under the sky and on the "soil'd world" (we're certainly not in a funeral parlor). If the narrator is heard, then, as one of the black soldiers who so often placed the white dead in coffins and buried them, he now finds that his labors of gathering death from the "soil'd world" of shallow graves strewn across the Southern landscape provides him a moment to express affection in a charged kiss on the lips of "the white face in the coffin," and the double emphasis on *white* captures the amazement of the former slave at this newfound liberty to kiss (and, as Faust reminds us, to "honor") the dead white soldier.[52] Whether that dead white soldier was a Union or a Confederate corpse, it would have been—for most of American history—the black's "enemy," but now, in this moment of intimate confrontation with the corpse, the experience of being a soldier unites rather than separates the black speaker from his dead white enemy, allowing this powerful (if macabre) experience of reconciliation. This is one Whitman poem for which we have no manuscripts, so it is impossible to determine, as we can in "The Sleepers" manuscript, if there is an erased black presence, even an erased black speaker, here. But the manuscript evidence for other such charged passages is strong enough to allow us to entertain the possibility of a ghost-black speaker in "Reconciliation" as well and to imagine this poem as another of the ways Whitman transformed his notes of what soldiers told him into a haunting and lasting poem. In this case, those soldiers would have been black soldiers who had been on grave detail, burying white soldiers and finding themselves again and again in the position of the speaker in this poem, drawing near to the coffin with the dead "enemy," all too familiar now with what it feels like to touch a white-faced corpse with affection.

I am suggesting, finally, that in those years at the end of the Civil War, Whitman was imagining, gathering evidence for, and occasionally inscribing a stunning new vision of a racially healed nation, a vision that we can now glean only through his erasures and discarded writings. His disillusionment with postwar America became so intense, his fear of black equality eventually trumping his hopes for a transformed nation, that his later writing suffers from a kind of stunted growth, a truncated sense of how America could learn to cope with, build on, and build *with* its tortured racial past. While attending the congressional debates that were deciding the extent to which blacks would be allowed entry into the reconstructed nation, Whitman looked at the changed world about him: "We had the greatest black procession here last Thursday—I didn't think there was so many darkeys, (especially wenches,) in the world—it was the anniversary of emancipation in this District."[53] The tone of this April 1866 letter to his mother is tricky to read: he has just experienced the first Emancipation Day celebration, which would take place annually in Washington in April throughout the rest of the century (Lincoln signed the Compensated Emancipation Proclamation, freeing enslaved people in the District of Columbia, on 16 April 1862, over eight months before issuing his general Emancipation Proclamation), and Whitman sees the procession as "great," but his description of the new black citizens as countless "darkeys" and "wenches" betrays a concern very different from the inspiring "new styles of physiognomical pictures" the faces of black soldiers had presented to him just a year earlier. As his vision of a multiracial society dimmed, his decisions about what to print and reprint and what to silently erase have, over time, occluded our ability to see the brief flowering of Whitman's multiracial hopes.

By 1868, when Washington held the first mayoral election in which blacks could vote, Whitman's multiracial hope had evaporated. As the "darkeys" took to the streets more and more frequently, he responded with some disdain and a growing alarm; in June 1868, he wrote again to his mother:

We had the strangest procession here last Tuesday night, about 3000 darkeys, old & young, men & women—I saw them all—they turned out in honor of *their* victory in electing the Mayor,

Mr. Bowen—the men were all armed with clubs or pistols—besides the procession in the street, there was a string went along the sidewalk in single file with bludgeons & sticks, yelling & gesticulating like madmen—it was quite comical, yet very disgusting & alarming in some respects—They were very insolent, & altogether it was a strange sight—they looked like so many wild brutes let loose—thousands of slaves from the Southern plantations have crowded up here—many are supported by the Gov't.[54]

Sayles Jenks Bowen (1813–96), one of the most controversial mayors in Washington's history, was elected in 1868. A radical Republican who fought bravely and tirelessly for black civil rights, he carried virtually all of the black votes as African Americans voted for the first time, and he pulled off a razor-thin victory over his Democratic opponent, who contested the results. Bowen wanted to fully integrate DC public schools and, unable to accomplish that, worked tirelessly (and contributed substantial sums of his own money) to develop a network of schools for blacks. He appointed African Americans to high administrative posts, and during his term blacks were elected to the city council. After the city's debt increased dramatically, he failed in his reelection bid in 1870.[55] Whitman had no sympathy for Bowen and worried that the new black citizens would now vote only in a block, undermining the independent individualism necessary for a democracy to function. The admirable marching black troops with guns on their shoulders had now, from his perspective, transmuted into a swarm of madmen with clubs, pistols, bludgeons, and sticks. Again, Whitman would never publish these impressions, but he clearly was beginning to doubt the promise of a racially integrated nation.

It was during the two years of Bowen's administration that Whitman wrote *Democratic Vistas*, his long prose meditation on the current state and future prospects of American democracy, a project he initially conceived of as a response to Thomas Carlyle's racist diatribe in his 1867 essay, "Shooting Niagara—and After?" Whitman set out to address the burning issue in America of black suffrage, but by the time the essay was published, just after Bowen had been soundly defeated in his bid for reelection,

African Americans were absent, once again erased, and the issue of suffrage was reduced to a whisper in an after-note, where race was perhaps implied but not explicitly mentioned. ("As to general suffrage, after all, since we have gone so far, the more general it is the better. I favor the widest opening of the doors. Let the ventilation and area be wide enough, and all is safe.")[56] And then, when he reprinted *Democratic Vistas*, he removed even that note and buried it deep in his "Notes Left Over" section of *Collect*.[57] The only mentions of his encounters with black troops that make it into his collected writings didn't get published until he collected some old fragments in *November Boughs* in 1888.[58]

Erasing race from his work during the final twenty-five years of his life was one of Whitman's occupations, as he became increasingly silent about one of the defining issues of American history. He left behind, however, enough traces that we can still glimpse the beginnings of his brave vision, his attempt to imagine a democratic subjectivity open enough to speak black experience in often subtle and moving ways, a vision that began with his first notes toward *Leaves of Grass* but lasted, sadly, only until soon after the Civil War ended, when the real work of building a multiracial society was just getting under way.

NOTES

1. For discussions of Whitman's racialist scientific theories, see Geoffrey Sill, "Whitman on 'The Black Question': A New Manuscript," *Walt Whitman Quarterly Review* 8 (Fall 1990): 69–75; Kenneth M. Price, "Whitman's Solutions to 'The Problem of the Blacks,'" *Resources for American Literary Study* 15 (Autumn 1985): 205–8.

2. See Beth Kolko, "Erasing @race: Going White in the (Inter)Face," in *Race in Cyberspace*, ed. Beth Kolko, Lisa Nakamura, and Gilbert B. Rodman (New York: Routledge, 2000), 213–32; Margaret Chon, "Erasing Race? A Critical Race Feminist View of Internet Identity-Shifting," *Journal of Gender, Race & Justice*, May 2000, 439–73.

3. Kenneth M. Price, *To Walt Whitman, America* (Chapel Hill: University of North Carolina Press, 2004), 11.

4. David Remnick, Talk of the Town, *New Yorker*, 15 October 2001, 53.

5. Walt Whitman, *Leaves of Grass*, Comprehensive Reader's Edition, ed. Harold W. Blodgett and Sculley Bradley (New York: New York University Press, 1965), 67.

6. "Autobiographical Data" notebook, in *Notebooks and Unpublished Prose Manuscripts*, ed. Edward F. Grier, 6 vols. (New York: New York University Press, 1984), 1:215–16. Whitman may be recalling the experience of witnessing the huge fire that wiped out a good part of the printing district in New York City in 1835, when Whitman worked there as a printer. One news report at the time describes the victims, including "a colored man, name unknown; was buried under the ruins of one of the fallen walls" (*New-York Spectator*, Thursday, 13 August 1835).

7. Whitman, *Notebooks*, 1:209.

8. See, for example, "New-York" in the *New-York Mirror: A Weekly Gazette of Literature and the Fine Arts*, 7 September 1833, where the author discusses "the state of society in New-York" and comments on "the badness of the servants," who are "chiefly people of colour, habituated, from their cradle, to be regarded as an inferior race, and consequently sadly wanting both in moral energy and principle." He goes on to note that the master of the house thus must never trust the keys to his wine cellar to a servant: "He would much rather know that the keys of his cellar were at the bottom of the Hudson, than in the pocket of black Caesar." For other examples, see "The Inheritance: The Author of Marriage," *Republic of Letters: A Republican of Standard Literature*, 1 July 1836; and "Chronicles of Ashley River—No. 5," *Southern Literary Gazette*, 15 October 1829.

9. Andrew C. Higgins, "Wage Slavery and the Composition of *Leaves of Grass*: The 'Talbot Wilson' Notebook," *Walt Whitman Quarterly Review* 20 (Fall 2002): 69. Higgins argues that Whitman's focus on slavery in his notebook has less to do with black chattel slavery than with white wage slavery.

10. Ibid., 76n36.

11. There has been a long controversy over the dating of this notebook. For a good summary of this debate, see ibid., 55–61.

12. Whitman, *Notebooks*, 1:67.

13. Karen Sánchez-Eppler, *Touching Liberty: Abolition, Feminism, and the Politics of the Body* (Berkeley: University of California Press, 1993), 50, 52.

14. Whitman, *Notebooks*, 1:67; a digital scan of the notebook (Notebook #80) is available on the Library of Congress "American Memory" website, http://www.memory.loc.gov.

15. Price, *To Walt Whitman*, 12–13.

16. See Whitman, *Leaves of Grass*, 48.

17. Martin Klammer, *Whitman, Slavery, and the Emergence of "Leaves of Grass"* (University Park: Pennsylvania State University Press, 1995), 115.

18. Martin Klammer, "Slavery and Race," in *A Companion to Walt Whitman*, ed. Donald D. Kummings (Malden, MA: Blackwell, 2006), 114.

19. Ed Folsom, "Lucifer and Ethiopia: Whitman, Race, and Poetics be-

fore the Civil War and After," in *A Historical Guide to Walt Whitman*, ed. David S. Reynolds (New York: Oxford University Press, 2000), 45–95.

20. Walt Whitman, *Leaves of Grass: The First (1855) Edition*, ed. Malcolm Cowley (New York: Viking, 1959).

21. Ibid., 111, ellipses in original.

22. Keith Wilhite, "'His Mind Was Full of Absences': Whitman at the Scene of Writing," *ELH* 71 (Winter 2004): 922. Christopher Beach examines how more conventional antislavery poets like John Greenleaf Whittier and Henry Wadsworth Longfellow wrote *of* the slave but not *as* the slave, failing to provide "a poetic space for the interiority of the slave's experience," unlike Whitman, who discovered "various alternatives to the exteriorizing and conventionalizing poetic discourse of Whittier and Longfellow"; see Beach's *The Politics of Distinction: Whitman and the Discourses of Nineteenth-Century America* (Athens: University of Georgia Press, 1996), 68.

23. Whitman, *Leaves of Grass*, 628n.

24. Wilhite, "'His Mind,'" 932.

25. Whitman, *Leaves of Grass: The First (1855) Edition*, 62.

26. Paul Outka, in "Whitman and Race ('He's Queer, He's Unclear, Get Used to It')," *Journal of American Studies* 36 (August 2002): 293–318, explores how, for Whitman, "racism in fact provided a poetic possibility, the sort of internalized social taboo shot through with repressed eroticism that the poetic voice loved to work against," releasing in the poetry "eroticized political energies" and offering "an opportunity for daring intimacy." I find Outka's analysis compelling, and his examination of Whitman's excitement at breaking the taboo of racial crossing supports my own sense of how Whitman's covering up (or erasing) of these taboo moments still allows the energy of the violation to infuse the poetic lines that remain, even when those lines may no longer seem to be about racial crossing.

27. See Folsom, "Lucifer and Ethiopia."

28. See Walt Whitman, "Ethiopia Saluting the Colors," in *Leaves of Grass*, 318–19.

29. Walt Whitman, *Specimen Days*, in *Prose Works 1892*, ed. Floyd Stovall, 2 vols. (New York: New York University Press, 1963), 1:92.

30. Ibid., 1:94.

31. W. T. Bandy, "An Unknown 'Washington Letter' by Walt Whitman," *Walt Whitman Quarterly Review* 2 (Winter 1985): 25.

32. Whitman had been fascinated with the building of the Capitol dome, and he worked through a series of metaphors to describe it, calling it in 1863 a "huge and delicate towering bulge of pure white," then shifting to "a vast eggshell, built of iron and glass, this dome—a beauteous bubble, caught and put in permanent form" (*New York Times*, 4 October 1863, 2), but his association of the newly completed dome with a female breast, complete with

the newly installed female Statue of Freedom serving as nipple, is a remarkable imaginative leap.

33. Kenneth M. Price, "The Lost Negress of 'Song of Myself' and the Jolly Young Wenches of Civil War Washington," in *"Leaves of Grass": The Sesquicentennial Essays*, ed. Susan Belasco, Ed Folsom, and Kenneth M. Price (Lincoln: University of Nebraska Press, 2007), 232–33. For the sake of clarity, I have removed Whitman's numerous manuscript deletions and have incorporated his numerous insertions; Price offers a more detailed and precise transcription.

34. Ibid., 233.

35. Whitman, *Leaves of Grass: The First (1855) Edition*, 35.

36. Whitman, *Specimen Days*, 1:113–14. Whitman's hospital visits to black soldiers remained a continuing source of sustenance to him late into his life. At his seventieth birthday dinner celebration in Camden, New Jersey, the frail Whitman, as he entered the hall, was seen being embraced by "the negro cook," who had come out to greet the poet because Whitman had nursed her husband in a Civil War hospital; see Horace Traubel, *With Walt Whitman in Camden* (Carbondale: Southern Illinois University Press, 1964), 5:250.

37. Whitman, *Notebooks*, 535.

38. "Colored Men in the Navy," unidentified newspaper clipping in the Thomas Biggs Harned Collection of the Walt Whitman Papers, Library of Congress.

39. Charles I. Glicksberg, ed., *Walt Whitman and the Civil War* (Philadelphia: University of Pennsylvania Press, 1933), 187n. See pp. 183–92 for a list of all of Whitman's saved newspaper clippings.

40. Clipping from the *Washington Chronicle*, dated by Whitman 26 May [no year], Harned Collection.

41. Whitman, "Last of the War Cases," in *Prose Works 1892*, 2:625–26.

42. Whitman, *Leaves of Grass*, 336.

43. Vivian R. Pollak, *The Erotic Whitman* (Berkeley: University of California Press, 2000), 175, 176.

44. Walt Whitman, *Correspondence*, ed. Edwin Haviland Miller (New York: New York University Press, 1961), 1:261.

45. Drew Gilpin Faust, *This Republic of Suffering: Death and the American Civil War* (New York: Alfred A. Knopf, 2008), 226–27.

46. One clipping, held at the Harry Ransom Humanities Research Center at the University of Texas, reads "Giving Burial to the Dead.—For some days past details have been made from the colored troops, who have been sent out with intrenching tools, to the battle fields around Richmond, and employed in the burial of the Union dead lying there exposed for a year past. Several hundred skeletons were put under the sod upon the battle grounds

of Gaines' Mill and Cold Harbor, and other battle fields are being attended to in their turn." Whitman annotated this clipping as from the *Richmond Whig* and dated it 2 May 1865.

47. Quoted in Gilpin, *This Republic of Suffering*, 57.

48. Glicksberg, *Walt Whitman and the Civil War*, 122; Whitman, *Notebooks*, 2:668. One other example of this irony of racial shifting in death that would no doubt have intrigued Whitman had he known about it is the description of Abraham Lincoln's face soon after he died. Daniel Mark Epstein describes what he calls "the very peculiar matter of the President's skin. As the funeral cortege had passed through Harrisburg and Lancaster, coal country, Lincoln's face had turned, curiously, black. It would have been unseemly for the President to appear in the rotunda of New York's City Hall as the silent interlocutor of a minstrel show. So the morticians had covered the President's face with a paste of white chalk." When Lincoln's casket was opened in 1887 (on the very day Whitman gave his Lincoln Lecture in New York City), the white chalk "had dissolved, leaving the dark lineaments dusted with a faint white powder." In death, the Great Emancipator had turned black. See Daniel Mark Epstein, *Lincoln and Whitman: Parallel Lives in Civil War Washington* (New York: Ballantine, 2004), 333–34.

49. Whitman, *Leaves of Grass*, 321.

50. David W. Blight, *Race and Reunion: The Civil War in American Memory* (Cambridge, MA: Harvard University Press, 2001), 23.

51. Natasha Trethewey, "On Whitman, Civil War Memory, and My South," *Virginia Quarterly Review* 81 (Spring 2005): 53.

52. Faust, *This Republic of Suffering*, 226.

53. Whitman, *Correspondence*, 1:273–74.

54. Ibid., 2:34–35.

55. See William Tindall, "A Sketch of Mayor Sayles J. Bowen," in *Records of the Columbia Historical Society, Washington, D.C.* (Washington, DC: Published by the Society, 1915), 18:25–43.

56. See my analysis of how Whitman forgot to answer Carlyle in "Lucifer and Ethiopia," 77–80. The note on suffrage can be found in *Democratic Vistas*, 83, in *Two Rivulets*, by Walt Whitman (Camden, 1876). Whitman published the first two parts of *Democratic Vistas* in the magazine the *Galaxy* in December 1867 and May 1868; the first essay, called "Democracy," did contain a section that more directly grappled with Carlyle's "Shooting Niagara," albeit in three tortured paragraphs that at once seem to mock Carlyle for his "spasms of dread and disgust" (and for his "comic-painful hullabaloo and vituperative cat-squalling") and to counsel him to be calm and "confront, embrace, absorb, swallow (O, big and bitter pill!) the entire British 'swarmery,' demon, 'loud roughs' and all. . . . [I]ncorporate them in the State as voters, and then—wait for the next emergency." As for what will

"become of 'nigger Cushee,' that imbruted and lazy being—now, worst of all, preposterously free," Whitman is characteristically much more evasive, and he shifts the question quickly to the need to extend "to full-grown British working-folk, farmers, mechanics, clerks, and so on . . . the privilege of the ballot." But these three paragraphs at least directly mention the race problem, and they were excised by the time Whitman published the book version of *Democratic Vistas* in 1871. For the excised material, see *Prose Works 1892*, 2:748–57. I explore Whitman's reactions to postwar Washington, DC, with its huge influx of freed slaves, in "The Vistas of *Democratic Vistas*," my introduction to *Democratic Vistas: The Original Edition in Facsimile* (Iowa City: University of Iowa Press, 2010), xv–lxvii.

57. See Walt Whitman, "Notes Left Over," *Collect*, in *Prose Works 1892*, 2:531.

58. See Walt Whitman, "Paying the 1st U.S.C.T.," in *Prose Works 1892*, 2:587; and Whitman, "Last of the War Cases," in *Prose Works 1892*, 2:625–26.

The "Creole" Episode

Slavery and Temperance in Franklin Evans

AMINA GAUTIER

Midway through Walt Whitman's temperance novel *Franklin Evans, or The Inebriate* (1842), the eponymous Franklin Evans finds himself traveling to Virginia on a journey that seemingly disrupts a narrative that has previously been mostly concerned with his travels between rural and urban northern spaces. Although Michael Warner has compellingly observed that "*Franklin Evans* seems more than anything else to narrate its title character into as many disparate social spaces as possible," I see Evans's stint in the South as something more than a trip made to heighten the picaresque quality of his peripatetic wanderings.[1] Rather, Evans's journey to Virginia and his extended stay on a southern plantation afford him a firsthand account of slavery, and the southern, or "Creole," episode of *Franklin Evans* becomes the ideal place for Whitman to explore the parallels between intemperance and slavery that many temperance writers drew upon to encourage reform. While Whitman's portrayal of Evans as a man figuratively enslaved to alcohol draws upon an already familiar trope, his decision to locate Evans, his figurative slave, on an actual slave plantation in the "Creole" episode of *Franklin Evans* introduces and integrates Evans into the culture of slavery, thus complicating the ways in which the narrative's conflation of slavery and intemperance is fully realized.

Published as a newspaper segment two years after the inception of the Washingtonian movement, which focused mainly on the individual alcoholic, relied upon the public sharing of one's experiences with alcohol, and encouraged total abstinence, Whitman's Washingtonian-influenced temperance novel draws connections between slavery and intemperance that reiterate the conventional wisdom on the part of most temperance reformers who found obvious similarities between slavery and intemperance and who relied upon such arguments to aid them in decrying the evil effects of alcoholism.

On 4 July 1828 Heman Humphrey, president of Amherst College, delivered a lecture entitled "Parallel between Intemperance and the Slave Trade," in which he used the occasion of an Independence Day celebration to offer a rationale to ban the sale and consumption of alcohol: "For however cruel and debasing and portentous African servitude may be, beyond the Potomac, there exists, even in New-England, a far sorer bondage, from which the slaves of the South are happily free. This bondage is intellectual and moral as well as physical. It chains and scourges the soul, as well as the body. It is a servitude from which death itself has no power to release the captive."[2] In his lecture, Humphrey draws an analogy between American chattel slavery and the "far sorer bondage" of intemperance to show the horrors of alcohol consumption and to predict that intemperance will cause the fall of the American empire. Intemperance, alternately deemed a "domestic tyrant," "tempest of fire in all our borders," "western bondage," and "the sorest plague that ever visited our country," threatens American liberty by dismantling the nation, crippling its citizens, and "enslaving" them to alcohol consumption.[3] In Humphrey's extended metaphor, intemperance has its own middle passage, a journey that every drunkard takes: he starts out in "health and freedom and happiness" and then goes through "the most grinding and crushing bondage that ever disgraced and tortured humanity," ending up in "his final rotting place."[4] For the African slave, the Middle Passage ends with forced disembarkation on foreign soil; for the intemperate drinker, the "middle passage" ends with death. In Humphrey's address, slavery first begins as a simile but ultimately becomes a metaphor. The two are elided so that intemperance is no longer simply like the thing to which it has been compared but has instead become the thing itself.

Though Humphrey's comparison downplays the negative effects of slave trading, his goal of "comparing intemperance with some terrible scourge of humanity, which has fallen under deep and universal reprobation," illustrates a familiar tactic within temperance discourse.[5] For example, Humphrey's comparisons echo those put forth two years earlier by Lyman Beecher in 1826: "We execrate the cruelties of the slave trade—the husband torn from the bosom of his wife—the son from his father—brothers and sisters separated forever—whole families in a moment ruined! But are there no similar enormities to be witnessed in the United States? None indeed perpetrated by the bayonet—but many, very many, perpetrated by intemperance."[6] Beecher asserts that intemperance also features its own "middle passage of slavery, and darkness, and chains, and disease, and death," and he refers to intemperance as a "moral miasma" spreading and infecting the health of the nation.[7] Frequently conflating the inebriate with the slave, temperance writers generally depicted alcohol as "a form of tyrant, resembling slavery in depriving people of their ability to act as morally responsible creatures"; succumbing to intemperance symbolized the "destruction of one's autonomy."[8] The intemperate man is always in danger of becoming "enslaved" to the demon drink, the serpent in the cup.

The inebriate faces not only the loss of agency but also a loss of whiteness. Temperance writers often represent the drunkard's body and skin undergoing epidemiological change due to inebriation, and these effects of excessive drinking cause a change in the drunkard's skin color that results in a loss of the inebriate's whiteness. Inebriation causes the drunkard's face to be perpetually "red" or flushed, and living in squalor darkens his skin, turning it "brown" from the dirt and grime among which he lives.[9] Although temperance narratives are deeply complicated by race and gender, and intemperance itself is neither a distinctly white nor a male behavior, temperance advocates and writers primarily focused their attention and recuperative efforts on the white male drunkard. This is especially true of the Washingtonian-influenced temperance narrative, of which *Franklin Evans* is a prime example.

In this essay, I will deliberately restrict my focus to the male inebriate because the Washingtonian brand of temperance, which heavily influenced the writing of Whitman's narrative, was especially dedicated to rehabilitating the male drunkard. Although

AMINA GAUTIER

large numbers of women signed the temperance pledge, female participation in Washingtonian meetings was greatly limited, and women were not allowed to testify publicly at the meetings. Although sentimental fiction and temperance narratives frequently used women to reproach male drunkards for the ways in which their alcohol consumption brought destruction and grief into the household or domestic sphere, women were rarely the focus of redemption in temperance narratives. This is especially true in *Franklin Evans*, where the female inebriates who do appear are not rehabilitated. Evans clearly understands the problem of intemperance as a distinctly male endeavor: "It is a terrible sight, I have often thought sure, to see *young men* beginning their walk upon this fatal journey."[10] In *Franklin Evans* Whitman primarily depicts homosocial relationships among men leading to inebriation. He shows Evans and other white men (first Colby and later Bourne) bonding over alcohol in public spaces, musical drinking halls, saloons, and taverns, forging bonds of friendship and transacting business, and often living to recount the tale and rehabilitate themselves, unlike the women he depicts who drink and die alone.

The status of the African slave was often compared to that of the inebriate and found to be similar. Inebriation, or alcoholism, signaled a loss of agency, the enslavement to one's passions, a weakness and vulnerability indicative of an inability to self-govern. Gretchen Murphy has argued that the frequent conflation of intemperance with slavery "upsets the raced and gendered conventions of domestic antebellum fiction, creating a narrative problem of a figuratively 'enslaved' white male."[11] Dubbing an inebriate a "slave" was a means of symbolizing man's struggle with his desires, his tendency to succumb to his basic instincts rather than practice discipline and willpower, and the negative and destructive results of man's failure to control his body, desires, and passions. It also paved the way for future discourse on addiction. Michael Warner has argued that the temperance movement's evolution represented a shift from a movement in which addiction was first understood as "a legal term describing the performative act of bondage" to one in which addiction came to be discussed as "a metaphor to describe a person's self-relation," thereby virtually inventing the modern notion of addiction.[12] Like the chattel slave, the figuratively enslaved inebriate's liberty is not his own. He is powerless, not in full possession of himself. The drunkard has no self-control; he can master neither his body nor his will.[13] Most typically represented as white and male and, thus, representative of the American body politic and its voting citizenry, the figuratively enslaved inebriate poses a threat to democracy.[14] Historian Thomas Augst has argued that "the drunkard's story taught individuals and communities to govern themselves and one another in new ways, helping to transform an ancient virtue of moderation into a distinctively liberal practice of freedom."[15] Following this logic, one could argue that if the drunkard's addiction could threaten the stability of the nation and render its citizens virtually synonymous with its enslaved population, so too could the drunkard's renunciation of alcohol be understood as a nationally redemptive endeavor. The inebriate's renunciation of alcohol dependency, generally evidenced by the voluntary signing of a temperance pledge, in which he promises either to abstain from consuming hard spirits or to abstain from all alcohol, signals "the drunkard's liberation from his excessive embodiment," which "is not only a passage to manhood, but also a passage from slavery to freedom."[16] Following this line of reasoning, temperance advocates and writers often concluded that "drunkenness was a worse national evil than slavery and that doing away with alcohol would uplift America, Americans and the world."[17]

Later in life, Whitman would excuse his writing of *Franklin Evans*. Ironically, among his disclaimers for writing the "rot of the worst sort," as Whitman would call the novel, was his own inebriation.[18] Although Whitman would later devalue his writing of the temperance novel and excuse it away as something written only for commercial purposes, claiming to have written the text while drunk over a period of "three days of constant work" and only for the "offer of 'cash payment,'" biographer Gay Wilson Allen suggests that Whitman was indeed earnest at the time of his writing.[19] Taking their cue from Whitman, critics have generally followed suit and deemed the text "rot." Among its flaws has been noted the inclusion of tales that seem to have little to no textual synthesis with the rest of the novel, such as the tale of Windfoot, Little Jane, and the temperance dream in which the Last Slave of Appetite is freed. Allen, who describes *Franklin*

AMINA GAUTIER

Evans as "rapidly and certainly carelessly written," suggests that Whitman inserted tales he had previously written to lengthen or pad the story. Allen characterizes the novel as comprised of an "interminable soap opera plot" and a "melodramatic, maudlin story."[20] David S. Reynolds describes Whitman's temperance literature as "long on sensation and short on moralizing" and argues that much of Whitman's novel "has little to do with temperance."[21] Michael Warner suggests that "when he is talking about alcohol in *Franklin Evans*, Whitman often seems to be thinking of something else" and Jerome Loving has deemed the text "a maudlin and superficial drama."[22] Despite the disclaimers and disavowals of Whitman and critics alike, *Franklin Evans* stands as a compelling examination of the manner in which race complicates temperance discourse. Unlike most temperance narratives that simply reiterate the presumed connective similarities between slavery and intemperance, Whitman explores the metaphoric juncture of the two. In *Franklin Evans*, Whitman convenes the literal denotations and the metaphorical connotations of slavery and intemperance in his eponymous protagonist's experiences on a southern plantation.

Franklin Evans begins with its protagonist leaving his Long Island home to make his fortune in the city. There, in New York, Evans accompanies newfound friend Colby into a musical drinking hall, where the two imbibe heavily in what turns out to be Evans's first downward step toward alcoholism. Each of Evans's ensuing interactions drags him further down the spiral, illustrating his increasing loss of control in his battles for self-mastery. As his drinking progresses, Evans neglects his responsibilities, resulting in the loss of employment and the death of his wife, Mary. Evans then turns to criminal activity, which results in his arrest. Following his arrest, Evans signs the temperance pledge and is rehabilitated. Here, after a sequence of improbable and sensational events, the narrative seems to take a pause, suggesting that Evans has suffered the worst effects of intemperance. Intemperance has cost him his livelihood, his love, and his liberty. The respite, however, is but temporary. In the latter portion of the novel, where Evans travels south, also known as the "Creole" episode, Evans experiences what Whitman describes as his worst moments.

Evans's interlude in the South serves as a sobering wake-up call for the protagonist. It brings about the novel's most significant change, causing Evans to repent of his inebriation and renounce alcohol. Despite the chronological brevity of Evans's stay in Virginia, a visit that lasts a mere "four or five weeks," instead of glossing over Evans's brief time in the South, Whitman focuses a disproportionate amount of narrative attention to this section of the novel. Dubbed by Glenn Hendler "the weirdest and most Gothic episode of the novel," the "Creole" episode ushers in a series of improbably linked events that heighten the text's sensationalism and are often overlooked in criticism or simply read as bizarre and unusual.[23] Martin Klammer finds the very inclusion of the "Creole" episode superfluous and unnecessary to *Franklin Evans*.[24] In this portion of the novel, Evans travels to Virginia, befriends a plantation owner, imbibes heavily, marries a slave woman, takes a mistress, engages in a love triangle that results in the deaths of both women, and weathers a plague. Whitman depicts Evans's stint in the South as the nadir of his alcohol-induced experiences. His southward journey, therefore, represents both his literal and his figurative descent, a geographic descent that is also a moral one. Whitman depicts Evans's trip to the South and his marriage to the Creole slave Margaret as the culminating effect of intemperance. The "Creole" episode is the literal and figurative end of the road for Evans's debauchery. Though it may well seem episodic or incongruous, the "Creole" episode reveals the ways in which Whitman's elision of slavery and intemperance is further complicated by Evans's act of miscegenation and his ensuing experimentation in slave trading. The ways in which Evans interacts with the slaves Margaret and her brother Louis and distinguishes himself from them reveal the ultimate failure of the comparison between slavery and intemperance and the emptiness of the rhetoric that would position the two as similar.

Whitman depicts Evans's trip south as his lowest moral point, a time when Evans's "evil genius was in the ascendant" (79). Evans's marriage to Margaret is presented as the climax in a series of progressively worsening drunken follies, a cautionary event that demonstrates the vulnerability to which the drunkard is susceptible. Succumbing to drink leaves the drunkard with impaired judgment and allows the inebriated man to be exploited

AMINA GAUTIER

for intents and purposes other than his own; drunkenness figuratively turns white men into "slaves," depriving them of their humanity, agency, and will. During his first encounter with Margaret, Evans's intoxicated state impairs his judgment to such an extent that he entertains the thought of marrying her. Impressed by her beauty, he objects not to their racial difference but to her slave status, deeming her unsuitable because "her very liberty was owned by another" (82). However, Margaret's "loveliness" and Evans's own attraction to her cannot sufficiently overcome the slave woman's lack of "liberty." Despite his desire, Evans asks, "What had I to do with such as she?" (82). In order to promote the marriage and placate Evans's objections, Bourne (the plantation's owner) removes the impediment of slavery by manumitting Margaret so that the two may marry. After the marriage, Evans recovers from his "lethargy" (83), or inebriation, and regrets his actions, believing his marriage to be the "crowning act of all my drunken vagaries" (82). Excusing his marriage as an act of "drunken rashness" (85), Evans blames his behavior on inebriation and impaired judgment: "There seems to be a kind of strange infatuation, permanently settled over the faculties of those who indulge in strong drink. It is as frequently seen in persons who use wine, as in them that take stronger draughts. The mind becomes *obfusticated*, and loses the power of judging quickly and with correctness. It seems, too, that the unhappy victim of intemperance cannot tell when he commits even the most egregious violations of right; so muddied are his perceptions, and so darkened are all his powers of penetration" (82).

Evans argues that only drunkenness could have prompted him to commit "the most egregious violations" in marrying a slave, but his extreme horror, disgust, and repentance are hyperbolic compared to his other infractions committed while drunk, which include the far more serious charges of robbery and attempted murder. Regarding interracial marriage as worse than criminality, claiming that "a man with his senses about him would never have acted in so absurd a manner" (82), Evans distances himself from the stigma of miscegenation. Opting to deny responsibility for his actions, he displaces the blame onto Margaret, whom he accuses of attempting to "entrap" him (83), an accusation Whitman corroborates.[25] In order to present Evans as a sympathetic victim devoid of blame because he is enslaved by alcohol and manipulated by his wife, Whitman transfers the blame for Evans's marriage and all of the calamities it inspires from Evans to Margaret, whose "heart had still a remnant of the savage" (99). Once Evans has transferred his affection to a visiting widow, he recants his prior assessment of Margaret.[26] Previously depicted as a virtuous heroine full of "loveliness and grace," Margaret is no longer seen by Evans as "a very woman" but is now "devilish" (85).

Margaret's racial ancestry becomes the basis for Whitman's increasingly villainized depictions of her. Initially described as racially ambiguous to the naked eye, with a "complexion just sufficiently removed from clear white" (80), Margaret seems to grow increasingly darker and is later described as identifiably African and "dark and swarthy," in stark contrast to the "wonderfully fair" widow Conway (85).[27] Concomitant with the darkening of her skin is the darkening of her motives for marrying Evans. Margaret initially appears in the text as a chaste and virtuous damsel in distress who rejects the plantation overseer's licentious overtures and who marries Evans out of love. She is soon recast as a strategic seductress who deliberately manipulates Evans, trapping him into marriage in order to further her own goals and bring about her freedom. There is, however, no textual evidence for this imagining on Evans's part and much more textual evidence to suggest that Margaret's nemesis, the sexually mature widow Conway, who is a "woman of the world" with "but one aim, the conquest of hearts" (84), is far more strategically minded and invested in manipulating Evans in order to avenge the humiliation visited upon her cousin, the overseer whom Margaret scorned. Whitman's indemnification of the slave woman justifies Evans's defection and his subsequent affair with the widow.

Whitman's contrast of Evans, the figurative slave, against Margaret, the slave in fact, shows that Evans is ultimately capable of gaining a self-mastery unavailable to Margaret. The criminal acts Evans commits are represented as the results of his enslavement to inebriation; Evans's criminality is temporary rather than inherent and thus forgivable. In contrast, Margaret is depicted as one who is biologically predisposed to criminal behavior and crimes of passion. Whitman ultimately blames Margaret's murder of the widow and her instrumentality in Evans's "ruin" upon

AMINA GAUTIER

the "fire of her race" (80). Convicted and punished for having the heart of a savage, Margaret becomes the vehicle that gives rein to the feelings and emotions Evans would express; she commits acts Evans only imagines. In this way, Margaret's actions unite earlier and seemingly disparate portions of the novel, bringing certain events such as Evans's attempted murder and his fear of pestilence full circle. There is a textual cohesiveness between Evans's and his wife's murderous behaviors. Both Evans, in his earlier attempt to murder his friend Colby, and Margaret, in her murder of the widow Conway, opt for strangulation, thereby textually yoking their two criminal acts together by the manner in which they attempt to kill. Though their methods are similar, husband and wife differ in that Evans's attempt at murder fails and Margaret's attempt succeeds, such that Margaret functions as one who not only stands in as the foil for Evans's baser desires but is eventually made to embody them and is consequently punished for them. Similarly, Margaret's involvement in spreading a plague-like malady across Bourne's plantation brings to life Evans's earlier premonition and fear of contagion by explicitly showing her to be the embodiment of Evans's fears.

In *Franklin Evans* Whitman consistently represents alcohol not only as a form of enslavement but also as a form of contagion, corroding both body and will. After his first drink, Evans compared alcoholism to pestilence: "It would have been better for me had he ushered me amid a pest-house, where some deadly contagion was raging in all its fury" (28). When the pestilence that Evans earlier deemed preferable to inebriation sweeps over Bourne's plantation, Margaret uses its arrival to avenge herself upon her husband's mistress by orchestrating the widow Conway's illness. Margaret has her brother Louis lead the widow to an infected cottage, where she contracts the disease and falls ill. Then, upon news of her impending recovery, Margaret strangles the widow and masks the cause of her death. Shortly afterward, Margaret's brother also succumbs to the epidemic. In addition to drawing parallels between intemperance and slavery, associations between intemperance and pestilence or contagion were frequently drawn by temperance advocates and writers. In their addresses against intemperance, both Humphrey and Beecher conflated intemperance not only with slavery but also with pestilence. Describing intemperance as a pestilent epidemic capable of dismantling a nation, temperance discourse also frequently depicts victims of alcoholism not only as figuratively enslaved but also as diseased and infected. First depicted as bloated, inebriates are then eventually described as wasting away. Just as Whitman convened the metaphorical and literal representations of slavery in Evans's marriage to Margaret, so too does he convene the metaphorical and literal depictions of plague and pestilence in Margaret's person. Whitman attributes the spread of the contagion and its multiple deaths to Margaret's jealousy, which is further evidence of the "savagery" of her race. Whitman's portrayal of Margaret as the embodiment of pestilence suggests that Evans has been contaminated by his act of miscegenation, "infected," as it were, by his relationship with a slave woman.

Whitman's revision of Margaret from heroine to villainess comes at the significant expense of textual continuity and cohesion. In chapters 19 through 21 of *Franklin Evans*, Whitman makes the textual mistake of recounting the widow Conway's death on more than one occasion, thereby effectively killing the same character twice. The two scenes in which her death appears are not presented as continuations of one another. In fact, an entire chapter on an unrelated subject separates the two scenes of her death. The configuration of chapters 19 and 20 prompts readers to assume that the widow died of the epidemic with which she was infected, as chapter 19 ends with the widow's faint after she discovers that she has visited an infected cottage, and chapter 20 begins with her death. Importantly, neither chapter mentions Margaret's instrumentality in the widow's death. Chapter 20 announces that it is "some days after Mrs. Conway's death" (94), yet in chapter 21 Evans begins by asking: "Could it be possible that the widow might escape the fatal effects of her visit to the cottage?" (98), a question that proves unnecessary, since it has already been answered in chapter 20 and is further confirmed by Evans's usage of the word "fatal." Chronologically, at the conclusion of the "Creole" episode, Evans returns north, is reunited with his former benefactors, and signs a temperance pledge, renewing his vow of sobriety. The novel ends with Evans leading a wealthy life after inheriting money. Textually, the "Creole" section concludes, is followed by Evans's temperance dream, and then is

AMINA GAUTIER

returned to once more without explanation, effectively disrupting the narrative's sequencing of events.

Whitman's rekilling of the widow cannot be fully explained by the claim that *Franklin Evans* was rapidly and carelessly written. In order to reiterate Margaret's guilt and villainy, Whitman manipulates the text and returns the reader to a scene he has already concluded.[28] Whitman's return to the "Creole" episode after Evans's temperance dream offers a full and sensational recounting of the widow's death at Margaret's hand. When Whitman returns the reader to the scene, his descriptions of the widow's death in graphic and minute detail heighten the sensationalism of the murder. The widow is not merely killed twice; the second narrative iteration of her death informs the reader of Margaret's guilt and heightens the sensationalism of the "Creole" episode by providing a graphic rendering of the actual murder. The reader is invited to voyeuristically follow the violent struggle between the two women, which, incidentally, never awakens the nearby sleeping Evans. Whitman's return to the widow's death forces the reader to witness her murder and follow along as "her throat is clutched by a pair of tight-working hands" and to watch as "she turns, and struggles, and writhes" until she succumbs to the "deadly fingers" and "her convulsive writhings cease" (101). Deliberately shielding the reader from graphic scenes of illness, Evans initially refuses to describe the widow's bout with the plague out of a desire to forgo sensationalism, deeming the topic not "worthwhile" and finding it beneath him to give "a minute account" of a scene that "few love to look upon, or have pictured for them" (98). Yet Whitman's act of revisiting the scene nevertheless exposes the reader to "a minute account" of a graphic murder, thus violating Evans's earlier dignified refusal. Whitman's revisiting of a scene whose conclusion has already been foretold and confirmed reiterates Margaret's responsibility for the widow's death. Similar to his earlier revisions of Margaret's skin color and denigration of Margaret's positive traits, Whitman revises his description of the widow's death to reinforce Margaret's villainy and reiterate Evans's passive innocence. Inebriation absolves Evans of guilt, robs him of agency, and renders him as passive as "a ship upon the ocean, without her mainmast," so that he is "tossed about by every breeze of chance" (88), while Margaret's behavior is attributed to her African blood and the "fire of her race," which are ironically presented as both cause and excuse for her behavior.

Because Margaret's actions appear to be readily explained by Evans's accusation of jealousy, critics who have turned their attention to Whitman's portrayal of Margaret in the "Creole" episode of *Franklin Evans* rarely examine the part that Evans's own human trafficking plays in provoking his wife's violent responses, and the significance of Evans's slave ownership has been largely left unexplored. Critics have downplayed Louis's status as Evans's slave, often referring to him as a "servant" or "page," preferring instead to focus on the sensationalism of Margaret's murder of the widow Conway and her own subsequent suicide. The result of such readings is that Evans is either exonerated or only partially indicted as "the oblique cause of his wife's death," whereas Margaret is read as a fully culpable opportunist.[29] Margaret's act of murder has been generally interpreted as an act of "jealousy" caused by her status as a woman who has been "spurned."[30] Anne Dalke adopts Evans's stance that Margaret's behavior stems from jealousy and fear: "Margaret is outraged by his behavior, not only because it entails a loss of pleasure for her, but because it challenges as well her new-found freedom from slavery. An ambitious woman, she had exulted in her marriage as a means of rising above her fellow slaves."[31] Klammer makes a similar claim, reading Margaret as a "violently jealous" woman who acts out of a "mad frenzy."[32] Though Hendler, who reads Whitman's inclusion of the "Creole" episode as part of the novel's sensationalism, blames Evans for the death of both wives and mistress, most readings of the "Creole" episode that critically examine Margaret's role in the murder of the widow largely accept Evans's biased assessment of his wife's motivations and guilt at face value, with little to no interrogation of Evans's deliberate attempts to excuse and rationalize his own behavior.

Ignoring the actions that precipitate Margaret's murder of the widow diminishes the complexities of her motivation, thereby making allowances for readings that synch with Evans's biased assessment that Margaret merely displays the savage tendencies of her race. It is not only Evans's abandonment that arouses Margaret's retribution but, more importantly, the gifting of Louis to the widow that elicits her violent response. It is important to re-

AMINA GAUTIER

member that Margaret does not initially seek retribution upon learning that Evans prefers the widow Conway to her. Secure in the legality of their marriage and the knowledge that Evans is "bound to her by indissoluble ties" (85), she opts to keep silent out of "pride" (84) and displays no outward anger, much to Evans's amazement. It is when Evans discloses his intention to give Louis away that Margaret responds with "a kind of stunning sense of surprise, almost incredulity," which is followed by an awakening of all her "fearful propensities" (87). It is Evans's callous act of giving away his brother-in-law more than his adultery that fuels Margaret's desire for revenge. Thus it is an oversight to view Margaret's response as composed only of feminine jealousy. Interpreting her behavior only as that of a woman scorned dismisses the complexity of her actions and distorts the significance of what she is responding to. This dismissal and distortion prevent us from seeing Margaret not merely as an ignored wife but also as a woman and former slave in a precarious position of powerlessness. Though Margaret is a newly freed slave who now enjoys the fruits of freedom, her only relative, her brother, is still enslaved and is subject to Evans's arbitrary and vacillating behavior. In the "four or five weeks" during which Evans resides on the Bourne plantation, Margaret is threatened with rape by an overseer she humiliates, granted a freedom that is denied her brother, discarded as a wife, and then made to witness the transfer of her brother to the relative of a man whose power she narrowly escaped. The widow Conway is not merely Margaret's romantic rival for Evans; she is the overseer's cousin. As such, she is also the potential conduit by which Margaret's brother may be used to exact retribution for Margaret's rejection of the overseer. After all, the widow does not seduce Evans out of love for him but out of familial loyalty in order to avenge the humiliation her overseer cousin suffered at the hands of Margaret and Evans. Though Whitman depicts the slaves who reside on Bourne's plantation as happy, Evans's threat to gift Louis to the widow is also a threat to separate brother and sister, since the widow is merely visiting the plantation in order to see her cousin, the overseer. Presumably, had she and Louis lived, she would have taken him away with her when she left the plantation. Evans's threat palpably extends beyond the romance and jealousy, threatening to disrupt Margaret's family by separating her from her brother Louis and provoking justifiable fears within a woman with limited power to act.

Whitman's use of a southern plantation as the setting for the novel's dramatic action furthers the metaphoric conflation of slavery and intemperance. Though little examined, one of the most significant results of Evans's marriage is its transformation of Evans into a slave owner. Evans's time spent in the South serves as an apprenticeship in slavery during which he imbibes not only Bourne's wine but also his slaveholding principles and beliefs. Evans is no mere observer on the plantation, he becomes an active participant in its running: "My residence and walks about the plantation, made me familiar with all its affairs; and I even took upon myself, at time, the direction of things, as though I were upon my own property. I cannot look upon this period of my life without some satisfaction" (79). Not only does Evans assume a position of authority that seems to lie somewhere between plantation owner and overseer, in Louis he also receives his own slave to free, gift, or retain as he sees fit. During the "four or five short weeks" Evans spends in Virginia, he becomes infected by the system of American chattel slavery and acculturated to the idea of slaveholding, as evidenced by his consequent behavior toward Louis. Bourne's gift of Louis effectively renders Evans a slaveholder. Though presented as a formality, a courtesy to keep Evans from the stigma of having a relative or "connection" (82) who is a slave, Bourne's transfer of Louis to Evans is nevertheless legal, binding, and transformative. The fact that money does not exchange hands between Bourne and Evans does not diminish the significance of the transaction or mute its depiction as a moment of human trafficking wherein Evans receives absolute ownership of Louis and, later, arbitrarily gives him away rather than give him his freedom. The irony of this change in Evans's status is clear; Evans, the inebriate who has been a figurative "slave" to alcohol, is now the master of his own personal slave. The transfer of property that gifts Evans with Louis frees Evans from the stigma of enslaved relatives while simultaneously transforming him into a slaveholder.

Bourne gives Louis to Evans under the assumption that Evans will manumit his brother-in-law or that Louis will enjoy the relative freedom of being a slave in name only. Evans, however,

AMINA GAUTIER

never manumits his wife's brother, and the exact nature of Louis's status becomes a point of contention when the widow Conway requests to have Louis serve as her "page" (87). Though the widow regards Louis as her "page," this euphemistic title romanticizes his true status as chattel and downplays his status as first Evans's and then the widow's slave. Usage of the more ambiguous terms "page" and "servant" in reference to Louis's status erroneously shifts the focus away from the enormity of Evans's transaction, discounts Evans's human trafficking, and downplays Evans's own culpability. Evans never refers to Louis as his brother-in-law, he never thinks of him as a relative or "connection," and he does not view Louis's enslavement to be merely nominal. Because Evans sees no ambiguity in his relationship to Louis, he primarily regards Louis as his property and easily rationalizes the act of slave trading inherent in making a gift out of a human being: "Why should I not do with my own property as I liked, and bestow it as I listed?" (87). Unlike Bourne, who presents Louis as a relative by marriage, Evans regards his brother-in-law in terms of property, reminding himself, "He was mine" (87). He makes a gift of Louis as much as if Louis were a bouquet of flowers or a promise ring in order to prove his romantic devotion to the widow. Evans's dual position of being both a slave's master as well as a figurative "slave" himself (to alcohol) enables him to use Louis as a vehicle to recoup his own agency. In order to free himself from his figurative enslavement, Evans asserts his own agency by giving Louis away. Whitman shows that Evans's own self-mastery is ultimately dependent upon his ownership of Louis, and, thus, his agency can only be fully realized by his act of giving Louis away. Giving Louis away disrupts the metaphoric juncture of slave and inebriate, thereby permanently distinguishing Evans from his wife and her slave "connections" and certifying that his own "liberty" is not "owned by another." Thus Evans's decision to confer Louis onto the widow Conway becomes a recuperative endeavor that symbolizes his own "emancipation" from figurative enslavement.

The narrative portrayal of Evans in an episode in which he travels south, befriends a slave owner, and marries a slave woman appear for cautionary and punitive reasons. Evans's experience in the South proves to be ultimately curative. In Virginia, Evans regains his agency, renounces his "slave" status, and puts himself back on the road to sobriety. Evans, the figurative "slave," proves the inviolability of his body by literally becoming a slave master, an act Whitman implies no chattel slave can accomplish. As Evans himself reminds us, "The drunkard, low as he is, is a *man*. The fine capacities, the noble marks which belong to our race, those glorious qualities which the Great Builder stamped upon his masterpiece of works, are with him still" (56). This manhood, which intemperance ever threatens, is what disrupts the parallel between intemperance and slavery, for the slave, low as he is, is but a slave and not legally a *man*. Though the drunkard may become enslaved to alcohol, he possesses the potential to redeem himself and make a full recovery. Accordingly, the man who gives himself over to alcohol, thus becoming a "slave," will ultimately be "emancipated" when he chooses sobriety. Consequently, abstention and sobriety return Evans to his former state none the worse for wear, while those around him succumb and die. By the novel's end, Evans is no longer a "slave"; he is free. He is a wealthy and productive citizen, no longer a threat to democracy. After a harrowing experience in the South, he has reclaimed his liberty and denounced drinking. Once he returns to New York, he further cements his freedom by signing the temperance pledge of total abstinence, which symbolized "a second, personalized declaration of independence."[33] After having sunk to the lowest forms of debasement, Evans returns to the city, where he inherits his old employer Stephen Lee's fortune and reforms for good.

Although Evans follows many of the steps deemed necessary for self-mastery, he oddly fails to confess his guilt or assume responsibility for initiating the chain of events on Bourne's plantation that led to the deaths of many people. Ironically, Evans consistently fights the very confession, acknowledgment of guilt, and acceptance of blame that characterize the very public Washingtonian temperance experience, whose rhetoric infuses *Franklin Evans*. Rather than mimic his temperance dream, in which his symbolic counterpart, the Last Slave of Appetite, capitulates and confesses, Evans instead disavows his time spent in the South: "Thinking over what had taken place, as I prepared for my journey back to New York, I sometimes fancied I had been in a dream. The events were so strange—and my own conduct, in respect to some of them, so very unreasonable, that I could hardly

AMINA GAUTIER

bring myself to acknowledge their reality" (104). Unlike the inebriates who must stand publicly at a Washingtonian meeting and
recount their stories, cleanse themselves with cathartic tears, and
then, reborn, sign the temperance pledge, symbolizing a visible
renunciation of their old ways, Evans shies away from accept-
ing responsibility for what transpired in Virginia. Displacing the
blame onto others and disavowing the events in the South in a
refusal to "acknowledge their reality," viewing them instead as a
"dream," Evans ultimately manages to dissociate himself from his
actions. Ultimately, then, Evans's earlier premonition has come
true. Contagion did rage on the Bourne plantation, and it was indeed better for Evans to have been amidst it, because he emerged
unscathed, while the debilitating obstacles and seductive tempta-
tions of the South to which he fell prey and that he held responsible for undermining his will (beautiful slave women, seductive
widows and mistresses, and the power of slave ownership) were
all done away with.

In presenting the parallel between slavery and intemperance,
Whitman shows that the similarities go only so far. Although
being an inebriated man may be akin to being a chattel, it is not,
however, one and the same. While the inebriate remains intoxicated, he is certainly enslaved to the serpent in the cup, yet as
soon as he decides to embrace sobriety, he removes the shackles
of his enslavement. He does not need to wait passively for another to manumit him, as does the slave; either his signing of the
temperance pledge and his embrace of sobriety or his mastery
over another may act as a process of manumission. Such agency
is denied the chattel slave, as the two transfers of ownership on
Bourne's plantation make demonstrably clear. Margaret cannot
free herself nor bring about Louis's manumission and freedom.
She can only stand by and watch as Evans transfers ownership
of Louis to the widow Conway. Thus, this gifting of Louis, while
downplayed by critics and softened through the use of romanti-
cized language, is a stark moment wherein Whitman reveals the
juncture where the parallels of intemperance and slavery do not
and cannot meet.

Evans's transfer of Louis is key and complicated. Beginning as
an act Evans commits because he is not strong-willed enough to
deny the widow Conway's request, his act nevertheless becomes

an action Evans takes credit for, defends, and eventually exalts in. It is also here in the "Creole" episode that we see a reversal of Evans's primary complaint. On numerous occasions, Evans has bemoaned the lack of human sympathy and attributed this lack to the main reason for the inebriate's downfall.[34] Evans attributes the absence of human compassion and sympathy to the downward spiral of the inebriate, yet it is his withholding of compassion from Louis and Margaret and his cold indifference to the feelings of his wife that provoke Margaret's attack on the widow. By bringing together these parallels of slavery and intemperance on an actual plantation where the similarities between the two can be fully played out, Whitman presents his audience with an alternative pathway to sobriety that complicates the simple Washingtonian method of the inebriate man breaking his bonds by signing the temperance pledge. Signing the temperance pledge and abstaining becomes but one path to self-mastery, while subjugating another and exerting one's dominance over another person proves to be an equally viable path to self-mastery. For Evans is not only one who is enslaved but also one who is capable of enslaving another, and it is his mastery over Louis, proven when he transfers ownership in an undeniable act of slave trading, that signals his mastery over his own body and self and his freedom from inebriation, enslavement, and ensnarement. By exploring the presumed parallels between intemperance and slavery on a slave plantation, Whitman adapts this familiar trope to show how dissimilar and faulty the comparison actually is.

NOTES

I am grateful to Richard Fusco and Vivian Pollak for their careful readings of this essay and their valuable comments.

1. Michael Warner, "Whitman Drunk," in *Breaking Bounds: Whitman and American Cultural Studies*, ed. Betsy Erkkila and Jay Grossman (New York: Oxford University Press, 1996), 37.

2. Heman Humphrey, *Parallel between Intemperance and the Slave Trade* (Amherst: J. S. and C. Adams, 1828), 1.

3. Ibid., 4, 5, 23, 35.

4. Ibid., 19.

5. Ibid., 6.

6. Lyman Beecher, "Six Sermons on Intemperance" (1826), in *The Radical Reader: A Documentary History of the American Radical Tradition*, ed.

AMINA GAUTIER

Timothy Patrick McCarthy and John McMillian (New York: New Press, 2003), 62.

7. Ibid.

8. Ronald G. Walters, *The Antislavery Appeal: American Abolitionism after 1830* (Baltimore, MD: Johns Hopkins University Press, 1976), 128.

9. Warner provides an alternative reading of the drunkard's flushed skin, associating it with depictions of onanism in reform literature; see "Whitman Drunk."

10. Walt Whitman, *Franklin Evans, or The Inebriate* (1842), ed. Chris Castiglia and Glenn Hendler (Durham, NC: Duke University Press, 2007), 42. Subsequent references to this edition will be cited with page numbers in parentheses in the text.

11. Gretchen Murphy, "Enslaved Bodies: Figurative Slavery in the Temperance Fiction of Harriet Beecher Stowe and Walt Whitman," *Genre* 28 (1995): 96–97. Glenn Hendler, Gretchen Murphy, and Karen Sánchez-Eppler have shown temperance narratives to be complicated by race and gender. Both Hendler and Murphy point to the racialization of the drunkard as evidenced in the progressive darkening of his skin. See Hendler, "Bloated Bodies and Sober Sentiments: Masculinity in 1840s Temperance Narratives," in *Sentimental Men: Masculinity and the Politic of Affect in American Culture*, ed. Mary Chapman and Glenn Hendler (Berkeley: University of California Press, 1999); Sánchez-Eppler, *Touching Liberty: Abolition, Feminism, and the Politics of the Body* (Berkeley: University of California Press, 1993); and Murphy, "Enslaved Bodies." Certainly it is in the "Creole" section of *Franklin Evans* that the racialization of the narrative is fully articulated.

12. Warner, "Whitman Drunk," 32. For more information, see David S. Reynolds, who divides temperance literature into four categories: conventional, dark temperance, ironic, and transcendental ("Black Cats and Delirium Tremens: Temperance and the American Renaissance," in *The Serpent in the Cup: Temperance in American Literature*, ed. David S. Reynolds and Debra J. Rosenthal [Amherst: University of Massachusetts Press, 1997]). Conventional temperance literature was didactic in nature, focusing on the rewards of virtue and avoiding sensationalism. It was followed by dark temperance, which was influenced by the Washingtonian movement and was highly sensational in nature. Dark temperance, which aptly describes Walt Whitman's *Franklin Evans*, "placed new emphasis on the pathological behavior and diseased psychology associated with alcoholism" (ibid., 23). For further reading on the basis and evolution of the temperance movement in the United States, see chapter 6 of Ronald G. Walters, *American Reformers, 1815–1860* (New York: Hill and Wang, 1978), which, in addition to providing the historical evolution of the formation of the temperance movement in nineteenth-century America, summarizes the main arguments of each main

group as well as the cause and effect of the decline of the American Temperance Society, the increasing popularity of the Washington Temperance Society, and, ultimately, the emergence of the Sons of Temperance.

13. As has been noted, women figure in temperance novels as the victims of drunkard husbands, or, when women are depicted as inebriates, they are condemned and consigned to death. No sympathetic friend or husband rehabilitates them. Ian Tyrrell has shown that even Martha Washingtonians, the female branch of the Washingtonian movement, focused mainly on reforming men and not women (*Sobering Up: From Temperance to Prohibition in Antebellum America, 1800–1960* [Westport, CT: Greenwood, 1979], chap. 7). For more information about the gendered implications of the Washingtonian experience meetings, see Hendler, "Bloated Bodies."

14. Jerome Loving, *Walt Whitman: The Song of Himself* (Berkeley: University of California Press, 2000), 70.

15. Thomas Augst, "Temperance, Mass Culture, and the Romance of Experience," *American Literary History* 19, no. 2 (Summer 2007): 298.

16. Hendler, "Bloated Bodies," 133.

17. Walters, *American Reformers*, 129.

18. Gay Wilson Allen, *The Solitary Singer* (New York: New York University Press, 1967), 57.

19. Ibid. In describing Whitman being commissioned to write *Franklin Evans* for print as an octavo newspaper segment, Allen puts Whitman's disclaimers about writing the novel into perspective. Whitman made his disclaimer late in life, at a time when he wanted to distance himself from the narrative, but Allen believes Whitman did not write the text drunk and instead was a sincere temperance man at the time of his writing of *Franklin Evans*.

20. Ibid., 58–59.

21. Reynolds, "Black Cats," 48–49.

22. Warner, "Whitman Drunk," 31; Loving, *Walt Whitman*, 74.

23. Hendler, "Bloated Bodies," 135.

24. Martin Klammer, *Whitman, Slavery, and the Emergence of "Leaves of Grass"* (University Park: Pennsylvania State University Press, 1995), 9. My argument diverges from Klammer's in key ways. Klammer reads the introduction of the "Creole" episode as a place where "the text changes from a conventional temperance novel into another type of conventional antebellum literature, that of the proslavery romance." I find it hard to make this argument, as the most popular proslavery novels, which would make the literature "conventional," would not be written until the 1850s, that is, several years after the publication of *Franklin Evans*. Instead, I do not see the "Creole" episode as a textual change that represents a diversion from the conventional temperance novel. As I have shown, Whitman's conflation of slavery

and temperance in the "Creole" episode is a conventional trope belonging to the temperance novel. Second, I do not read Margaret as a tragic mulatto, as Klammer does, since many of the key elements Klammer describes as necessary to define her as such are missing, such as discovery of her black blood after having been raised white, which, of course, does not apply to Margaret. I also do not read Evans as being proactively instrumental in saving Margaret from the overseer. Since Evans merely intends to come to her aid, but the need for him to do so never arises because Margaret's appeal to her owner, Bourne, is sufficient, I cannot find any textual evidence that depicts Evans as a "rescuing Northerner" who "intercedes on her behalf" (ibid., 16).

25. Evans's claim, of course, is unsubstantiated. Aside from the initial interview between Margaret and Bourne, where Evans first meets her, the two have no other contact prior to their marriage, giving her little opportunity to ensnare him. Further, although Evans claims that he will intercede with Bourne on Margaret's behalf and take her side against Phillips, the overseer, he never actually does so. As Margaret is already a favorite of Bourne's, there is never a need.

26. Leslie Fiedler has also written on Whitman's contrasting of the two women as evidence of the recurring archetypes of the "Dark Lady" and the "Fair Maiden" (*Love and Death in the American Novel* [New York: Criterion Books, 1966], 300–301).

27. In reference to Whitman's darkening of Margaret's skin, Sánchez-Eppler argues that the lengthy treatment of the "Creole" episode in *Franklin Evans* is less about temperance than about Whitman's desire to "represent intoxication itself as an issue of color" (*Touching Liberty*, 58).

28. Although the widow dies in chapter 19, it is not until chapter 21 that Margaret's instrumentality is mentioned.

29. Anne Dalke, "Whitman's Literary Intemperance," *Walt Whitman Quarterly Review* 2, no. 3 (1985): 18.

30. Vivian Pollak, *The Erotic Whitman* (Berkeley: University of California Press, 2000), 51; and Loving, *Walt Whitman*, 75.

31. Dalke, "Whitman's Literary Intemperance," 18–19.

32. Klammer, *Whitman, Slavery*, 7.

33. Augst, "Temperance, Mass Culture," 305.

34. Evans, who has blamed the demise of many drunkards on indifference and lack of human sympathy, nevertheless proves to be quite selfish at the novel's end. Upon his return north, Evans encounters his old friend Colby drunk and begging on the streets. However, neither the sight of Colby's bloated face nor Evans's acknowledgment of the similarities shared between them prompts him to offer help.

Kindred Darkness

Whitman in New Orleans

MATT SANDLER

In early 1848 Walt Whitman traveled by steamboat down the Ohio and Mississippi Rivers to New Orleans, where he had found work as an editor for the *New Orleans Daily Crescent*. He arrived just after the signing of the Treaty of Guadalupe Hidalgo, which ended the Mexican-American War and expanded the southwestern territory of the United States by over half a million square miles. Whitman had recently been fired from the *Brooklyn Daily Eagle* for his support of the Wilmot Proviso, which would have prevented the extension of slavery into the newly acquired frontier. The founders of the *Crescent*, Sam McClure and A. A. Hayes, hired Whitman for his knowledge of northeastern journalism. In the first issue, published on 5 March 1848, they took a risky position that must have appealed to him: they began advertising their editorial perspective as "divested of all party politics." Whitman recalled the moment in his old age:

> Probably the influence most deeply pervading everything at that time through the United States, both in physical facts and in sentiment, was the Mexican War, then just ended. Following a brilliant campaign (in which our troops had march'd to the capital city, Mexico, and taken full possession), we were returning after our victory. From the situation of the country, the city of New Orleans had been our channel and entrepot for everything, going and returning. . . . [N]o one who has never seen the society of a city under similar circumstances can understand what a strange vivacity and rattle were given throughout

by such a situation. I remember the crowds of soldiers, the gay young officers, going or coming, the receipt of important news, the many discussions, the returning wounded, and so on.[1]

Always a booster, Whitman recalls New Orleans's promise as a hub of commerce and military deployment, as well as the public feeling of national triumph. "Divested of all party politics" himself by the time of these reminiscences, he leaves out certain facts: that New Orleans served crucially as an entrepôt for slaves, that sectional conflict over slavery cut deeply into the period's imperialistic fervor, and that his presence in the South paradoxically had been the result of his opposition to the extension of slavery. The poet of American freedom repeatedly revised the story and the meaning of his spring in New Orleans, building layers of ambiguity around his time in what was then the largest slave market in antebellum North America.[2]

Often in his postbellum recollections, Whitman associates New Orleans with sensual indulgence. Answering John Addington Symonds's queries about his homosexuality, Whitman retorted that he had fathered illegitimate children down south:

My life, young manhood, mid-age, times South &c: have all been jolly, bodily, and probably open to criticism—

Tho' always unmarried I have had six children—two are dead—One living southern grandchild, fine boy, who writes me occasionally. Circumstances connected with their benefit and fortune have separated me from intimate relations.

I see I have written with haste & too great effusion—but let it stand.[3]

This decisively silly confession has stirred up endless controversy. Early twentieth-century research attempted to substantiate this claim through what little is known about his trip to New Orleans.[4] More than a few Whitmaniacs hoped weakly to confirm his heterosexuality by substantiating his claims to Symonds via New Orleans. One early commentator, for instance, conjectured that his children's mother was "a French Creole or Spaniard . . . a Southern woman, belonging to some noble family."[5] In the decades that have intervened since this conversation began, historians of racialization have begun to make clear that the Louisiana

Creoles, born out of permissive local attitudes toward *métissage*, only became "white" by a complex process of political, sexual, and cultural assimilation that lasted well into the twentieth century.[6] Emory Holloway, the critic most responsible for most of the early work on this period of Whitman's life, hypothesizes that Whitman's reticence in the above passage stems from the likelihood that his female lover was a "Creole octoroon."[7] In his 1926 study, Holloway reads Whitman's sympathy for prostitutes (throughout *Leaves of Grass*) as inflected by New Orleans culture while carefully pointing out differences between the practice of *plaçage* in New Orleans (where white men kept black or mixed-race women as mistresses in common-law marriages) and more conventionally defined prostitution.

The humorous bluster with which Whitman recalls his "jolly, bodily" spring in the South evaporates when one considers the "circumstances" that might have "separated" the poet from his illegitimate children. Rather than protecting the honor of some noble European woman, Whitman may have been hinting at his patronage of legally circumscribed institutions of interracial mixture like the quadroon balls and plaçage. This specifically southern libertinage depended on the system of slavery. Holloway claimed that "all evidence points to New Orleans as the place where he learned what can be taught by romantic passion" (65). What can we say now about relations between this "romantic passion" and the "strange vivacity" of New Orleans as a site of imperial ambition?

Métissage, and the French and Spanish Louisiana institutions that supported it, paradoxically took on new purpose after the transfer of rule to the United States. Because New Orleans came to prominence after the United States outlawed the African slave trade in 1808, the traffic in slaves there was putatively domestic.[8] The growth of the southern system relied significantly on the sexual reproduction of slavery. The so-called fancy trade of the New Orleans slave market had as much to do with demographic necessity as with the licentiousness of the place as such.[9] Following Edward Brathwaite, historian Gwendolyn Midlo Hall claims that the Afro-Creole culture of Louisiana can be seen "radiating outward from the slave community."[10] The phrase is deliberately abstract, accounting for the myriad ways that an Afro-Creole might find his or her genealogy leading back to slavery. Whitman's view of the historical background of New Orleans sexual culture and of the connections between slavery and Afro-Creole culture was abstract, associative, and Romantic. However, with a poetic sensitivity to the "rattle" of national transformation happening on the streets of late 1840s New Orleans, Whitman heard auguries of an inchoate black America.

The poet's declarations, especially regarding his paternity, are fundamentally dubious, and so the stakes in Whitman's revisions of the New Orleans period are a bit unclear. Eve Kosofsky Sedgwick has argued for the queerness of the lush array of denials and boasts in the letter to Symonds but has also expressed disappointment at the loss it represents for then-emerging gay identity.[11] Whitman's longtime companion Peter Doyle was an Irish southerner, a fact that may have contributed to Whitman's notion of the South as a place of languid sexuality. Arguments have been made that "Once I Pass'd through a Populous City"—a key poem that reworks the New Orleans period—is actually about an affair with a man (the manuscript of the poem has "a man" in place of "a woman" as the person "who passionately clung to me"),[12] and the rhetoric of "romantic passion" that hangs around the New Orleans period does little to foreclose the likelihood of Whitman's homosexuality. One might wonder further whether he slept with a man of some African descent. *Leaves of Grass* certainly contains moments in which Whitman appears to revel in the visual pleasures of black male bodies. However, queer theorists, Sedgwick chief among them, have argued the futility of seeking "proof" of real-life homoerotic acts in pre-twentieth-century textual archives. Tackling this already impossible historical problem on the shaky terrain of the New Orleans racial landscape does not help matters.

Research into Whitman's life and work has begun to deemphasize the importance of the short period he spent in New Orleans in the face of these confusions. Citing "mixed evidence," David S. Reynolds writes: "Any thesis about the supposedly transforming effect of the New Orleans period is suspect."[13] However, the so-called mixed evidence is hard to escape: Reynolds acknowledges that New Orleans expanded Whitman's sympathy for the South, his ideas about American English, and his exposure to black culture. He also agrees with the scholarly consensus that Whitman's self-identification, in an early notebook, as "the poet of slaves and of the masters of slaves" provided the stylistic starting point for the free verse of *Leaves of Grass*.[14] Since Whitman likely wrote this private declaration in the years immediately following his Louisiana journey, it makes sense to reevaluate his experience there in terms of its local black culture. After all, the city offered the largest slave market in the United States and had become home to what Midlo Hall calls "the most Africanized slave culture in the United States."[15]

In what follows I return to the record of Whitman's time in New Orleans. I do not finally establish the race or gender of his hypothetical southern lover(s). I also leave unsettled the questions of Whitman's political attitudes toward slavery or his periodic racism toward people of African descent. Instead, I argue that the "Creole" and "Africanized" cultures of New Orleans informed Whitman's poetics. The two main discoveries of my research are simple enough: Whitman saw the city's famed Mardi Gras festivities and engaged, in some way, with New Orleans voudou. I submit that these two facts are just as important as the nonce possibility of his illegitimate children and the nuances that city may have carved into his antebellum politics. If New Orleans displaced American ideas of race, it did so not only legally and politically but also significantly in the form of syncretic rituals. To tell the story in this way requires returning to Whitman's Romanticism: his secular spirituality, its connection to his ideas of freedom, and the continuity he saw between subjective love and the project of nation building. New Orleans's Carnival and New Orleans's voudou express the uneven processes of assimilation that the city had undergone for almost half a century before Whitman's arrival. New Orleans's status as an entrepôt for the coalescing forms of African diasporic culture forms a crucial part of what Emerson surmised was the "long foreground" of Whitman's formation as a poet.[16] Through New Orleans's stylized performances of mixed faith and "liberated" sexuality, African slaves transformed into African Americans and provided strange possibilities for what would become Whitman's poetics of "merging."

In proposing to rethink the New Orleans period, I take my departure from Jonathan Arac, who has made a case for rethinking

Whitman's language as "creole," emphasizing the poet's international sympathies. Arac points to the comparatively significant presence of foreign words in proportion to local colloquialisms in *Leaves*, ranging from Whitman's occasional use of neologisms like "camerado" to the rare use of words like "trottoir." Arac contends that *Leaves* relies much more often on discursive juxtapositions than on some "autochthonous" American voice. He cites Ralph Waldo Emerson, who called Whitman's poetry "a remarkable mixture of the *Bhagavat-Geeta* and the *New York Herald*."[17] Arac uses the term "creole" in a strictly sociolinguistic sense, meaning a mixed but stable language arising out of colonial encounters and migrations.[18] His choice is polemical and aimed at arguing against the "hypercanonization" of Whitman as the representative of a unified vernacular. Arac does not pay significant attention to the local culture of New Orleans, though his choice is useful for delinking the significance of the New Orleans period from myopic discussions of Whitman's possible offspring. Furthermore, if Whitman's writing is properly "creole," his meditations on people of African descent might extend beyond their role in the drama of antebellum American politics.

In *An American Primer* (1904), Whitman writes what might be called a "proto-creole" theory of national language. He praises the retention of Native American place-names and argues that "the nigger dialect has hints of the future modification of all the words of the English language, for musical purposes, for a native grand opera in America."[19] Whitman associates the euphony of African American English with "the old English instinct for wide open pronunciations—as *yallah* for yellow—*massah* for master."[20] The surprising comparison with the British accent supports Arac's case for Whitman's internationalism. On the other hand, this kind of orthographic dialect never really appears in his poetic language. In his notes for this work, Whitman expands on the passage about black and white "tributaries" to American English, suggesting that they might mix sexually to produce this "native grand opera": "Then we should have two sets of words, male and female as they should be."[21] He figures the pliability of American English pronunciation as a kind of miscegenation. The language of the hypothetical "native grand opera in America"—

a phrase by which Whitman may or may not have meant *Leaves of Grass* itself—should be creole, born out of both cultural and sexual mixture.

Oddly enough, Whitman's most significant use of the word "creole" took place years before his trip to New Orleans. In 1842 Whitman had written a temperance novel entitled *Franklin Evans, or The Inebriate*. The eponymous protagonist, a virtuous young man from the provinces of Long Island, is corrupted by the loose morals of Manhattan. During the years of his greatest dissipation, Evans moves to Virginia and marries a slave, Margaret, whom Whitman describes repeatedly as "creole." He endows Margaret with a stereotypically emotive sensuality: "The fire of her race burnt with all its brightness in her bosom." The young Whitman, like his contemporaries, associated slavery and blackness with sins of the body. Elsewhere, Evans construes himself as the "Last Slave of Appetite."[22] Reynolds has convincingly shown that *Franklin Evans* makes an example of what he calls "immoral reform," insofar as it describes the social ills it seeks to vanquish in richly ambivalent detail, thus implicating the author and the reader in temptation.[23] Thus, it might be said that Whitman was tempted to identify in himself that blackness that he also associated with sin. New Orleans attracted him with its reputation as an American Sodom where he could explore the connections between chattel slavery and overindulgence in physical pleasure. When Whitman was offered the job at the *Crescent*, he must have anticipated experiences that would clarify the moral and political turbulence of his day.

Whitman's first publication in the *Daily Crescent* was a poem entitled "The Mississippi at Midnight," which appeared in the 7 March 1848 issue. The poet narrates a steamboat trip along the river, a "dense black tide" on which the night falls like a "phantom army": "A murky darkness on either side, / and kindred darkness all before us!"[24] Whitman later revised the poem for inclusion in *Collect*, balancing the blackness of night with a didactic message:

But when there comes a voluptuous languor,
Soft the sunshine, silent the air,
Bewitching your craft with safety and sweetness,
Then, young pilot of life, beware.[25]

MATT SANDLER

The "pilot of life" metaphor advertises the ethical freight of the poem, and yet Whitman never quite makes clear the meaning of the "murky darkness." The poem offers a kind of excursus on the moralized color symbolism that American Renaissance authors used to construe racial issues.[26] It recalls the racially and topographically symbolic language of Franklin Evans's self-diagnosis: "The unhappy victim of intemperance cannot tell when he commits even the most egregious violations of right; so muddied are his perceptions, and so darkened are all his powers of penetration."[27] One suspects that the young Whitman had not taken the poem's retrospective warning against the "voluptuous languor" of the subtropics. Franklin Evans certainly did not. One might also more simply say that Whitman's boasts of an illicit paternity hint at a sort of "kindred darkness." In *Leaves of Grass*, Whitman would present the interlocking issues of race, miscegenation, and sensual indulgence as important to the fulfillment of American national promise.

As a much older man writing in *November Boughs* (1888), Whitman admits to partaking of the alcoholic luxuries of southern living and at the same time draws an even more direct connection between the alcoholic aspects of New Orleans decadence and slavery: "About nice drinks, anyhow, my recollection of the 'cobblers' (with strawberries and snow on top of the large tumblers,) and also the exquisite wines, and the perfect and mild French brandy, help the regretful reminiscence of my New Orleans experiences of those days. And what splendid and roomy and leisurely bar-rooms! particularly the grand ones of the St. Charles and St. Louis. Bargains, auctions, appointments, business conferences, &c., were generally held in the spaces or recesses of these bar-rooms."[28] Somehow, he looks back fondly, across forty years of sectional conflict, on a scene whose pleasures were inextricable from slavery. In *Soul by Soul: Life inside the Antebellum Slave Market*, Walter Johnson uncovers an informal "network" that ran from the bars of New Orleans to the "peculiar institution": "Every bartender was a potential broker."[29] The "slavery of appetite" was not just a figure of speech; it was a way of representing the total insinuation of the slave system into every aspect of moral and physical life. Whitman thus saw in New Orleans a luxuriant society that depended completely on and thrived in the grip of slavery. He appreciated New Orleans's apparent lack of northeastern moral fussiness. He had grown suspicious of the dogmatism of the temperance advocates and resisted abolitionism, though he remained antislavery. The city thus acted as a moral experiment in which "romantic passion" was brought to a fevered pitch by the cultures of slavery. Its local practices offered an imaginative resolution of the dynamic of freedom and slavery he had seen differently in New York.

While at the *Crescent*, Whitman wrote a series of urban sketches, a new form that allowed him to capture New Orleans's "strange vivacity" in language.[30] These feuilletons, or "little leaves," as they were known in the French newspapers, also allowed Whitman to avoid the hackwork editorializing that got him into trouble at the *Brooklyn Daily Eagle*. Walter Benjamin suggested that the speculations of the feuilletonist might be thought of as "botanizing on the asphalt," and New Orleans certainly provided Whitman with opportunities for amateur genealogical research.[31] In one sketch, he writes of a mixed-race woman who sells flowers: "[Dusky] Grisette is not a 'blue' by any means, rather a *brune*, or, more prettily, a *brunette*—'but that's not much,' the vermillion of her cheeks shows straight through the veil, and her long glossy hair is *nearly straight*. There are many who affect the *brune* rather than the *blonde*, at least when they wish to purchase a bouquet—and as 'Night shows stars and women in a better light,' they have a pleasant smile and bewitching glance thrown in for the bargain."[32] In *Franklin Evans*, Whitman had described Margaret in similar confusion, "doubtful whether he is gazing on a brunette, or one who has indeed some hue of African blood in her veins."[33] Here Whitman avoids the standard tripartite racial classifications of New Orleans society—he makes no mention of "creoles" or "octoroons," for instance. Instead, he offers "faint clews and indirections," focusing on the woman's "*nearly straight*" hair and the sanguinity of her "vermillion" cheeks.

Whitman further aestheticizes the encounter with Dusky through a complex series of references. The first of these, "but that's not much," is a short misquotation from Shakespeare's *Othello* (3.3.270), specifically, the monologue in which Othello wonders whether his blackness has driven Desdemona to unfaithfulness: "Haply for I am black, / and have not those soft

MATT SANDLER

parts of conversation . . . yet that's not much." Here, Whitman's half-comic inferences about Dusky's race echo the Moor's much more serious deliberations about race and sexuality. Further into the passage, Whitman quotes Lord Byron's *Don Juan* (1819–24): the line "Night shows stars and women in a better light" is taken from Canto 2, in which the main character falls for Haidee, the exotic but innocent daughter of a Greek pirate and slaver. In this case, Whitman borrows from the European tradition to overturn some of the aesthetic prejudice around night and the color black. He suggests that all of this learning is unavailable to Dusky herself—she may be a "brunette," but she is "not a blue," as in "bluestocking," a woman inclined to intellectual pursuits. The sketch is fundamentally and copiously allusive and treats the rich racial complexity of New Orleans life with a kind of winking discretion. Rather than describing Dusky in realistic exactitude, Whitman adds to her mystique, setting her within a dance of literary, cultural, and political references.

Finally, Whitman hints that Dusky's customers have an economic interest in *her* as much as they do in her flowers: "There are many who affect the *bruno* rather than the *blonde*, at least when they wish to purchase a bouquet." He suggests that some of her customers might desire a particular color of flower seller as much as they worry over the color of the flowers. Benjamin claimed that prostitutes appeared in the feuilletons frequently because they form a "dialectical image" embodying "both seller and sold in one" and thus provide a window onto messianic cultural and political possibilities.[34] Whitman points to Dusky's role in the local sexual economy through a series of elevating cultural references. He saw in the mixed-race women of New Orleans a thick network of signification and later realized his difficulty in articulating what they synthesized for him. In conversation with Horace Traubel, Whitman depicted the Creole women as offering predecessors to his own "loafing," claiming that their "habits" are "indolent, yet not lazy as we define laziness North." He goes on to suggest (partly now using Traubel's socialist language) that the Afro-Creole women are "a hard class to comprehend . . . fascinating, magnetic, sexual, ignorant, illiterate: always more than pretty—'pretty' is too weak a word to apply to them."[35] In another of his sketches for the *Crescent*, Whitman would confront a more formal, public incarnation of the messianic politics he saw in the Afro-Creoles.

Near the end of his stay in New Orleans, Whitman went on Maundy Thursday of the Catholic Holy Week, the evening of the Last Supper, to Saint Louis Cathedral in Jackson Square. In reporting the scene, he takes note of its "solemnity" and again finds himself drawn to the beauty of New Orleans's "duskier" female residents: "Our dark-eyed Creole beauties, with their gilt-edged prayer books in their hands, would walk in with an air that seemed to say that beauty was part of religion."[36] This remark has a very specific context. The transition from French and Spanish to considerably more racist American Catholic stewardship stirred up controversy in the Saint Louis Cathedral; through the first half of the nineteenth century, Afro-Creole congregants found it an increasingly inhospitable place to worship.[37] In Armand Lanusse's 1845 anthology of Francophone Afro-Creole poets, *Les cenelles* (The hollyberries), Mirtil-Ferdinand Liotau wrote a poem about the conflict entitled "An Impression":

> Church of Saint-Louis, old temple shrine,
> You are today empty and deserted!
> Those who were entrusted in this world to your care,
> Scorning the needs of the sacred tabernacle,
> Have led the Christian army elsewhere.[38]

Liotau takes a different turn on the doctrinal conflict, figuring the church as "empty" to represent its abandonment of the Afro-Creole flock. The conceit relies on poetic license, since the church remained the center of Catholic worship in the city as Irish immigrants replaced the Afro-Creole congregants. However, the poem also hints at the increasing popularity of voudou and spiritualist practices through the 1840s, which drew worshipers away from the Catholic Church. Liotau's use of the French idiomatic expression *ici bas*, which Regine Latortue and Gleason R. W. Adams translate here as "in this world" but which literally means "down here," has some idiomatic resonances worth remarking both within the Christian tradition and in Creole traditions of African diasporic religion. The related expression *là-bas*, meaning "down there," can connote hell or earthly damnation, as in French symbolist J. K. Huysmann's novel about Satanism entitled *Là-*

MATT SANDLER

Bas (1891). In Haitian *vodou*, the name of the spirit Papa Legba comes out of the homophony between the French *là-bas* and the Yoruban orisha Eshu Elegbara. Papa Legba, in Haitian vodou cosmology, acts as the main liaison between the *loa*, or deities, and humanity; in this office, he is addressed at the beginning and end of most vodou services. His phonemic legibility in the poem suggests that if the "Christian army" has been led "elsewhere," that "elsewhere" has distinctly African diasporic dimensions. The "air" of Whitman's "dark-eyed Creole beauties" thus stirred up energies well beyond their luxuriant sexuality. They stood for an aestheticized Catholicism, an alternative to capitalist conformity, and a political courage inextricable from African diasporic religion. For Whitman, they may also have stood for a new union of body and soul through poetic language.

Contemporary African American writers also saw rich possibilities in the spiritually inflected culture of the Afro-Creole women of New Orleans. Martin Delany, in his novel of black revolution, *Blake, or The Huts of America* (1859–62), depicts a street life sparked with fleeting interracial harmonies: "Here might be seen the fashionable young white lady of French or American extraction, and there the handsome, and frequently beautiful maiden of African origin, mulatto, quadroon, or sterling black, all fondly interchanging civilities, and receiving some memento or keepsake from the hand of an acquaintance. Many lively jests and impressive flings of delicate civility noted the greetings of passersby. Freedom seemed as though for once enshielded by her sacred robes and crowned with cap and wand in hand, to go forth untrammeled through the highways of the town."[39] Surrounded by absolute bondage, the city provided some of its black residents with an extravagant, seemingly metaphysical liberty. Here "freedom" appears as conversational ephemera ("flings of delicate civility"), then becomes a gift ("some memento or keepsake"), and finally emerges as a long-cloistered goddess. Delany defines the freedoms offered by New Orleans in terms of access to relations across racial categories, even though elsewhere in the novel he is careful to note legalistic restraints on black sociability. The image of the goddess casts this freedom in some kind of "pagan" messianism. It has a peculiarly New Orleans context—the goddess recalls the so-called allegorical floats that first appeared in

Carnival parades during the decade before Whitman arrived in New Orleans. The figuration of Liberty as a goddess would also become a centerpiece of the poet's cosmology.

In the *Crescent*, Whitman calls New Orleans "a remarkably free city."[40] Even Delany, one of the most radical black public intellectuals of the nineteenth century, felt this periodic freedom. How could a city that was notorious for its slave markets, in which "free" young black women were forced by necessity into totally dependent romantic relationships, and in which negotiations over chattel could begin anywhere, be "remarkably free"? Here we hit upon an extraordinary contradiction: New Orleans produced both freedom and slavery simultaneously. Throughout the Mississippi Valley, masters terrorized slaves by warning them that they would be "sold down the river." This threat implied the breakup of families and unknown horrors at the hands of harsher masters. Harriet Beecher Stowe and Mark Twain both use this idea of New Orleans as a narrative device in their famous novels of slavery. To be bought by residents of New Orleans, however, meant avoiding plantation labor and sharing in the city's more developed black culture. Readers of *Uncle Tom's Cabin* will recall the idylls of Augustine St. Clare's city mansion as an apotheosis of this idea. Solomon Northrup and William Wells Brown, among others, have mentioned that they preferred slavery in New Orleans to slavery elsewhere.

The slave market remained the fixed point around which the ambiguously momentary epiphanies of freedom circulated in New Orleans. Whitman often witnessed the proceedings of the major slave markets on Exchange Place and in the Saint Louis Hotel, all within blocks of the offices of the *Daily Crescent* on St. Charles Avenue. He chose to represent this scene in *Leaves of Grass*, rather than the free Afro-Creole women in whom he had read so much significance.[41] In "I Sing the Body Electric," he bombastically interpolates the motormouth speech of the slave auctioneers into his grandiose and distinctly northern reformist argument:

A slave at auction!
I help the auctioneer . . . . the sloven does not half know his
    business.

MATT SANDLER

Gentlemen look on this curious creature,
Whatever the bids of the bidders they cannot be high enough
    for him,
For him the globe lay preparing quintillions of years without
    one animal or plant,
For him the revolving cycles truly and steadily rolled.

In that head the allbaffling brain,
In it and below it the making of the attributes of heroes.[42]

Whitman makes of the mode of the auctioneer an appeal to the shared humanity of the audience and the slave. He maintains the auctioneer's proprietary air, assuring his reader that the male slave will be involuntarily displayed for his gaze: "Examine these limbs, red black or white . . . . they are very cunning in tendon and nerve; / They shall be stript that you may see them."[43] Where, in Delany, freedom can only appear in public "enshielded by her sacred robes," in this fiery passage, the slave must be denuded so that his humanity can be made apparent. Whitman accords the anonymous slave the transhistorical implication he often reserves for himself. In "Crossing Brooklyn Ferry," the poet calls his own brain "baffled," like the slave's here.[44]

When Whitman turns his auctioneer persona toward the female slave, he praises her potential genealogy: "A woman at auction, / She too is not only herself . . . . she is the teeming mother of mothers."[45] Whitman fails to make clear whether the woman's "teeming" encompasses the racial amalgamation of which New Orleans life was emblematic; the anxieties that such miscegenation catalyzed across the antebellum political spectrum do not register in Whitman's celebratory poetic argument. According to Arac, we might think of his auctioneering as "creole" because of the discursive juxtapositions it enacts. Here Whitman pits British and northeastern proto-Darwinism against the means-ends rationality of southern chattel slavery. What's more, in spite of all the scientific attention to bodies in "I Sing the Body Electric," Whitman actually borrowed his conceit from Henry Ward Beecher, who in April 1848 staged an "auction" to buy the freedom of two slave girls, Mary and Emily Edmonson.[46] A fellow Brooklynite and, like Whitman, trying to bridge a compromise between antislavery and antiabolition, Beecher addressed his congregation: "Gentlemen, they say she is one of those pray-ing Methodist niggers, who bids? A thousand—fifteen hun-dred—two thousand—twenty-five hundred! Going, going! Last call! *Gone!*"[47] Where Beecher literally "sells" the freedom of the Edmonson girls, Whitman's lyric rendering lays bare the rhetori-cal paradox of an antislavery advocate auctioning a slave. While the preacher worries about salvation, the poet aims at a mixture of political, metaphysical, and biological transcendence. Whit-man's language is more scientific, more careful; the word "nigger" certainly doesn't appear in *Leaves*. However, Beecher described the scene he caused with a favorite word of the poet's, as a "panic of sympathy." And both consider the ramifications of slavery be-yond the life of the individual slave.

Whitman's and Beecher's much-discussed reticence about radical abolitionism frames the strange and ironic combination of protest, collaboration, and identification of the mock slave auction. Both Beecher and Whitman play on regional and eco-nomic divisions within their white audiences, on liberal guilt, and on northern mercantile self-regard. In this effect, they drew on their source material; Johnson argues that the transactions of the slave market defined the entire southern class hierarchy. The pageantry of the slave market served symbolic capital, promising whites access to the leisure, distinction, and luxury of plantation ownership. The process distinguished auctioneers as well—from traders, for instance, who were looked upon with some disdain by planter families.[48] The auctioneers worked on commission and were licensed by the state of Louisiana, which limited their num-bers. Traders, on the other hand, made their money by specula-tion on the market itself, which was seen as less dignified by the more settled planter class. Large audiences ennobled the auction-eers, while the traders operated in the dark recesses of barrooms and hotel parlors. Beecher's and Whitman's personae draw on the professional objectivity of the auctioneer to make space for their ambivalence about abolition. Emerson heard these tones in Whitman's catalog method more generally and qualified his offer of a copy of *Leaves* to Thomas Carlyle: "If you think, as you may, that it is only an auctioneer's inventory of a warehouse, you can light your pipe with it."[49] Even in his sensitivity to the fail-ings of market capitalism, Whitman believed in its potential to

MATT SANDLER

provide freedom.[50] The strange poetic spectacle he puts on here anticipates ongoing historical debates about the relation between capitalism and slavery. By playing the slave auctioneer in a poem about the way the body "balks account," Whitman draws his poetics into dangerous and dialectical complicity with a social system that took brutal account of bodies.

Whitman manages to argue the humanity of slaves and take their inventory at the same time. Former slaves occasionally dwelled on moments of forced complicity with the "peculiar institution" in ways that contrast intriguingly with Whitman's mixture of political attitudes and professional ethics in "I Sing the Body Electric." William Wells Brown in 1853, for instance, gives an account of working in the New Orleans slave pens as a barber. He claims, with cutting ambivalence, that the experience gave him "opportunities, far greater than most slaves, of acquiring knowledge of the different phases of the 'peculiar institution.'" Brown writes: "William had to prepare the old slaves for market. He was ordered to shave off the old men's whiskers, and to pluck out the grey hairs where they were not too numerous; where they were, he coloured them with a preparation of blacking with a blacking brush. After having gone through the blacking process, they looked ten or fifteen years younger. William, though not well skilled in the use of scissors and razor, performed the office of the barber tolerably."[51] Brown abets the cosmetic deceptions of the slave market. Johnson points out that this practice concealed the debilitating aspects of plantation labor, thus buttressing the symbolic capital accrued to slave buyers. Slaves were dressed in fine garments, suggesting the supposed gentility of plantation life, before being stripped. Johnson also argues that slaves were forced to substantiate the conventions of scientific racism; they "were made to demonstrate their saleability by outwardly performing their supposed emotional insensibility and physical vitality."[52] Solomon Northrup, in his account of being sold at the New Orleans market, emphasizes the slavers' interest in his "musical attainments": "We were paraded and made to dance."[53] Indeed, Joseph Roach hypothesizes that the "highly theatrical spectacle" of the slave market marks the birthplace of African American comic and musical performance.[54]

Brown refers to himself in the third person, defusing the carnivalesque drama of slave sales through coldly diagnostic writing. This technique, drawn from the tradition of spiritual autobiography, could not be more removed from Whitman's "barbaric yawp."[55] Bravado has no place in Brown's account and points at the cold rationalism of the traders' tricks. He creates a sense of formal distance different from Whitman's calling the slave auctioneer a "sloven." Where Whitman's slaves are stripped of even their skin, exposing their "tendons," and so on, to make the case for their universal humanity, Brown must add blacking where their blackness has faded. While Whitman tries to expand the temporal scope of the slaves' potential by pointing to their ancestors and descendants, Brown must try to shrink the apparent age and experience of the slaves. However, both Brown and Whitman view the market in totalizing, millennialist terms. Brown sees the trader he works for "amassing a fortune by trading in the bones, blood, and nerves, of God's children."[56] They each approach the politics of slavery with a scientific attention to bodies, divining from physical particularity to cosmological judgment, from the body parts of slaves to their unrecognized infinity. Both marshal a "creole" myriad of discourses—scientific, religious, as well as political—in their rhetorical attacks on slavery.

New Orleans had other, more popular "creole" cultural events that addressed the tensions wrought by the slave market. Early Mardi Gras celebrations expressed interclass resentment between whites through racially charged ritual gestures. Mardi Gras brought New Orleans's license, always rich with racial implications, to fevered pitch before the renunciations of Lent. On Wednesday, 8 March 1848, the *Crescent* ran an unsigned item concerning the previous day's Mardi Gras celebration:

> Yesterday was the famous day for those who wished to see the colors of the rainbow in streets and squares. All the principal avenues were filled with persons dressed in the most grotesque costumes. The "turbaned Moor" had his face indelibly made lily white by a dash of flour thrown by the hand of some inelegant imp who had less brains than wit. . . . The celebration of "Mardi Gras" is very pretty, but throwing flour in the face of a man whose imagination is not flowery is an unpoetic act, and moreover, a diabolical abomination.

MATT SANDLER

In early, "promiscuous" masked processions in New Orleans, packets of flour were among the first "throws," and like many such items, they made talismanic reference to the city's complex racial makeup. The flour ruins the blackface of the "turbaned Moor," a popular costume for white men. New Orleans street celebration displaces dualistic American race relations with Mediterranean characters and Renaissance comedy. Here Whitman saw an act of racial mimicry that would have struck him with more deep cultural-historical dimensions than had the plantation stereotypes of blackface minstrelsy. Roach extrapolates a comparison between New Orleans and Venice inasmuch as both cities acquired reputations as dreamscapes through their bustling ports and markets.[57] He argues that the local cultural practices of New Orleans memorialize the racial violence of transatlantic history. An incident like this acts as "a release of pent-up furies, a publicly enacted dream of escape from race hatred's waking nightmares."[58] Roach reads the city as a spatial unconscious, saturated with the effects of the Middle Passage, in which history cuts enjoyment at every turn. His work offers an apt way of viewing the most climactic moments in Whitman, which so often intensify the present with the spiritual history of generations. The young poet certainly saw Mardi Gras celebrations during his visit—he may even have written the above-cited report—and he could not have avoided the enervations of the scene.[59]

In his auctioneer persona, Whitman combined his awareness of slaves' ancestors with hope for their descendants: "This is not only one man . . . . he is the father of those who shall be fathers in their turns, / In him the start of populous states and rich republics."[60] These lines allude vaguely to the forms of black nationalism that had begun to take root in the Americas much earlier. Whitman knew, of course, of the Haitian revolution, which had made New Orleans strategically less attractive to French imperial ambition and which confirmed fears of slave rebellion throughout the hemisphere.[61] His most explicit imagination of black revolution never made it into *Leaves of Grass*. The 1855 version of the poem that would become "The Sleepers" contains traces of a persona that appears to be an enraged slave, stalking the streets and fantasizing violent revenge on his master for breaking up his family:

Now Lucifer was not dead .... or if he was I am his sorrowful
    terrible heir;
I have been wronged .... I am oppressed .... I hate him that
    oppresses me,
I will either destroy him, or he shall release me.

Damn him! how he does defile me,

. . . .

How he laughs when I look down the bend after the
    steamboat that carries away my woman.[62]

This passage, deleted in the final edition of *Leaves of Grass*,
leaves inchoate the context of slavery. However, in drafts of the
poem, Whitman expanded on this character significantly, following the boat to rescue the slave's family: "I burst the saloon doors
and crash a party of passengers."[63] He draws on the milieu of
antebellum Louisiana, where the specter of slaves stalking the
streets at night intimidated the white population. American ad-
justments made to the *Code Noir* required slaves to return home
before a nightly curfew, and a cannon was fired nightly in the
Place d'Arms to signal its onset. Delany sets the key scenes in
the New Orleans chapters of *Blake* after dark to suggest the danger of such associations. Whitman returns to the "darkness" of
the "Mississippi at Midnight," but now in the persona of a black
man separated from his family by the trade. He imagines himself
interrupting his master's drunken leisure and losing himself in
sadistic punishment: "His very aches are ecstacy."[64]

Whitman works through richer figures for his embodiment of
the slave:

I am a curse: a negro thinks me;
You cannot speak for yourself, negro;
I lend him my own tongue;
I dart like a snake from your mouth.[65]

This passage represents an early and particularly raw moment
in Whitman's career-long project of commingling his own voice
with "many long dumb voices."[66] Indeed, in many respects it
is a much more audacious example than we find in the published verse. Whitman's critics have long associated his voice
with American regional vernaculars like southwestern tall talk

MATT SANDLER

and Bowery b'hoy slang, but this moment indicates that he may have also been influenced by the more cosmopolitan culture of 1840s New Orleans. Roger D. Abrahams, in *The Man-of-Words in the West Indies*, points to "talking broad" as an important social function in Afro-Creole culture. The oratorical occasions of Caribbean life—rites of passage, Carnival, and so on—mix high and low, English and African speech in ritualized argument. He notes that this tradition involved "the use of talk to proclaim the presence of self." Abrahams quotes a British traveler to Antigua, Mrs. Lanigan, whose 1844 account of the phenomenon might have appealed to Whitman: "The negroes were indefatigable talkers, at all times and in all seasons. Whether in joy or in grief, they ever find full employment for that little member, the tongue."[67] In giving voice to slaves, Whitman also gained something for his own voice.

What if Whitman's project of speaking for "long dumb voices" owes something to voodoo spirit possession as well as to William Wordsworth's "Preface to Lyrical Ballads"? The souls of drunks, prostitutes, and slaves bring the poet to his limits; they constitute the ecstatic quality of his verse, and he cries out: "O Christ! My fit is mastering me!"[68] The ritual context of Whitman's "Lucifer" passage is almost certainly New Orleans voodoo; his vocal and bodily metempsychosis in the snake-tongue simile draws unmistakably on the voodoo concept of spirit possession.[69] An organized religion in nineteenth-century New Orleans, voodoo worship centered on Damballah, a deity drawn from Haitian vodou and Dahomeyan cosmology whose signature, or maidservant, is a snake. Robert Farris Thompson writes that the name Damballah plays on the Ki-Kongo word for "sleep," and its Haitian *veve* (an iconic symbol drawn on the floor in powder as a beacon to the *loa*) icon often represents two serpents entwined in romantic embrace around a palm tree.[70] Catholicism acted as a vessel for African diasporic religious practices, and Damballah was associated with Saint Patrick driving the snakes from Ireland and the story of Moses and the brazen serpent. Some interpreters inevitably associated the snake with the incarnation of Satan in the Garden of Eden, especially those who, like Whitman, drew parallels between the vengeance of the slave and that of Lucifer. Zora Neale Hurston notes that in Haitian vodou, Damballah "never does bad work" and that he "guards domestic happiness."[71] Thus, in casting himself through the snake as "the God of revolt," Whitman draws clumsily on a very specific African diasporic religious and political context.[72] Nevertheless, Hurston also reports that Damballah is "the great *source*" of all creation, the oldest spirit in a tradition based on ancestor-worship.[73] When Whitman describes his embodiment of the rebellious slave as "deathless, sorrowful, vast," he is not entirely off the mark.[74]

The presence of long-dead spirits among the living had transformative political implications in the Caribbean. Vodou rituals played an integral role in fomenting the Haitian revolution. C. L. R. James writes that "voodoo was the medium of the conspiracy," citing the incendiary rituals conducted in 1791 by Dutty Boukman, who exhorted his followers to "throw away the symbol of the god of the whites who has so often caused us to weep, and listen to the voice of liberty, which speaks in the hearts of us all."[75] Boukman, whose name means "dirty book man" in Jamaican patois, here mixes Enlightenment and sentimental political tropes with African diasporic spirit possession. Many practitioners of Haitian vodou ended up in Louisiana in the aftermath of the revolution either as the slaves of fugitive plantation owners or as bourgeois free people of color seeking asylum. Whitman might have been sympathetic to the Haitian revolution, to its Hegelian fulfillment of the promise of Enlightenment ideals beyond their contemporary practice. If he felt this way about it, he left no indication. On the other hand, New Orleans voodoo certainly represents an example of what Whitman called, in *Democratic Vistas*, "New World metaphysics."[76]

Contemporary New Orleans newspaper reports of voodoo ceremonies often emphasized a rank hedonism rather than a spiritual doctrine:

> This kind of meeting appears to be rapidly on the increase. . . . Carried on in secret, they bring the slaves into contact with disorderly free negroes and mischievous whites, and the effect cannot be otherwise than to promote discontent, inflame passions, teach them vicious practices, and indispose them to the performance of their duty to their masters. . . . The public may have learned from the [recent] Voudou disclosures what takes

place at such meetings—the mystic ceremonies, wild orgies, dancing, singing, etc. . . . The police should have their attention continually alive to the importance of breaking up such unlawful practices.[77]

The passage displays an awareness of the organization of New Orleans voodoo "practices," their communicability, performativity, teachability, and ability to "promote discontent." Marie Laveau and Doctor John, the most popular practitioners in the mid-nineteenth century, were also canny entrepreneurs, often selling their services and gris-gris at fantastic prices. New Orleans voodoo catalyzed fears of black political organizing and black capitalism, and the occasional participation of whites in its rituals also raised concerns about intemperance and miscegenation. Whitman sought, like the voodoos, to "inaugurate a new religion."[78] His rebellious slave hardly constitutes an organized group; rather, he is a bit like the angry drunken slave who, in Delany's *Blake*, mistakenly gives away the protagonist's plot to start a revolt in New Orleans.[79]

Through the oral and phallic sensuality of the image of the snake tongue, Whitman torques public anxieties about the perceived sexual dangers of voodoo but also works through its intergenerational cosmology. In her fieldwork on New Orleans voodoo, Hurston recorded a curse against "one's enemies" attributed to Marie Laveau by her informant:

Oh Lord, *I pray that their fathers and mothers from their furthest generation will not intercede for them before the great throne*, and the wombs of their women shall not bear fruit except for strangers, and that they shall become extinct; and pray that the children who may come shall be weak of mind and paralyzed of limb, and that they themselves shall curse them in their turn for ever turning the breath of life in their bodies. . . . *I pray that their tongues shall forget how to speak in sweet words, and that it shall be paralyzed*, and that all about them will be desolation, pestilence and death.[80]

The punishments sought in this curse resonate with the genealogical disruptions of slavery; it seeks to wreak vengeance across generations, and it leaves its target mute. Like Hurston's curse, the drafts of "The Sleepers" are not primarily political. In another fragment, Whitman writes of the masters:

> May the genitals that
>   begat them rot
>
> . . . .
> They shall $\overset{\text{not}}{\wedge}$ hide themselves
>   in their graves
> I will pursue them thither
> Out with their [illegible] coffins—
> Out with them from their
>   shrouds![81]

Whitman's "Lucifer" persona avenges the genealogical disruptions of slavery with a kind of *lex talionis*—he disturbs the graves of the master's dead ancestors and "rots" the "genitals" of the living. This eye-for-an-eye justice would affect the history and present of the white slaveholding South. The curse points not to the fecundity of the subtropical South but to its moral decay and violence. It also clearly references the Haitian vodou concept of the "zombie" or "zambi." The confusion that attends Whitman's late-in-life boasts about his "six children" might be thought of as haunted by "Lucifer."

Whitman's decision to excise the slave character from "The Sleepers" represents a loss to American poetry that extends beyond the circumstances of the poem itself. The choice to delete the character meant sacrificing a personal protest against slavery that contrasts with the reasoned objectivity of his ironic embodiment of the slave auctioneer. The poetry he has influenced, by African Americans and everybody else, could certainly have used the elaboration of this fiery voicing. How would Langston Hughes and Sterling Brown, for starters, have responded to the inclusion of these lines? The poetic argument that lies inchoate in the drafts would have provided a substantial addition to the body of Romanticisms (from Hegel and Goethe to Poe and Melville) that comprise the associations between Satanism, modernity, and black rebellion. By not associating the "Lucifer" passage with New Orleans, critics have missed a key connection between Romanticism and African diasporic tradition. The city's stylized and carnivalesque rituals comprise a specifically black contribution to Whitman's poetics. What he saw in the black people of New Orleans was not simply an index of the brutality of slavery but also the birth of a national culture that he could only call his own by reaching a long ways. To borrow again from Martin Delany, he saw a people desperately, angrily, and gracefully catching and throwing the "flings" of freedom and culture.

NOTES

This essay has benefited from the generous attentions of Jonathan Arac, Jacob Rama Berman, Paul Rand Dotson, Ed Folsom, Solimar Otero, Stefanie Sobelle, Courtney Thorsson, and Ivy Wilson.

1. Walt Whitman, *November Boughs*, in *Poetry and Prose*, ed. Justin Kaplan (New York: Library of America, 1982), 1200.

2. Walter Johnson, *Soul by Soul: Life inside the Antebellum Slave Market* (Cambridge, MA: Harvard University Press, 1999), 2.

3. Walt Whitman, *Correspondence*, ed. Edwin Haviland Miller (New York: New York University Press, 1969), 5:73.

4. The key biographies are Henry Bryan Binns, *A Life of Walt Whitman* (London: Methuen and Company, 1905); and Léon Bazalgette, *Walt Whitman: The Man and His Work*, trans. from the French by Ellen FitzGerald (Garden City, NY: Doubleday, Page and Company, 1920). Novelizations of Whitman's life have also focused on this episode with similar intentions; see Grant Overton, *The Answerer* (1921); and John Erskine, *The Start of the Road* (New York: Frederick A. Stokes, 1938).

5. Bazalgette, *Walt Whitman*, 83.

6. See Arnold R. Hirsch and Joseph Logsdon, eds., *Creole New Orleans: Race and Americanization* (Baton Rouge: Louisiana State University Press, 1992).

7. Emory Holloway, *Whitman: An Interpretation in Narrative* (New York: Knopf, 1926), 67.

8. The federal government often failed to prevent smuggling in the region. W. E. B. Du Bois cites naval officers complaining about lax enforcement in the Gulf Coast region through the 1840s. See W. E. B. Du Bois, *Writings: The Suppression of the African Slave Trade* (New York: Library of America, 1987), 162.

9. Johnson, *Soul by Soul*, 113.

10. Gwendolyn Midlo Hall, *Africans in Colonial Louisiana: The Development of Afro-Creole Culture in the Eighteenth Century* (Baton Rouge: Louisiana State University Press, 1995), 158.

11. See Eve Kosofsky Sedgwick, *Between Men: English Literature and Male Homosocial Desire* (New York: Columbia University Press, 1985).

12. See Fredson Bowers, *Whitman's Manuscripts: Leaves of Grass (1860)* (Chicago: University of Chicago Press, 1965), 64–65.

13. David S. Reynolds, *Walt Whitman's America* (New York: Vintage, 1996), 121.

14. Whitman, *Notebooks and Unpublished Prose Manuscripts*, ed. Edward F. Grier (New York: New York University Press, 1984), 1:67. The "Talbot Wilson" notebook has been dated everywhere from 1847 to 1854; more recent scholars tend to prefer the 1850s, thus accommodating the case for the decisiveness of the New Orleans period. For a recent overview of the issues in dating it, see Matt Miller, *Collage of Myself: Walt Whitman and the Making of "Leaves of Grass"* (Lincoln: University of Nebraska Press, 2010), 2–8.

15. Midlo Hall, *Africans in Colonial Louisiana*, 161.

16. From Emerson's famous 21 July 1855 letter to Whitman, in *Poetry and Prose*, 1350.

17. Jonathan Arac, "Whitman and Problems of the Vernacular," in *Breaking Bounds: Whitman and Cultural Studies*, ed. Betsy Erkkila and Jay Grossman (New York: Oxford University Press, 1996), 54.

18. Kirsten Silva Gruesz uses Whitman's trip to New Orleans and the likelihood of his engagement there with the city's international newspapers as a point of departure for a history of the literature of the Americas more broadly ("The Mouth of a New Empire: New Orleans in the Transamerican Print Trade," in *Ambassadors of Culture: The Transamerican Origins of Latino Writing* [Princeton, NJ: Princeton University Press, 2002]).

19. Walt Whitman, *An American Primer* (Boston: Small, Maynard, and Company, 1904), 24–25. Whitman does not acknowledge the existence of African survival words that move American English further toward becoming a proper creole.

20. Ibid., 24.

21. Walt Whitman, *Daybooks and Notebooks*, ed. William White (New York: New York University Press, 1978), 3:748.

22. Walt Whitman, *Franklin Evans, or The Inebriate*, in *Early Poems and Fiction*, ed. Thomas Brasher (New York: New York University Press, 1963), 82, 80, 98. The poet's brother Jeff, who accompanied him on his journey south, writes in a letter to their mother about the licentiousness of New Orleans's denizens: "They never meet a friend but you have to go and drink and such loose habits." He tries to reassure her with an allusion to the young poet's temperance: "You know that Walter is averse to such habits, so you need not be afraid of our taking it" (Whitman, *Correspondence*, 1:31). Throughout the spring of 1848, the *Crescent* reported daily on the progress of the New Orleans Temperance Society. The phrase "slavery of appetite" was popular among antebellum temperance advocates who sought to draw on

MATT SANDLER

the rhetorical power of the abolition movement. I discuss Whitman and the slavery of appetite in my book manuscript "Self-Help Poetics: Genealogies of an American Vernacular."

23. Reynolds, *Walt Whitman's America*, 75.

24. Whitman, "The Mississippi at Midnight," in *Early Poems and Fiction*, 42.

25. Whitman, "The Mississippi at Midnight," in *Poetry and Prose*, 1133–34.

26. See Toni Morrison, *Playing in the Dark: Whiteness and the Literary Imagination* (New York: Vintage, 1992).

27. Whitman, *Franklin Evans*, in *Early Poems and Fiction*, 82.

28. Whitman, *November Boughs*, in *Poetry and Prose*, 1201.

29. Johnson, *Soul by Soul*, 52.

30. Whitman, "New Orleans in 1848," *November Boughs*, in *Poetry and Prose*, 1200.

31. Walter Benjamin, *Writer of Modern Life: Essays on Charles Baudelaire* (Cambridge, MA: Belknap Press, 2006), 68.

32. Walt Whitman, *Uncollected Poetry and Prose*, ed. Emory Holloway (Garden City, NY: Doubleday, Page and Company, 1921), 1:203.

33. Whitman, *Franklin Evans*, in *Poetry and Prose*, 80.

34. Ibid., 41.

35. Horace Traubel, *With Walt Whitman in Camden* (New York: D. Appleton and Company, 1908), 2:283.

36. Whitman, "The Old Cathedral," in *Uncollected Poetry and Prose*, 1:222.

37. Caryn Cossé Bell, *Revolution, Romanticism, and the Afro-Creole Protest Tradition in Louisiana, 1718–1868* (Baton Rouge: Louisiana State University Press, 1997), 65–89.

38. Armand Lanusse, ed., *Les cenelles*, trans. Regine Latortue and Gleason R. W. Adams (Boston: G. K. Hall, 1980), 89.

39. Martin Delany, *Blake, or The Huts of America* (Boston: Beacon Press, 1970), 99.

40. Whitman, "Timothy Goujon, V.O.N.O. (Vender of Oysters in New Orleans)," in *Uncollected Poetry and Prose*, 1:211.

41. This choice can best be read as another revision of the New Orleans experience. The only reference to miscegenation in *Leaves* is the account of the marriage of a "trapper" and a "red girl" in "Song of Myself" (Whitman, *Poetry and Prose*, 35). For a poet so preoccupied with issues of race, genealogy, and sexuality, this is surprising, but it does support my argument that Whitman sought to draw political, religious, and poetic significance from miscegenation more than he sought to confront it.

42. Whitman, "I Sing the Body Electric," in *Poetry and Prose*, 123.

43. Ibid.

44. Whitman, "Crossing Brooklyn Ferry," in *Poetry and Prose*, 312.

45. Whitman, "I Sing the Body Electric," in *Poetry and Prose*, 124.

46. See also Debby Applegate, *The Most Famous Man in America: The Biography of Henry Ward Beecher* (New York: Doubleday, 2006), 225–29, 284–85, 317.

47. William Beecher and Samuel Scoville, *A Biography of Rev. Henry Ward Beecher* (New York: Charles Webster, 1888), 293.

48. Johnson, *Soul by Soul*, 54.

49. Ralph Waldo Emerson and Thomas Carlyle, *Correspondence of Emerson and Carlyle*, ed. Joseph Slater (New York: Columbia University Press, 1964), 509, letter dated 6 May 1856.

50. Mikhail Bakhtin associates the bodily and intellectual freedoms of Renaissance carnival festivities with the emergence of the urban market in ways that are particularly relevant to the New Orleans spectacles like the slave sale and Mardi Gras. He points out that "the billingsgate idiom," the language of the marketplace, "is a two-faced Janus" that inverts "praise and abuse" (*Rabelais and His World* [Bloomington: Indiana University Press, 1984], 165).

51. William Wells Brown, *Clotel, or The President's Daughter*, ed. Robert S. Levine (Boston: Bedford/St. Martin's, 2000), 51, 52.

52. Johnson, *Soul by Soul*, 130.

53. Solomon Northrup, *Twelve Years a Slave* (Auburn: Derby and Miller, 1853), 79–80.

54. Joseph Roach, *Cities of the Dead: Circum-Atlantic Performance* (New York: Columbia University Press, 1996), 211.

55. Whitman, *Leaves of Grass* (1855), in *Poetry and Prose*, 87.

56. Brown, *Clotel*, 50.

57. Roach, *Cities of the Dead*, 179.

58. Ibid., 243.

59. A good portion of the material in the *Crescent*, including pieces Holloway attributed to Whitman in the 1920s, ran without a byline. The author refers elsewhere to Byron, Whitman's reading for the spring of 1848, and takes a visibly northeastern, moralizing tone.

60. Whitman, *Leaves of Grass* (1855), in *Poetry and Prose*, 123.

61. Michel Rolph-Trouillot has argued that the "silences" around the Haitian revolution stem from the inability of Enlightenment philosophy to fully comprehend it (*Silencing the Past: Power and the Production of History* [Boston: Beacon Press, 1995], 70–108). In Whitman, one hears a low murmuring below the silence. He might just as well have been thinking of the various colonization schemes that cropped up among advocates for abolition. New Orleans would have provided an intriguing vantage on such plans, given its proximity to Texas and Central America, two popular poten-

tial sites for such plans in the American imagination (see Floyd J. Miller, *The Search for a Black Nationality: Black Emigration and Colonization, 1787–1863* [Urbana: University of Illinois Press, 1975]).

62. Whitman, "The Sleepers" (1855), in *Poetry and Prose*, 113.

63. Whitman, *Notes and Fragments*, ed. Richard Maurice Bucke (London, ON: privately printed, 1899), 19.

64. Whitman, *Notes and Fragments*, 19.

65. Ibid.

66. Whitman, "Song of Myself," in *Poetry and Prose*, 50.

67. Roger D. Abrahams, *The Man-of-Words in the West Indies: Performance and the Emergence of Creole Culture* (Baltimore, MD: Johns Hopkins University Press, 1983), 29, 28.

68. Whitman, *Leaves of Grass* (1855), in *Poetry and Prose*, 69.

69. In their notes on the poem in the Comprehensive Reader's Edition, Harold Blodgett and Sculley Bradley argue that "The Sleepers" is "the only surrealist American poem of the nineteenth century" (*Leaves of Grass*, Comprehensive Reader's Edition [New York: New York University Press, 1965], 424). Reynolds attributes this phenomenon to Whitman's thorough knowledge of spiritualism (*Walt Whitman's America*, 275–76). I submit that New Orleans voudou is at least as important a context for this passage. For New Orleans voudou under the rubric of spiritualism, see Bell, *Revolution, Romanticism*; and Carolyn Morrow Long, *Spiritual Merchants: Religion, Magic, and Commerce* (Knoxville: University of Tennessee Press, 2001).

70. Robert Farris Thompson, *Flash of the Spirit: African and Afro-American Art and Philosophy* (New York: Vintage, 1983), 177–79.

71. Zora Neale Hurston, *Tell My Horse: Voudou and Life in Haiti and Jamaica* (New York: Harper Perennial, 2008), 118–19.

72. Whitman, *Notes and Fragments*, 19.

73. Hurston, *Tell My Horse*, 119.

74. Whitman, *Notes and Fragments*, 19.

75. C. L. R. James, *The Black Jacobins: Toussaint L'Ouverture and the Santo Domingo Revolution* (New York: Vintage, 1989), 86–87.

76. Whitman, *Democratic Vistas*, in *Poetry and Prose*, 1008.

77. *Daily Picayune*, 31 July 1850, 2, cited in Long, *Spiritual Merchants*, 42.

78. Whitman, "Starting from Paumanok," in *Poetry and Prose*, 180.

79. Delany, *Blake*, 106–7.

80. Zora Neale Hurston, "Hoodoo in America," *Journal of American Folklore* 44, no. 174 (October–December 1931): 337 (emphasis added).

81. Ed Folsom, "Walt Whitman's 'The Sleepers,'" *The Classroom Electric*, accessed 1 January 2012, http://www.classroomelectric.org.

4

Walt Whitman,
James Weldon Johnson,
and the Violent Paradox
of US Progress

CHRISTOPHER FREEBURG

C. L. R. James found himself possessed by Whitman's "craving to mingle with all his fellow-men," his rejection of standardized poetic forms, and his refusal merely to put the modern world in "individual terms." In James's eyes, Whitman bravely faces "the mass of things which dominate modern life."[1] Some of James's important writing on Whitman was published in close proximity to the origination of W. E. B. Du Bois's *Phylon* magazine. In one of the early issues, *Phylon* published an article on Whitman's ideas about racial equality in the United States by Charles Glicksberg called "Whitman and the Negro." While not refuting James's praises about Whitman's verse, Glicksberg focuses on how Whitman nearly neglects the topic of racial inequality. Glicksberg, unlike James, found it remarkable that Whitman missed the opportunity to depict the Negro as "the touchtone of democracy" or to muse on the American Dream deferred as blacks were "kept in bondage, chattel or economic, or discriminated against" without official political redress. Whitman, Glicksberg insists, nowhere explicitly denounced "the evil of racial discrimination and racial intolerance."[2]

Despite Glicksberg's insistence on Whitman's failures to unequivocally denounce racism, Ed Folsom shows that Whitman thought seriously about slavery and racial difference. Additionally, Folsom asserts that Whitman was careful and even strategic about what views he published on blacks and US racism. Whitman, in Folsom's view, wanted to coerce slave masters into recognizing the humanity in slaves and "to voice the subjectivity of slave."[3] Yet neither Folsom's reading of the slave nor James's adoration of Whitman's democratic idealism fully attend to the racial critique Glicksberg emphasizes. Though one can challenge Glicksberg's inability to nuance Whitman's thinking on race by examining published and unpublished works alike, as Folsom's work certainly does, Glicksberg's remarks remain relevant insofar as Whitman's published writing is concerned. To this point, given Whitman's interests in reconciling the most troubling American divisions after the Civil War, why did racialized social inequality fall off his radar entirely? Whether Whitman was an actual racist, ignored racial difference, or thought carefully about racial politics while revising his work, it is important to think broadly about how racial difference figures in Whitman's notion of US postbellum progress. What is more, I submit, it is actually the centrality of race to Whitman's strident commitment to US progress and national unity in postbellum America that encourages us to see connections between him and black writers such as James Weldon Johnson, whose work reflected the nation's turbulent uncertainty, violence, and need for progressive social transformation.[4]

The ongoing crisis of racial violence in the United States after the Civil War, the most violent time in the United States outside of war, was one crisis that Whitman appeared to watch from a distance in his published work. Whitman's absence is striking but also compelling for a comparison with Johnson. It is because of Whitman's deep commitment to national unity and to sociopolitical and historical progress that he actually shares much with black writers such as Johnson, even though Whitman is mum on racial conflict and violence, while Johnson explicitly engages it. What I want to emphasize is Whitman's and Johnson's shared focus on the idealistic fulfillment of US democracy, social equality, and the centrality of race to it, even if their approaches appear to contradict one another.

Racial violence between whites and blacks in the South replaced the regional violence of the Civil War. More importantly, the ever-growing racial conflict in the American themes that

Whitman famously found interesting—life and death, sexuality, the nude body, mutilated bodies, US equality, and the future unification of the nation—were absent from his well-recognized revisions and expansions of *Leaves of Grass*. This absence makes the minute presence of black figures more interesting. In this vein, I want to demonstrate how Whitman's "Ethiopia Saluting the Colors" (1871–72), while bereft of physical violence, points to racial difference as a stagnating obstacle to the movement toward nationalist consensus, a fulfillment of absolute history. Johnson, while certainly driven by political conflict, was also interested in revealing how the historical promises of US democracy could be fulfilled. Just after the turn of the century, Johnson published *The Autobiography of an Ex-Coloured Man* (1912), which contains a famous lynching scene that invokes the question of masculinity, violence, and progress at the heart of Whitman's aesthetics. Johnson was also an accomplished poet with works such as "Fifty Years" and "God's Trombones," which deal with challenges of white supremacy, but they do not capture the bodily mutilation of lynching as *Ex-Coloured Man* does. And it is lynching specifically that Amy Louise Wood and Jacqueline Goldsby find so enmeshed in dramatic scenes of spectatorship in the South and public fantasies in the North after the Civil War and that allows me to think about Whitman and Johnson together.[5]

While it is true that Whitman was complicit with white supremacist attitudes and perhaps felt them deeply, the white supremacy that became more apparent at the end of slavery was part and parcel with the ideological push for national unity that shaped the writing of both Whitman and Johnson. Both Johnson and Whitman, the former facing the brutal tragedies of racial violence and the latter missing them, I argue, are aligned by their commitment to an ideology of US progress as well as a sense of contradiction and even limitation that defines this commitment. Focusing on why racial conflict is an obstacle for both authors, I submit, reveals the paradoxical import of it for both writers. Whitman, in my view, abnegates all violence in his idealistic language of "Passage to India" without dealing with the pressing realities of race and social conflict that compel the bearded poet to want so desperately to move beyond violence. Johnson directly addresses lynching and the dehumanization of blacks that many

CHRISTOPHER FREEBURG

whites in the North deny or ignore, but, like Whitman, his future is also plagued by a sense that progress cannot actually be made without confronting the violence of the present; his protagonists try unsuccessfully to avoid the haunting social effects of racial conflict, and his narrative contains an impasse. Whitman and Johnson appear to absorb contradiction, to convert it into absolute harmony, but I demonstrate here that an impasse remains, that there is movement but no progress—in Whitman's words, a "lingering of the night, indeed just as the dawn appear'd."[6] What ultimately unites Whitman and Johnson is not violence but their mutual and compelling insistence on utilizing the present for progress without realizing that their aesthetic expressions reveal further pressing disturbances that challenge and even thwart their endeavors.

There are several reasons why this type of odd pairing is fruitful. Critics interested in race often discuss the degree to which Whitman reproduced the racist ideas of his day, but this essay uses Whitman's race thinking to create a dialogue with African American writers such as Johnson to recalibrate what they share in the turbulent moments after the Civil War. To this end, I use Johnson's literary expression to transform and even enrich conversations about Whitman's concepts of poetic forms and history. In this vein, this study does not shun racial violence but rather uses it as a vehicle for thinking about how seemingly divergent figures share in seemingly inevitable forces of history.

———

The Civil War broke the United States in two, and the end of the war, which brought the North and South together, did not reconcile the over half-million dead, the troubled economies, and the decades of regional resentment. Walt Whitman's postwar poetry charts a new and more powerful future through its insistence on a national unity. By Whitman's own account, his expression produced the idea of a unified nation.[7] Whitman opens the 1871–72 edition of *Leaves of Grass* with "One's-Self I sing, a simple separate Person; / Yet utter the Democratic, the word En-Masse," celebrating "the need of comrades" moments later and encouraging the unification and collection of democratic individuals with the line "all gather, and all harvest."[8] Whether in masculine or feminine figurations, the mutuality of the individual and the collective as a vessel of the nation remains consistent across Whitman's corpus. While Whitman always emphasizes the chant of the nation/self, after the Civil War new conditions placed different demands on the poet. "Whitman," writes Sandra Gustafson, offers "his poetic persona and lyric voice as means to achieve a more perfect union."[9] But did this "more perfect union" include confronting the interracial conflict in the ailing nation?

Michael Moon advances the idea that in Whitman's *Drum-Taps* (1867) "Whitman strives to come to terms with . . . the catastrophic division by the violence of war."[10] This is not surprising, since Whitman witnessed the effects of mangled and brutalized bodies firsthand when he nursed the ill and wounded and confronted slain soldiers. He dressed soldiers' wounds, wrote as a journal correspondent, and knew a lot about the politics of the southern region.[11] This action, without a doubt, brought him closer to his fellow man, but this closeness was rooted in graphic scenes of postbattle surgeries. These scenes unveil despair, gore, and heroism. Whitman's gift, as James recognized it, was transforming this personal and local scene into a larger vision of the struggle for life and dignity in the face of death.[12] Peter Coviello explains that in *Memoranda during the War* (1876) "Whitman relates without censure the cruelties of both sides, the torture and dismemberment of men, and the ruthlessness with which even the crawling wounded are picked off."[13]

Even more telling, Whitman's speaker in "The Wound-Dresser" (1881–82) depicts an "amputated hand," a "crush'd head," and pictures of the war's carnage. The speaker displays unmatched empathy, honoring the soldier's "priceless blood—'I could not refuse this moment to die for you, if that would save you.'"[14] Whitman endured these violent intimacies and pondered the mortal challenges that ravished individual soldiers. So many of the soldiers were working-class people who revealed the brutal face of a democratic ideal. For Whitman, their bodies make concrete the poetic sense of a pluralistic collectivity. Whitman, no doubt, also challenged himself by such intense moments of identification. Betsy Erkkila explains that Whitman intensified the spiritual idealization that characterizes his revisions throughout *Leaves of Grass*.[15] Yet along with spiritualization, Whitman's poetics simul-

CHRISTOPHER FREEBURG

taneously kept the male body in close view, exulting the aftermath of bloody conflict as a kind of blood sacrifice that ultimately will yield a healed nation.

After the war, Whitman thought hard about its effect on him. He wrote to Horace Traubel: "The War saved me."[16] More specifically, it was the social being of the soldier and suffering in the face of death.[17] Yet the idea of suffering, removed from the actual scenes, contains an interesting relationship between torn male bodies and Whitman's own salvation. The saving power of the war corrects the actual violence, alleviating the traumatic interaction between wound-dresser and soldier and the real effects of the imagination. David S. Reynolds understands this personal realization, articulated to Traubel, as laying a different foundation for Whitman's ideal for national unity. The problem with this idea, Reynolds continues, is that the exemplary national consciousness that the war symbolized for Whitman "was not mirrored in the reality of postbellum America."[18] The postbellum United States was marked by a major transformation and technological developments in industrialization and mass culture. And Whitman, while celebrating these triumphs, as Whitman critics have pointed out, was selectively blind to others.

Hence, while Whitman certainly thought about national reconciliation and what to do with newly freed slaves, he actually mentions blacks less as his published works evolve. Perhaps this postwar absence continues from an important antebellum fact that while "Song of Myself" voices the subjectivity of the slave, no "black person utters a word."[19] This aspect worsens in Whitman's writings during and after Reconstruction. Discussing Whitman's *Memoranda during the War*, Coviello points out that "Whitman dramatically underplays the war's great failure: to secure for all Americans a just and equal freedom."[20] Much like white progressive writers such as Albion Tourgée and George Washington Cable, who addressed the troubling conflicts in the postbellum South, Whitman felt the pressures of the fractured nation and its changing social dynamics.[21] Unlike Tourgée and Cable, who were lauded by many black intellectuals for their courage in addressing the United States' escalating racial problems, Whitman was largely quiet. To this point, black men, having recently acquired the right to vote with the Fifteenth Amendment, were subject to more violent acts at the hands of white mobs. The national media reported on the violent treatment of blacks in both sympathetic and unsympathetic ways.[22] Hence, while Whitman began to emphasize the tragedy of mutilated and injured bodies as part of a Civil War past, black people experienced record numbers of physical injuries at the hands of white mobs.

Folsom depicts Whitman's 1870s verse and prose as filled with "confusion and ambivalence" surrounding the migration of southern blacks north.[23] Erkkila puts it in even starker terms, writing that in a poem such as "Ethiopia Saluting the Colors," the bard's verse actually perpetuated "racial violation."[24] Reconstruction efforts after the war became cantankerous, and the North's efforts to ensure that blacks could fully participate not only failed but became a second site of brutal violence—violence that was ultimately sanctioned by influential whites in the North and South.[25] Abolition won the battle against slavery but lost the war against white supremacy. Erkkila explains that Whitman's racial ideas progressed along similar lines. Before the war he advocated abolition, but this did not mean that he advocated social equality for blacks after the postbellum era.[26]

One could claim that Whitman's remarks about blacks or his reinforcement of white supremacist ideas made him socially complex at best and a racist hypocrite at worst. But in my view, his lack of attention to the major violent conflicts that affected the institutional and local conflict between races and classes in the Reconstruction era is the most striking. That is, Whitman's social acceptance of blacks or lack thereof is far less interesting than the glaring absences of the bodily terror that blacks were experiencing in the form of lynching and other forms of racial violence during Reconstruction and beyond. How did this historical reality, which plagued the nation, escape his personal, historical, and aesthetic sense of salvation?

The postbellum era in the South saw no end to violence. In this vein, Eric Foner depicts the vast diversity of political economy and social life in the South as surprisingly united by one thing: "unchecked racial violence."[27] Many of the violent massacres and contests for power were actually and symbolically against black men, their political influence, and the illusion of their sexual savagery. Actual riots and massacres across the South

CHRISTOPHER FREEBURG

focused on killing and maiming black men, and this destruction increased through the turn of the century. One may find it strange how much Whitman also focused on ideas of male anatomy, "the range and meaning of bodily experience."[28] But when it came to what blacks were experiencing at the hands of whites or to the subject of black experience at all, Whitman did not address one of his signature interests. Given Whitman's concerns during a time of rampant violence against the black male body, I find it odd that Whitman did not address the vast and dynamic changes occurring in race relations between blacks and whites.

Why didn't Whitman address blacks stripped of their clothing, families, literal flesh, and rights? Thematically, this would seem to fit Whitman's most specific interests and his broader determination to speak of a collective but unifying vision. Whitman was well aware of southern attitudes and protest against the specter of black domination. In fact, at one point he thought southern whites deserved this inferior condition early after the Civil War. It is not enough to say that Whitman neglected black experience or shared racist sentiments of white supremacy but rather that critics acknowledge further the severity of the paradox that Whitman's devotion to national progress poses. His desire for nationalized historical perfection in verse after the war might have caused him to lose sight of the role of aesthetic power in the deepest moral and political challenges the United States faced after the Civil War: lynching, and racial massacres against blacks.

What is more, in the closing decades of the nineteenth century, while Whitman continued to revise *Leaves of Grass*, the federal government's protections for freed slaves disintegrated.[29] The federal government loosened its safety precautions to protect blacks from white violence, while white elites tried to maintain social dominance over blacks legally, economically, and socially.[30] It is true, as Judith Stein shows, that portraying the entire post-Reconstruction moment as white domination and black suffering is reductive, and one thing about US progressivism after the Civil War that one should also recognize is the strategic political organization across racial lines.[31] Yet still, bursts of interracial populism in the aftermath of the war made way for a sea of racist violence. In the wake of a contested election in Colfax, Louisiana, a white militia overpowered the armed freedmen and the state militia in an attempt to control the courthouse. The white militia killed over one hundred freedmen and another fifty or more after the blacks had surrendered.[32] Abdul JanMohamed suggests that violence like this contributed to the "culture of death" that defines Jim Crow.[33] JanMohamed's view may be too prescriptive, but at the same time one cannot downplay the effects of violent episodes as an umbrella of racial contest and unrest. Charles Chesnutt captured what southern whites believed to be at stake in his novel *The Marrow of Tradition* (1901). Chesnutt's Captain McBane embodied feelings of white resentment that resulted in the cold violence to which blacks were exposed. McBane says: "All niggers are alike. . . . [T]he only way to prevent them from stealing is to not give them a chance."[34] Chesnutt's novel presented the black community with a few resources but mostly fully exposed them to white violence, burning, torture, and bodily injury.

The cascading violence in the South was defined by lynching. Black bodies, mutilated and destroyed, hanging from trees, saturated the public discourse. In fact, during Reconstruction and at the turn of the century, the number of lynchings surpassed legal executions.[35] Whitman never supported lynching, but, as Glicksberg said, he also never went out on a limb to support the protection of blacks against violence. Also, one does not have to repeat the litany of insulting phrases that Whitman used to refer to blacks or his view that "black domination" was a punishment that the white South deserved for seceding from the Union. Whitman was a racist, and he did subscribe to white supremacist ideas and attitudes. The most interesting of his remarks about blacks is contained in the following realization: "Blacks can never be to me what the whites are. Below all political relations, even the deepest, are still deeper, personal and emotional ones, the whites are my brothers & I love them."[36] When Whitman sang the poetry of the body, was he, despite a glance at the slave, always really thinking about a white master's body or one racial type? It is clear that he sings many selves and mentions blacks, but perhaps this is a perfunctory nod to the abolitionists or progressive whites in *Leaves*.

Still, Whitman never ceases engaging the body in verse, sculpture, and photography. Folsom shows that Whitman embraced the naked body in public and more private aesthetic ways, walk-

CHRISTOPHER FREEBURG

ing around openly nude in front of friends and posing for artists Thomas Eakins and Sidney Morse.[37] Nudity, maleness/femaleness, and the body resonate throughout his poetics, and again, there is no mention of the desecration of black men in civic and public life. Whitman's admitted affinity for white physiology, alongside the absence of blackness, speaks significantly to broader ideas about political unification and the US progress narrative. This is not to say that by excluding blacks from his major poems Whitman never thought about real racial history or the truth. In fact, the opposite is the case. He thought about it, as Folsom and others claim, and in doing so, he chose what he deemed was the best way to represent his vision, America's vision.

But what about when blackness appears in Whitman's verse? "Ethiopia Saluting the Colors" makes an important statement about black racial difference and the political future of the United States. If it is true that Whitman subscribed to Hegel's concept of history and believed that the United States had an ultimate fulfillment of it in the future, the enigmatic black woman in "Ethiopia" reflects a cog in the wheel of progress. Whitman begins with a dusky woman "rising by the roadside here, do you the colors greet?"[38] Surprisingly, after the woman tells the story of her capture and enslavement she silences herself. Whitman writes, "No further does she say, but *lingering all* the day," and this line never gets resolved, as her history and account of past, present, and future remain enigmas to the reader.[39] The "dusky woman" has been read as the future of the Negro, but it is the "Negro" who is central to the moral and political challenges of the American future.[40] The dusky woman intervenes as history itself, not figuring absolute knowledge but a "lingering all." This abstract way of being historical manifests itself materially as well in the woman's appearance and in the presentation of her words. Hence, what constitutes her as an irresolvable figure of impasse, of "lingering," is that her words are distinguished from the rest of the poem because they are italicized. She is even further distinguished, as Ivy Wilson observes, as exotic, wearing a "wooly-white and turban'd head."[41]

What is also interesting is Whitman's repetition of the phrase "hardly human" to depict her. The "hardly human" phrase seems like a direct assault on the woman's humanity and equality, and while I think this is a misreading, it corresponds to what the black woman symbolizes in this context.[42] Considering her import, she represents a time of racialized social conflict that is at once present and pertinent as well as universal for Whitman. The speaker is fascinated by time and mystery and the flow of history that the woman captures. Still, paradoxically, the black identity foregrounds the unanswered question with which Du Bois begins his *Souls of Black Folk* (1903): "How does it feel to be a problem?"[43] Temporality as an idea and the future, more specifically, are problems for the speaker in "Ethiopia," who is fascinated by time, not just by itself but because the speaker wants answers beyond himself that he believes the "dusky woman" may have. The poem, in this sense, gives the impression of stalling and, in this way, the future cannot answer; she and the speaker are mutually compressed into the obstruction of the present. "Ethiopia" opens up the reality of the present that limits the certainty of the future.

Whitman's "Passage to India," on the other hand, celebrates the historical present as the future's guarantee of absolute fulfillment. Henry Nash Smith claimed that this poem effectively made evident Manifest Destiny by proclaiming its completion.[44] Whitman, with his eyes on a literally broken past after the Civil War, imagining the nation in ruins, sees the past as broken and the present as evidence of the potential for a perfected healing. Whitman focuses on imperial pathways and US expansion as healing powers for national divisions. But the Suez Canal and proliferating railroads were very much about the destruction of land and people (labor and dispersion) as well as creation. Still, in Whitman, the former historical violence becomes the necessities of a gradual and harmonious "cosmic unfolding."

My point here is not just a historical one but a thematic and formal one as well. The "teeming gulf," the "sleepers and the shadows" impel the present and empower Whitman's speaker. The locomotives rushing and roaring are not corrupting machines but part of the fluidity of a US-led population fulfilling its absolute historical purpose. But even in this purpose, there is extreme violence. What was, the "Old," is not just passed but destroyed. Whitman finesses the disturbances of Indians, blacks, and laborers from brutal tragedies of modern production along with the "aged fierce enigmas" and "wrecks of skeletons."[45] Whit-

CHRISTOPHER FREEBURG

man appears hopelessly romantic, and I am sympathetic to that romanticism, but his spiritualization of material progress cannot absorb the lingering enigmas such as the black woman in "Ethiopia." In Whitman's professions of cosmic unfolding, he finds a way of constructing a beloved ideology that is certainly historical, but it is one that negates the crude violence this very history also produces. He abstracts violence and death into a grand unfolding.[46]

Interestingly enough, in "Passage" Whitman's romantic strategy also bespeaks its profound challenge to its progressive theme when he writes the "future" as "passage—immediate, passage."[47] In other words, the stark necessity of the imperative for progress and revelation for Whitman actually refers to the frustration of the lingering—of the stagnation expressed in "Ethiopia." So Whitman's imperative for absolute historical, aesthetic, political, and epistemic conglomeration actually reveals a repetition that points to the anxiety of time and political irreconcilability that Whitman decries. He has lost patience with enigmas and the unknown future, the deaths and tragedies of the immediate past, and that desperate declaration demands "*passage*, immediate, *passage*" (emphasis mine). Richard Rorty reads a progressive futurity in Whitman that triumphs over the past, violently if necessary, to ensure that it does not obstruct the future.[48] But while Whitman clearly immersed himself in the quotidian violence of wounded soldiers, mostly white men of the masses, and the gory tragedies of regional war, it is not clear that he had the same patience for violence in the ongoing racial contest during the decades after the Civil War.

If Whitman is in fact operating out of Hegel's influence upon him in both the individual and the world-historical senses, then his strident poetics suppress an important part of the emergence of enlightened consciousness engendered by crises. In Hegel's anecdote about the master and the slave, the subject must face death before he or she can realize freedom.[49] One cannot say that Whitman never faces death in the immediate sense here. Across his poetry he deals with the disintegration of bodies and the symbolic power of death. In the "Prayer of Columbus," which sits next to "Passage," turmoil of the body is central, but in the historical and transformational references in "Passage," Whitman removes ignorance, immobility, violence, and the aspects of social life that disturb progressive movement.

Whitman does not look past what Abraham Lincoln described as the "dead men dangling from the boughs of trees on every roadside."[50] He turned the everyday into an enfolding cosmic possibility without dealing with what James Baldwin calls "the price of the ticket," the dramatic bodily experiences of racial conflict and the effects of postbellum violence.[51] Still, as much as Whitman's verse could not reconcile this drama of the Negro problem, his poetry still reveals its presence as a factor in US progress in both everyday and world-historical, concrete, and abstract images. And in this vein, juxtaposing "Passage" with "Ethiopia" side by side, we see that, symbolically at least, the former suppresses the challenges of progressive transformations that haunt the latter.

Black writers focused on the types of graphic bodies that never made it into Whitman's work. Ida B. Wells's *Southern Horrors* (1892), for instance, shows that the lynch law not only was legal but had spread "its wings across the whole country." Wells writes that vigorous attacks on black families and black men especially were rooted in a fundamental belief that "this is a white man's country and the white man must rule." Northern whites from various ethnic backgrounds and classes excused the violence against blacks as "natural resentment" against the government and as ignorance.[52] It is uncomfortable for many critics to put Whitman in the same camp as those who advocated extreme violence against African Americans, yet it is not such a stretch to see that Whitman understood that whites would feel upset with something as disconcerting as black domination over whites. Violence and lynching, however impeding to US progress, were constitutive parts of it. Johnson depicted lynching as the "overthrow of the state" that was important for what Du Bois envisioned as "pushing onward" beyond "blood-filled paths" to complete enfranchisement of blacks as US citizens.[53] The "blood-filled" path Du Bois recalls is where James Weldon Johnson chooses to end his novel *Ex-Coloured Man*. Arguably the most important chapter in Johnson's novel begins with the narrator's discussion with different members of the American citizenry and their opinions

CHRISTOPHER FREEBURG

of the Negro problem. The chapter ends in a lynching. In the remaining part of this essay, I focus on the idea of black inferiority and whites' beliefs that blacks are behind or stalling progress because they are innately inferior and cannot be improved.

Johnson, like Whitman, sought to intervene in his readers' social and political awareness through verse. Johnson began to publish poetry after the turn of twentieth century, but his search for democratic possibility focused on the challenges of white supremacy and the failure of whites to treat blacks as social equals. While *Ex-Coloured Man* was the launch pad of Johnson's literary career, he flourished as a poet with poems such as "Fifty Years." This poem covers 1863 to 1913, the years of overlap that defined race relations for the twentieth century and that were formative for both Whitman and Johnson. Johnson calls for blacks to muster "Courage! Look out, beyond and see" the future after a past where their loyalty and sacrifice have been neither acknowledged nor appreciated enough to grant them equal civic participation. Johnson also emphasizes "new zeal, new courage, and new pow'rs" while confronting the seemingly intransigent position of blacks as legal and social "outcasts." The necessity of the poem, to protest "the staggering force of brutish might," comes from the feeling of immobility and desperation in what scholars call the nadir of black life in the United States.[54] The poem's historical view actually relies on naming a necessary future, but this future imperative points to what prevents it from occurring, and thus this moment reflects a pining for radical political transformation in the midst of little or no progress. Nothing reveals the failure of progress more than the quizzical sense Johnson expresses in "To America," where he returns to the uncertainty of black humanity, progress, and equality in two questions: "Rising or falling? Men or things?"[55]

In Johnson's poetry and prose, he refutes whites' devout beliefs in their supremacy and that blacks are beasts. The full humanity of blacks is not really a scientific question; instead, it is mostly a political one that concerns blacks convincing whites of their worthiness for democracy. If blacks had equal rights and protections under the law, then the human question would be less relevant. Still, the political problem and the human question mutually define one another, and thus the priority of Johnson is to change whites' "mental attitudes" about black humanity in hopes that that change will improve blacks' political traction.

Crucial to changing whites' attitudes was the production of a unique and authentic black culture. In *Ex-Coloured Man*, the protagonist goes south to learn more about black culture in order to enrich his musical career. After a long discussion with a black physician, the narrator is very impressed with the doctor's depth of knowledge about the Negro question of progress. The doctor ended their conversation by reiterating that the race ought to be judged "by the best it has been able to produce." The protagonist supports the former idea, yet in the previous moment the doctor had looked at some poor blacks and said, "They're not worth digging graves for."[56] The doctor's point concerns how whites see poor and uneducated blacks and stresses that whites should not judge all blacks by the less well-to-do; but Johnson, not the protagonist, points out the hollow elitism of the black physician; his statements about the value of the unsophisticated blacks mirrors the extreme statements that white supremacists express about blacks generally. Johnson shows the hypocrisy and depths of US racial logic even while showcasing the intelligence and other virtues of the black physician. Johnson ultimately proves his point about the "unconscious" effects of race that blacks can reproduce as well as whites.

While talking to an "old soldier and a Texan," the narrator discovers that the Texan's deepest fear is "having niggers over" whites. Negroes won't make good citizens, and "we buy 'em like so many hogs," says the Texan.[57] The Texan's likening blacks to animals reveals the dehumanizing logic Johnson wants to dispute. The protagonist concludes on a hopeful note by claiming that the conversation with the Texan need not appear so bad, since it is the "mental attitude of whites," not the conditions of blacks, that needs to be transformed in order for black progress to continue. This opposition between whites' racist attitudes and the "actual condition of blacks" is problematic because it not only obscures the largesse and complexity of the relationship between black people's conditions and whites' attitudes but also suggests that persuading whites is simply like waving a wand versus the reality of the near-impossible work of social transformation.[58]

CHRISTOPHER FREEBURG

All this is to say that Johnson sees whites' recognition of black equality and humanity as central to US progress, but his presentation of this conversation as one of just talk is apparent, because he ends the chapter with the crushing reality of lynching, which dwarfs the power of the discussion.

Before the lynching event, the protagonist exits the train and then continues to gather material for his work. Seeing the protagonist as an intellectual/artist is also important to Johnson's demonstrations of black social equality. The protagonist collects material for his music, and in doing so he becomes an ethnographer anthropologist, a discipline that, along with sociology, continued to have an increasing influence on the social sciences of the United States and Europe. Johnson intends to show that the protagonist is capable of making scientific observations and that blacks have their own culture that can be observed, collected, and analyzed.

Numerous critics have challenged black writers in this period for relying on the authenticity and exclusivity of black culture to produce an antiracist critique, and there is no escaping this contradiction. But it is not only the fact of having a culture but how the protagonist functions as the middle-class translator of the folk that Johnson emphasizes.[59] This translation occurs most poignantly when the protagonist goes to the "big meeting." The protagonist sees the poetic beauty of what he calls "primitive poetry" that moves the soul. He translates the movements, forms, and refrains of the black performance. The protagonist believes that he can convey the intellectual and spiritual meaning, structure, and pleasure and beauty of the religious meeting. For the benefit of his readers, he discusses a "treasured heritage of the American Negro" in terms of meter and harmony—as opposed to what may appear to whites and well-to-do blacks as "ridiculous" or chaotic, savage or hollow minstrel-like play. Johnson splits the difference by also emphasizing the Americanness of the specifically black religious practice. He does not emphasize God, morals, ethical substance, cultural value, and human ideas; instead, he focuses on the idea and fact of black culture, on understanding it, and on knowing that it is a crucial part of the black race's sense of historical advancement. He is not interested in individual discussions of church leadership, personalities, and economic transactions that also made it possible to service other social and ideological realities of the rural scene.

Although Johnson may be guilty of an overemphasis on rural culture, he certainly does not idealize the South. In fact, for him, the conditions of cultural work are also the conditions of brutal violence. Several moments after the big meeting, the protagonist witnesses the lynching of a nameless black man. The lynching itself and how Johnson depicts it are very important. The speed with which the text moves from the "big meeting" to the lynching suggests that Johnson wants readers to see the events not as separate snapshots but as a unified portrait that contains abundant contradictions.

Just before the protagonist went to bed, he "saw men moving in one direction and from the mutterings we vaguely caught the rumor that some terrible crime had been committed, murder! Rape! I put on my coat and hat." His impression was that there was a "quite orderly manner," yet the antics were passionate and violent at the same time. The protagonist himself feels impotent, "powerless"; the most salient part of this moment is the emphasis on the body: "I was looking at the scorched post, a smoldering fire, blackened bones, charred fragments sifting down through coils of chain, and the smell of burnt flesh—human flesh—was in my nostrils."[60] The protagonist is stalled, and so is all his talk and musing on progress. The way Johnson depicts the lynching crystallizes the social reality of the South: it is "bald, raw, naked." In the lynching, Johnson shows nakedness, violence, and the naked black body, which was not some random event but part of a new order and ritual of an "orderly manner" of the South.

Jacqueline Goldsby explains that lynching was a part of mass culture and technological circulation.[61] Johnson turns to the male body as his culminating image, and it immobilizes him and makes his character live with a melancholic and troubled life passing for white—a life of further immobility. Johnson writes: "Have you ever witnessed the transformation of human beings into savage beasts?" This transformation is twofold: it points to white action, yet it also points to what has to be done for blacks to turn into what whites think of them—"savage beasts."[62] Johnson's novel produces black humanity by also proving that whites treat blacks as less than human. Johnson must insist on black humanity while saying that whites still treat blacks and think of them as beasts.

But the entire novel complicates and even contradicts this. Johnson reiterates the intimacy between blacks and whites in the South—the black nursemaids and white children. In other words, the view that blacks are mistreated and seen as inferior, like an animal or a beast, is more rhetorical than literal. In my view, the beast rhetoric serves to show the intensity of the violence of lynching, though it does obscure the imperfect and racist but still very human interaction that occurs between races throughout the novel. Henceforth, the human question that violence against the black body provokes does not pertain to the everyday relations between blacks and whites but rather serves the political rhetoric of social equality and progress.

Johnson makes this point most succinctly when he makes the distinction between the "Negro race" and the "individual": "Southern white people despise the Negro as race, and will do nothing to aid in his elevation as such; but for certain individuals they have a strong affection, and are helpful to them in many ways. With these individual members of the race they live on terms of the greatest intimacy; they entrust to them their children, their family treasures and their family secrets; in trouble they often go to them for comfort and counsel; in sickness they often rely upon their care."[63] Johnson drops the racial designation when he uses the word "individual." He encourages readers to see both the Negro and the individual in the intimacy of interracial interaction, in which the political bipolarity of racist and antiracist critique often does not fit.

Thus, it is not that whites actually think of Negroes as inhuman but that Johnson's rhetoric of sociopolitical redress needs blacks to be conceived of as inhuman in order to chart the path toward humanity and full political inclusion. Additionally, Johnson's novel deems human social equality and progress as part of changing white attitudes on race, yet this is a gap between rhetoric and social practice that Johnson obscures. Demonstrating that whites think blacks are inhuman fulfills a strategy, but it hides or demurs the kinds of interactions between whites and blacks to which Johnson alludes but that he does not detail. Johnson wants to have it both ways. He wants to assert progress and possibility, yet he depicts the inhumanity and abuses that blacks are subject to as an unrelenting and indefatigable part of white supremacy. Johnson reaffirms the potentiality of progress, yet at the same time he displays what looks like its impossibility.

What I want to reiterate about putting together Johnson and Whitman is the cultural force of the ideological narrative of US progress. Johnson and Whitman both knew that people, for various reasons, wanted the United States to succeed in achieving its promise of social equality. I think Whitman believed, as many did in what Ernest Tuveson named "the redeemer nation," that the pitfalls of racism would end in the coming redemptive harmony even as the nation presently faced dramatic violence and social conflict.[64] Johnson, however, was faced with the immediate challenge of the utter denial of black social inequality and the rise of the Klan. Whitman and Johnson both saw race as a pressing concern, but Whitman, with a privileged sense of distance, felt comfortable enough to wait on the spirit of history, while Johnson saw history running over blacks. It is remarkable still that racial difference, the male body, the phallus, and violence were a part of both figures' published and unpublished thinking and writing, and yet their approaches and content appear to be so different. But despite this difference and their thematic similarities, they both drew upon the concept of human development and social transformation, even though these ideas are fraught with contradictions and a paralysis that made the prospects of fruition doubtful, even impossible.

NOTES

1. C. L. R. James, *American Civilization* (Cambridge, MA: Blackwell, 1993), 58, 66, 63.

2. Charles I. Glicksberg, "Whitman and the Negro," *Phylon* 9, no. 4 (1948): 331, 326.

3. Ed Folsom, "Lucifer and Ethiopia: Whitman, Race, and Poetics before the Civil War and After," in *A Historical Guide to Walt Whitman*, ed. David S. Reynolds (New York: Oxford University Press, 2000), 46–47, 52.

4. Peter Coviello discusses racial solidarity in Whitman's antebellum poetry. For Coviello, race is fundamental to the "secret tissue of relatedness" (*Intimacy in America: Dreams of Affiliation in Antebellum Literature* [Minneapolis: University of Minnesota Press, 2005], 141).

CHRISTOPHER FREEBURG

5. See Amy Louise Wood, *Lynching and Spectacle: Witnessing Racial Violence in America 1890–1940* (Chapel Hill: University of North Carolina Press, 2009); Jacqueline Goldsby, *A Spectacular Secret: Lynching in American Life and Literature* (Chicago: University of Chicago Press, 2005).

6. Walt Whitman, *Leaves of Grass* (Washington, DC, 1871–72), reproduced in *The Walt Whitman Archive*, ed. Ed Folsom and Kenneth M. Price, 280, http://www.whitmanarchive.org/works.

7. Coviello, *Intimacy in America*, xxx.

8. Whitman, *Leaves of Grass* (1871–72), 1, 6, 93.

9. Sandra Gustafson, *Imagining Deliberative Democracy in the Early Republic* (Chicago: University of Chicago Press, 2011), 29.

10. Michael Moon, *Disseminating Whitman: Revision and Corporeality in "Leaves of Grass"* (Cambridge, MA: Harvard University Press, 1991), 177.

11. David S. Reynolds, *Walt Whitman* (New York: Oxford University Press, 2004), 128.

12. James, *American Civilization*, 58.

13. Peter Coviello, introduction to Walt Whitman, *Memoranda during the War*, ed. Peter Coviello (New York: Oxford University Press, 2006), xlvi.

14. Walt Whitman, *Leaves of Grass* (Boston: James R. Osgood and Company, 1881–82), reproduced in Folsom and Price, *The Walt Whitman Archive*, 243.

15. Betsy Erkkila, *Whitman the Political Poet* (New York: Oxford University Press, 1989), 273.

16. Quoted in Reynolds, *Walt Whitman*, 125.

17. Ibid., 127.

18. Ibid., 133.

19. Michael Gilmore, *The War on Words: Slavery, Race, and Free Speech in American Literature* (Chicago: University of Chicago Press, 2010), 154.

20. Coviello, introduction, xlix.

21. Black writers and thinkers praised Tourgée's fictional works such as *A Fool's Errand* (1879) and *Bricks without Straw* (1880). Tourgée was often mentioned in the company of Harriet Beecher Stowe.

22. Douglas A. Blackmon, *Slavery by Another Name: The Re-enslavement of Black Americans from the Civil War to World War II* (New York: Doubleday, 2008), 244; Khalil Gibran Muhammed, *Condemnation of Blackness: Race, Crime, and the Making of Modern America* (Cambridge, MA: Harvard University Press, 2010), 116.

23. Folsom, "Lucifer and Ethiopia," 83.

24. Erkkila, *Whitman the Political Poet*, 242.

25. Philip A. Klinkner and Rogers M. Smith, *Unsteady March: The Rise and Decline of Racial Equality in America* (Chicago: University of Chicago Press, 1995), 74.

26. Erkkila, *Whitman the Political Poet*, 246; see also Coviello, introduction, xlix.

27. Eric Foner, *Reconstruction: America's Unfinished Revolution* (New York: Harper and Row, 1988), 119.

28. Moon, *Disseminating Whitman*, 173.

29. Ibid.

30. Ibid.

31. Judith Stein, "Of Booker T. Washington and Others: Political Economy of Racism in the United States," *Science and Society* 38 (Winter 1974): 422–63.

32. Lee Anna Keith, *The Colfax Massacre: The Untold Story of Black Power, White Terror, and the Death of Reconstruction* (New York: Oxford University Press, 2008), xi.

33. Abdul JanMohamed, *The Death-Bound Subject: Richard Wright and the Archaeology of Death* (Durham, NC: Duke University Press, 2005).

34. Charles Chesnutt, *Charles Chesnutt: Stories, Novels, and Essays* (New York: Library of America, 2002), 605; Bryan Wagner, "Charles Chesnutt and the Epistemology of Racial Violence," *American Literature* 73, no. 2 (June 2001): 311–37.

35. Klinkner and Smith, *Unsteady March*, 90–91.

36. Walt Whitman, *Notebooks and Unpublished Prose Manuscripts*, ed. Edward F. Grier (New York: New York University Press, 1984), 2160.

37. Ed Folsom, "Whitman's Calamus Photographs," in *Breaking Bounds: Whitman and American Cultural Studies*, ed. Betsy Erkkila and Jay Grossman (New York: Oxford University Press, 1996), 213.

38. Whitman, *Leaves of Grass* (1871–72), 357.

39. Ibid., 358.

40. Aldon Lynn Nielsen, *Reading Race: White American Poets and the Racial Discourse of the Twentieth Century* (Athens: University of Georgia Press, 1988), 15–16.

41. Whitman, *Drum-Taps*, in *Leaves of Grass* (1881–82), 249; Ivy G. Wilson, *Specters of Democracy: Blackness and the Aesthetics of Politics in the Antebellum U.S.* (New York: Oxford University Press, 2011), 95.

42. Erkkila and Vivian Pollak, among others, claim that Whitman's verse dehumanizes the dusky woman in "Ethiopia." See Erkkila, *Whitman the Political Poet*, 241–42; Vivian R. Pollak, "In Loftiest Spheres: Whitman's Visionary Feminism," in Erkkila and Grossman, *Breaking Bounds*, 95–96.

43. W. E. B. Du Bois, *The Souls of Black Folk*, in *W. E. B. Du Bois: Writings*, ed. Nathan Huggins (New York: Library of America, 1986), 363.

44. Henry Nash Smith, *Virgin Land: The American West as Symbol and Myth* (Cambridge, MA: Harvard University Press, 1950), 79–80.

45. Whitman, "Passage to India," in *Leaves of Grass* (1881–82), 322.

46. Karen Sánchez-Eppler discusses Whitman's ability to absorb racialized sexual conflict and division in *Leaves of Grass*. See *Touching Liberty: Abolition, Feminism, and the Politics of the Body* (Berkeley: University of California Press, 1993), 82.

47. Whitman, *Leaves of Grass* (1871–72), 15.

48. Richard Rorty, *Achieving Our Country: Leftist Thought in Twentieth-Century America* (Cambridge, MA: Harvard University Press, 1997), 25.

49. G. W. F. Hegel, *Phenomenology of the Spirit*, trans. A. V. Miller (New York: Oxford University Press, 1977), 117.

50. Abraham Lincoln, "Address before Young Men's Lyceum of Springfield," in *Abraham Lincoln: The Complete Works*, ed. John G. Nicolay and John Hay (New York: Century Company Press, 1894), 10.

51. James Baldwin, *The Price of the Ticket: Collected Nonfiction 1948–1985* (New York: St. Martin's Press, 1985).

52. Ida B. Wells, *Southern Horrors and Other Writings: The Anti-lynching Campaign of Ida B. Wells, 1892–1900*, ed. Jacqueline Jones Royster (Boston: St. Martin's Press, 1997), 60–61.

53. James Weldon Johnson, "Lynching—America's National Disgrace," in *James Weldon Johnson: Writings* (New York: Library of America, 2004), 727; W. E. B. Du Bois, "The Criteria for Negro Art," in *W. E. B. Du Bois: Writings*, ed. Nathan Huggins (New York: Library of America, 1986), 993.

54. James Weldon Johnson, "Fifty Years," in *Writings*, 814, 815.

55. James Weldon Johnson, "To America," in *Writings*, 816.

56. James Weldon Johnson, *Autobiography of an Ex-Coloured Man*, in *Writings*, 94, 100.

57. Ibid., 97.

58. Ibid., 101.

59. Kenneth Warren, "Troubled Black Humanity in *The Souls of Black Folk* and *The Autobiography of an Ex-Coloured Man*," in *The Cambridge Companion to American Realism and Naturalism* (New York: Cambridge University Press, 1995), 273–74.

60. Johnson, *Autobiography*, 113.

61. Goldsby, *A Spectacular Secret*, 25.

62. Johnson, *Autobiography*, 113.

63. Ibid., 104.

64. Ernest Tuveson, *Redeemer Nation: The Idea of America's Millennial Role* (Chicago: University of Chicago Press, 1968).

5

Postwar America, Again

IVY G. WILSON

Today in the "cold war" the picture of America which is being
presented to the world by the rulers of America is Whitman's picture.
Free individuals, free enterprise, science, industry, Democracy—that is
the Voice of America and this at a time when every thinking mind in
America is pondering over the outcome of precisely what these terms
signify for American and human civilization. The very attempt to
represent these as ideals for the whole world is no more an extension
of Whitman's *Salut au Monde* and *Passage to India*.

C. L. R. JAMES, *American Civilization*

In the wake of World War II, the Trinidadian intellectual
C. L. R. James and the African American writer Ralph Ellison
both turned to Walt Whitman in their respective examinations of
the meanings of the United States. In James's manuscript "Notes
on American Civilisation" (1950), he finds in Whitman's attempt
to "contain the multitudes" a larger crisis of how the two most
dominant world systems at the advent of the Cold War—Soviet-
style Communism and US laissez-faire capitalism—engaged the
notion of the "masses" to organize their respective polities. Ellison, writing in the same period, invokes the "Calamus" section of
Leaves of Grass in his epic novel *Invisible Man* (1952) to critique
the false pleasures of the poetics of an integrated America when
no corollary equivalency can be located in the politics of an interracial America.

The examinations undertaken by James and Ellison trace the
broader cultural maneuvers in the first half of the century that
were consolidating the United States specifically as "America,"

making them seemingly one and the same, and much of the work underwritten by this consolidation necessitated the establishing of a literary field discernible as classic literature. Critics like Van Wyck Brooks, Lewis Mumford, Newton Arvin, and especially F. O. Matthiessen all wrote monographs on key figures of what is now known as the "American Renaissance." And all of them, in exalting the pursuits of Ralph Waldo Emerson, Henry David Thoreau, Nathaniel Hawthorne, Herman Melville, and Whitman to write about the nineteenth-century foundations that undergirded an ostensible twentieth-century US democracy, evaded questions of blackness and racial formation by circumventing the traces of nineteenth-century chattel slavery and its residues in the twentieth century. In his phase as a Marxist-Leninist, James too shies away from deep reflections of race in "Notes on American Civilisation" (later to be published in 1993 as *American Civilization*), hewing instead to issues related to the particular US dialectic of individualism and collectivism that masked itself under the banner of liberal democracy. While James envisioned Whitman being more akin to the English Romantic poets, Ellison placed him in much the same lineage as did Brooks, Mumford, Arvin, and Matthiessen. But whereas they evaded the black presence in their studies of American literature, Ellison saw this presence as genetic to it, engendering the nation's cultural matrix and political maturation.

Much has been written about Ellison's own position in the genealogy of African American male writers, most notably as a node in the arc between Richard Wright and James Baldwin, as well as his relationship with white contemporaries, including Robert Penn Warren, Saul Bellow, and Norman Mailer, but appreciably less attention has been dedicated to analyzing Ellison's interpretation of the classic writers from the nineteenth-century United States. If Ellison's invocations of Melville and Whitman are primarily elliptical in *Invisible Man*, his nonfiction prose offers more explicit statements on his reception of nineteenth-century Anglo-American writers and, significantly, the mutual influence of blacks and whites in the creation of American culture. While Ed Folsom has correlated Whitman and Langston Hughes by examining their respective work on the edge of two national battles—the Civil War and the civil rights movement—

this essay stages Whitman as a central figure in the making of Ellison as a postwar writer and critic, with particular emphasis on the immediate aftermath of World War II.[1] In taking up the affinities as well as the divergences of their thoughts on language and culture, this essay focuses less on what Whitman's writings reveal about the nineteenth-century United States and more on what Ellison's engagement with Whitman divulges about the politics of his own cultural project, a project that could not yet announce "America" and "democracy" as convertible terms.

"It Would Be Many Years before I Was to Learn of My Father's Hope That I Would Become a Poet": Ellison and the Politics of Vernacular Style

If Ellison finds in Twain and Faulkner exemplary novelists, no less for their stylistic techniques than for how the African American presence instantiates the larger meanings of their most important fiction, he shares with Whitman the poet's preoccupation with language. Ellison's concern with language is twofold. On the one hand, from an anthropological perspective, Ellison understands language as an amalgam of cultures and, significantly, as one of the key sites where the contributions of African Americans can be readily discerned. On the other hand, from a sociological perspective, Ellison limns in language the promise of a national cohesion or bond engendered by a lingua franca that is underwritten by a number of idioms.[2] Underlying Ellison's view of language is his painful awareness of the perversities of US racial formation that place black and white Americans in ever closer proximity through the domains of culture (especially music and language) but continually segregated in the domain of formal politics.

In their estimation of the vernacular and the idiomatic, both Whitman and Ellison accentuate the modes of talk, dialect, and utterances that operate below the registers of normative speech in conceptualizing their theories of language. In this vein, Whitman's and Ellison's comments on language share striking similarities. Writing near the end of his life in the essay "Slang in America" (1888), with a retrospective pitch to his tone and perspective, Whitman delineates "language" from "slang" by distinguishing the latter as a kind of seed: "Slang, profoundly con-

IVY G. WILSON

sider'd, is the lawless germinal element, *below* all words and sentences, behind all poetry, and proves a certain perennial rankness and protestantism in speech."[3] Invoking the tenor of the geological sciences, Whitman uses language associated with botany to prefigure the etymological and philological impulses of his analysis of slang in America: "View'd freely, the English language is the accretion and growth of every dialect, race, and range of time, and is both the free and compacted composition of all. From this point of view, it stands for Language in the largest sense, and is really the greatest of studies. It involves so much; is indeed a sort of universal absorber, combiner, and conqueror."[4] Later in the essay, Whitman offers a range of examples of words (from Nevada, Virginia, and Mississippi, among states) that have come into the lexicon as language through their repeated enunciation as slang in everyday use. The role of language is important to Whitman's larger political project as a writer because he views slang's "attempt of common humanity" as a contest between the lexical and social boundaries of proper English.[5]

Ellison shared a similar perspective about language and confronted how best to use, and not simply deploy, it while writing his novel *Invisible Man*, in much the same way that Whitman did while writing (and rewriting) *Leaves of Grass*. One of Ellison's earliest statements on language came on 27 January 1953 in an address he delivered during the presentation ceremony for winning the National Book Award. In the address, Ellison acknowledges having turned to the "classical nineteenth-century novelists" but found that "something vital had gone out of American prose after Twain," save the notable exception of Faulkner, and language was as much a part of his concern as was form or theme: "Our speech I found resounding with an alive language swirling with over three hundred years of American living, a mixture of the folk, the Biblical, the scientific and the political. Slangy in one stance, academic in another, loaded poetically with imagery at one moment, mathematically bare of imagery in the next."[6] Ellison was intoxicated by the "rich babel of idiomatic expression" around him and wanted to find a way to have this idiomatic expression shape the language of his characters as well as the form of his novel, and he saw in this problem of artistry for the novelist a larger social dilemma for the country as a nation.[7]

Slang, for Ellison, cannot be reduced as simply the currency of the "lower frequencies," because it is as much about the specific words of a regional dialect as it is *how* conventional words from standardized English are inflected and reconstituted when enunciated by African Americans—and perhaps no better expression encapsulates Ellison's view than his phrase "freewheeling diction."[8] His preoccupation with tone and voice, then, is about expressing them equally on both the lower *and* upper frequencies.

While both Whitman and Ellison saw in the birth of the nation a necessary rescripting of English as a language for the American context, their perspectives differ in significant ways insofar as Whitman found these transformations as essentially a natural evolution, whereas Ellison understood them to be the alchemic products of a collision of many different cultures. In the preface to the 1855 edition of *Leaves of Grass*, Whitman articulates what amounts to a manifesto, one that includes his thoughts on the democratic possibilities of the nation, the role of the poet, and the function of language. For Whitman, the "grand American expression" is translated through the "English language" and ultimately transforms it:

> The English language befriends the grand American expression. . . . [I]t is brawny enough and limber and full enough. On the tough stock of a race who through all change of circumstance was never without the idea of political liberty, which is the animus of all liberty, it has attracted the terms of daintier and gayer and subtler and more elegant tongues. It is the powerful language of resistance. . . . [I]t is the dialect of common sense. It is the speech of the proud and melancholy races and of all who aspire. It is the chosen tongue to express growth faith self-esteem freedom justice equality friendliness amplitude prudence decision and courage. It is the medium that shall well nigh express the inexpressible.[9]

However much Whitman is at pains elsewhere to announce the newness of America as a society that has no discernible historical antecedent, here he latently acknowledges a lineal thread from England to the United States that connects the two countries. England is a political precursor, a country that "was never without the idea of political liberty," as much as English is a linguistic precursor. In this sense, Whitman understood America to be a version of England pushed to degrees beyond what that country, or any other, had yet realized. Importantly, this aspect of multiplication depends less upon exponentially heightening one privileged variable; instead, it is an illustration of introducing multiple variables of the English language (and in later poems, other languages) to create something recognizable as an American tongue. In Whitman's early estimation, this American tongue adopted and adapted high and low English, the "elegant" as well as the commonsensical.

If in the 1855 preface Whitman's understanding of language evinces an early articulation of his notion of internationalism (albeit initially through the linguistic registers of Anglo-Atlantic pathways), then Ellison's understanding of language evinces his notion of interracialism, or what he calls "cultural pluralism."[10] Both Whitman and Ellison wrestled with the idea of "e pluribus unum" and the dilemma of how to illustrate representativeness in their writings. Whitman's catalogs are only the most conspicuous aspect of his trying to register the multitudes in depicting the wide canvas of America. Whitman's near-schematic use of catalogs can be found throughout the various editions of *Leaves of Grass*, evident in such poems as "Song of Myself" and "Salut au Monde." He explicitly takes up the idea of "e pluribus unum," however, in "Poem of Many in One" from the 1856 edition (later titled "By Blue Ontario's Shore"). Here, Whitman deploys a number of techniques to create a sense of commonality without uniformity: the aural reverberations produced by anaphora; the listing of various states; and the naturalistic undertones of a political philosophy built around the "organic compact." Importantly, Whitman's engagement with the concept of "e pluribus unum"—translating the Latin "from many one" into the more idiomatic "many in one"—was also a moment to outline the role of language and the poet in America.

Ellison sought to illuminate the particular experiences of black America as representative for the nation writ large, and he saw in this mission the specific dilemma of what it means to be an American novelist. "In order to orient myself I also began to learn that the American novel had long concerned itself with the puzzle of the one-and-the-many," he offered in an address he gave before the Library of Congress in 1964, "the mystery of how each of us, despite his origins in diverse regions, with our diverse racial, cultural, religious backgrounds, speaking his own diverse idiom of the American in his own accent, is, nevertheless, American."[11] Ellison uses the genre of the epic novel for *Invisible Man* to correlate the transformation of his protagonist with that of the nation. In this sense, Ellison foregrounds a number of scenarios experienced principally by a single character with whom the reader may identify, unlike Whitman, who often privileges a multitude of types to engender his poetics of associative relationality. Ellison's complete oeuvre is underwritten by a desire to illustrate African Americans as simultaneously synecdochic and metonymic for the national subject-citizen.

In Ellison's vision, the "bond of language" unites US Americans across their different regional, class, ethnic, and religious particularities, and it is central to his notion of "cultural pluralism" that this language bears the tenor of blacks.[12] Ellison discusses this notion of cultural pluralism in a number of essays, but he specifically addresses its relationship to language in his "Haverford Statement," which he delivered to the college in May 1969: "There are many idioms of that language, and it is partially the creation of a voice which found its origin in Africa. Indeed, the language began to be influenced by this voice long before the American nation was formed. In the beginning was the word, and our voice sounded in the language with which the word was spoken. The American language owes something of its directness, flexibility, music, imagery, mythology, and folklore to the Negro presence."[13] For Ellison, like Whitman, language is a dynamic zone suspect to change, influence, and transformation, but Whitman is more concerned with how the United States as a new type of nation puts on demands to modify the English language and, more specifically, the literary enterprise of writing poetry. Ellison, by contrast, is primarily concerned with how language, as an iteration of cultural pluralism, manifests itself within the ecosystem of the nation. For Whitman, the emergence of the United States inaugurated new uses of language and new forms of poetry; for Ellison, these instances of what might be called linguistic interracialism, and the wider field of cultural pluralism,

IVY G. WILSON

would make the nation anew, pushing the United States closer to fulfilling its democratic promises.

To work through Ellison's interpretation of language in light of Whitman is to come to terms with how he conceived of the "Negro American idiom" as a cultural force that is both symptomatic of a past and symbolic of a possible future.[14] For Ellison, there are zones, places, moments, and events—the slave ship, the plantation, the nursery, the Pullman railcar, the jazz club, the sidewalk, among others—where black and white bodies come together, by force or volition, to produce something new called American culture. One such place in Whitman's nineteenth-century world would have been the Five Points neighborhood of New York City, where Irish, Protestants, and blacks mixed, sometimes clashing in degrees that resulted in violent riots. In Ellison's estimation, the contours of the "Negro American idiom" were to be found everywhere in US culture, from the commonplace expressions of the everyday to the formal diction of presidents. For example, in a quintessential moment of Ellisonian irony and insight while discussing the particular province of the spoken language as a site where the aurality of many different tongues began to merge, he calls upon the image of John C. Calhoun, the proslavery South Carolinian senator, to underscore this point: "So there is a *de'z* and *do'z* of slave speech sounding beneath our most polished Harvard accents, and if there is any such thing as a Yale accent, there is a Negro wail in it—doubtless introduced there by Old Yalie John C. Calhoun, who probably got it from his mammy."[15] Sometimes Ellison's phrase for these forms of continual cultural circulation is "acculturative process," but more often than not it is America's "vernacular" style.[16] In not a few respects, then, it becomes apparent why someone like Whitman, who is often thought of as a "vernacular" poet, would appeal to Ellison.

Another similarity in their thoughts on language—and, specifically, the making of new vernaculars, dialects, and idioms—is how both Whitman and Ellison circumvent the histories of conflict and contestation that ostensibly make the development of American English a veritable example of cultural pluralism. My earlier use of the phrase "dynamic zone" to describe Whitman's and Ellison's understanding of language, then, is meant to recall

Mary Louise Pratt's notion of the "contact zone" as a social space "where cultures meet, clash, and grapple with each other, often in contexts of highly asymmetrical relations of power, such as colonialism, slavery, or their aftermaths."[17] In the passage above where Ellison speaks of Calhoun, for example, his genteel affect precludes him from underscoring the violent histories of chattel slavery, similarly compelling him to avoid the inhumane trafficking of the Middle Passage (as Robert Hayden would do in his 1962 poem of the same name) or the lynchings in Jim Crow America (as James Weldon Johnson had portrayed in *The Autobiography of an Ex-Coloured Man* [1912]). Even in Whitman's essay "Slang in America," where he actually describes American English as "a sort of universal absorber, combiner, and conqueror," the histories of slavery and Manifest Destiny are seemingly rendered benign and unremarkable.[18]

If the parallels between Whitman's and Ellison's understanding of language are coincidental to their being US writers, then Ellison's particular attraction to Whitman comes into sharper focus through his more direct allusions to the poet. In an address on the novel, Ellison outlined that the classic American writers of the nineteenth century "enjoined us to experience nature and society to the hilt," forcing us to "interrogate ourselves, nature and the universe by way of realizing ourselves," and, importantly, that the "Whitmans were necessary to point out to us that this was a lyrical as well as a rugged experience."[19] While it seems unlikely that Ellison thought of Whitman as a lyric poet, he most likely intended to underscore the aurality, if not musicality, of Whitman's verse, as the broader field of sound, including cadence, rhythm, and tone, was intricately important to Ellison's crafting of *Invisible Man* as well as his writings about music. Justin Kaplan has noted the significance of the opera for Whitman, and it is crucial that Ellison himself uses Whitman's attraction to the opera as another avenue to discuss what he identifies as the history of the United States' acculturative process: "In reading, I came across Whitman, who was writing very early (I think 1848 or so), finding in the American Negro dialect—the dialect of slaves, as he put it—the possibility of an American grand opera, the possibility of a new music in speech."[20] Both Kaplan's and Ellison's estimations accentuate Whitman's impulse to take the high (European)

IVY G. WILSON

art form of the opera and have it opened and transformed by the vernacular. In Kaplan's estimation, the opera singer Marietta Alboni "liberated" Whitman from the "metrical, rhymed, 'ballad-style' of poetry"; in Ellison's view, African American dialect could itself constitute the high aesthetic.[21] Ellison's references to Whitman's thoughts on African American dialect here—followed by a second reference where he attributes Whitman's thoughts even further back to the 1830s—may have stemmed from his encounter with Whitman's *An American Primer*, initially edited by Horace Traubel and published in 1904. According to Traubel, Whitman began the *Primer* in the early 1850s but never finished it, although Whitman himself acknowledged that many of its ideas made their way into his other works. Even if Ellison misremembered the exact date and the actual language of Whitman's statement, his references to the *Primer* reveal that he read deeply into the corpus of Whitman's writings, including manuscripts beyond the central work of *Leaves of Grass*.[22]

Whitman in Ellison's Postwar America

Ellison's regard for Whitman and other nineteenth-century authors early in his career as a writer coincided with the movement by critics to identify and delineate a "classic" literature as a body of writing that exemplified, as much as it was a product of, the United States as a democratic horizon. As Ellison saw it, for a century from approximately the revolution to the Hayes-Tilden Compromise, the nation's political milieu had created an affective social milieu whereby writers could sympathize with African Americans: "We are reminded that from 1776 to 1876 there was a conception of democracy current in this country that allowed the writer to identify himself with the Negro, and that had such an anthology been conceivable during the nineteenth century, it would have included such writers as Whitman, Emerson, Thoreau, Hawthorne, Melville and Mark Twain."[23] Ellison's comments appeared in the *New Republic* in 1945, almost seven years before the publication of his first novel and within weeks of the conclusion of World War II. The United States would emerge from the war as a veritable hegemony, being installed as a military superpower and inaugurating an economic boom. An essential aspect of this consolidation of the United States as a cultural hegemony was endowing it with a "classical" past, and perhaps no single work was more important to establishing the literature of that classical past than F. O. Matthiessen's *American Renaissance*. Published in 1941 and subtitled *Art and Expression in the Age of Emerson and Whitman*, Matthiessen's tome was only one of many that apotheosized the mid-nineteenth-century era, an impulse that grew perceptibly stronger in the postwar years with such publications as Van Wyck Brooks's *The Times of Melville and Whitman* (1947), Richard Chase's *The American Novel and Its Tradition* (1957), Benjamin T. Spencer's *The Quest for Nationality* (1957), and Newton Arvin's books on Longfellow, Hawthorne, Melville, and Whitman written over more than forty years, among others. Although Ellison dedicated his most extensive reflections to Twain, Crane, Faulkner, and Hemingway, the writers from what is now identified as the American Renaissance surface often in his addresses and essays, with Whitman appearing again at least twice in 1967 and 1974.

If the essays intimate an image of Ellison as a critic of Whitman, then his invocation of the "Calamus" section of *Leaves of Grass* in *Invisible Man* registers a failed attempt at transposed equivalency, one where the homosocial bond among Whitman's men is stalled by the processes of racialization in Ellison's twentieth-century United States. Chapter 9 of *Invisible Man* finds the protagonist having just arrived in New York City, determined to make his way to Mr. Emerson's office, where he hopes his "recommendation" letter from Dr. Bledsoe will secure him employment. Although the invisible man is unsuccessful in gaining an audience with Mr. Emerson, he learns the sad truth that the letters are hardly endorsements from the younger Emerson. This Emerson, the son, is experiencing a sort of existential crisis; his language is indirect and mysterious, pushing the protagonist into a further state of disbelief, and Ellison uses literary references to underline this sense of confusion.

> "Some things are just too unjust for words," he said, expelling a plume of smoke, "and too ambiguous for either speech or ideas. By the way, have you ever been to the Club Calamus?"
>
> "I don't think I've ever heard of it, sir," I said.
>
> "You haven't? It's very well known. Many of my Harlem

friends go there. It's a rendezvous for writers, artists and all kinds of celebrities. There's nothing like it in the city, and by some strange twist it has a truly continental flavor."[24]

While it is not clear that Ellison's Club Calamus is actually located in Harlem (Emerson only says that his Harlem friends sometimes frequent it), the interwar period marked a time when the uptown section of Manhattan became a location where the color line, as well as that of sex and sexuality, were frequently crossed in places like clubs, cabarets, and dance halls. As scholars like Shane Vogel have noted, much of the literature of the Harlem Renaissance, from Johnson's *Autobiography of an Ex-Coloured* to Nella Larsen's *Passing* (1929), features episodes of transgressive queer politics where the lines between race, gender, and sexuality are traversed.[25]

While it is not surprising that the protagonist of *Invisible Man* has not heard of the club, Ellison nonetheless underscores the scene with a freighted irony by having his nearly college-educated protagonist fail to register the symbolism of the name "Calamus" and other literary references. Whitman's celebration of "adhesive" love as well as the manly "love of comrades" is forestalled in the "Emerson" episode, as it is for much of the novel, and not only prevented from materializing but precluded from emerging on the horizon of possibility altogether.[26] Ellison punctuates the scene by switching from allusions to queer relationships in *Leaves of Grass* to a different kind of "queer" relationship—that of a racialized infantilization—in Mark Twain's *Huckleberry Finn* (1884). The invisible man is confused when the younger Emerson declares himself to be "Huck," which necessarily positions the invisible man in a dialectic wherein he must be "Jim": "I was trying to tell you that I know many things about you—not you personally, but fellows like you. Not much, either, but still more than the average. With us it's still Jim and Huck Finn. A number of my friends are jazz musicians and I've been around. I know the conditions under which you live—Why go back, fellow?"[27] In Emerson's mind, he is breaking away from the expectations thrust upon his generation, but rather than figuratively slay the father in an Oedipal drama, he chooses to cross the color line as a form of rebellion. When Emerson implores the invisible man to not attempt a return to college, insisting that he will not find what he's looking for there, Emerson's reasoning is more existential than it is material; for, to actualize his own personal bildungsroman, he needs his own Jim. His recognition, then, of the "conditions" under which the invisible man and presumably other blacks live does not extend to an understanding of the historical materialism of how traces of nineteenth-century chattel slavery reemerged in the modern corporations of the twentieth century. For his part, the invisible man is equally ignorant of such connections and remains confused as to why Emerson insists upon talking about a "kid's story."[28] Far from representing interracial or same-sex love, Ellison marches his protagonist through any number of scenes where desire never develops into a genuine affective bond, and it is compelling that the story ends with the protagonist reduced to living alone in a basement, absent the "manly love of comrades" he experienced earlier with the Brotherhood, a multiracial doctrinaire organization the author loosely based on the Communist Party. Ellison invokes *Huckleberry Finn* and *Leaves of Grass* in his novel, set in Jim Crow America, to frame the limits of intimacy between black and white Americans as violent forms of racial inequity continue to persist in the postwar period.

Ellison's earlier account of Harlem in his 1942 essay "The Way It Is" bears little of the romanticism ostensibly embodied in such places as Club Calamus but rather displays catalogs to expose the contradictions of black life that, by force of the processes of racial formation in the United States, endure as antinomies. Whitman's frequent use of catalogs makes it nearly impossible to mention the term without conjuring his image. As a formal aspect of his poetry, Whitman employs the catalog to approximate a sense of rhythm while eschewing metrical conventions, engendering a sense of cadence that is produced by anaphora. As a thematic aspect of his poetry, Whitman's use of the catalog intimates a desire to denote the large inventory of America, a seemingly ever-expansive inventory that is often signaled by his use of ellipses. But the democratic impulse of Whitman's catalogs is commonly understood to be generated not only by his panoramic vision of inclusion but also by his exploitation of contradictions. In poems such as "Song of Myself," "Salut au Monde," and "The Sleepers,"

Whitman places seeming opposites side by side to create a sense of parity devoid of hierarchy within the lines of his stanzaic landscapes in an effort to describe America. In his efforts to describe the world of Harlem, Ellison too relies upon contradictions; but whereas Whitman deploys them to formulate a notion of equivalency, Ellison does so to illustrate inequities.

> It is an old story. Touch any phase of urban living in our democracy, and its worst aspects are to be found in Harlem. Our housing is the poorest, and our rents the highest. Our people are the sickest, and Harlem Hospital the most overcrowded and understaffed. Our unemployment is the greatest, and our cost of food the most exorbitant. Our crime is the most understandable and easily corrected, but the policemen sent among us are the most brutal. Our desire to rid the world of fascism is the most burning, and the obstacles placed in our way are the most frustrating. Our need to see the war as a struggle between democracy and fascism is the most intense, and our temptation to interpret it as a "color" war is the most compelling. Our need to believe in the age of the "common man" is the most hope-inspiring, and our reasons to doubt that it will include us are the most disheartening. (This is no Whitmanesque catalogue of democratic exultations, while more than anything else we wish that it could be.)[29]

Ellison's catalog appears "Whitmanesque" in the sense that it is a litany, but it functions quite differently because of the aural patterns produced by his morphological framing. Like Whitman, he makes use of anaphora through the repetition of the word "our." But, whereas the lines of Whitman's catalogs often feel and sound as if they could continue indefinitely, Ellison's sentences are framed by a contrapuntal structure that allows him to correlate the phonological registers of their sound to the sociological underpinnings of their meanings. More specifically, each sentence in Ellison's catalog feels as if it is bifurcated, split in half by the caesura that divides one part from the other, as if the morphological structure of each sentence itself encapsulates the binary racial logic of Jim Crow America. The meanings of Ellison's words here are accentuated by the fabricated quasi volta in each sentence that initializes a drastic turn in the second clause. Far from projecting a kind of apotheosis for the social realm, the second clauses can only be said to be counterpoints for their poetic or lyrical tonality. The hermeneutics of each sentence enacts a failure of complementarity or closure and puts into high relief a series of antinomies that evince how black life in Harlem, and perhaps the United States as a whole, is structured by the social processes of racialization that continually seek to naturalize this habitus of contradiction as inevitable, always-already, and foregone.

Whereas Whitman saw the regional sections of the nation melded together into one country forged in the fire of the Civil War, Ellison too thought of World War II as a historical moment where African Americans could be better integrated into a more egalitarian body politic. The black presence diminishes in Whitman's poetry after the Civil War, even while each subsequent edition of *Leaves of Grass* grows larger, causing some critics to wonder about how he interpreted the place of African Americans in the new republic. There are no images representing something resembling the Fifty-Fourth Regiment Massachusetts Volunteer Infantry or writer-activist Martin R. Delany depicting black soldiers in the Civil War in *Leaves of Grass*.[30] The one poem where Whitman does address race and the Civil War is "Ethiopia Saluting the Colors" (1871–72), which recounts a soldier's confusion as to why the black woman he passes would salute the flag. The soldier is perplexed by not being able to ascertain whether she can appreciate the symbolism of the Stars and Stripes or the meaning of the Union soldiers.[31] As Ellison saw it, blacks had been involved in fighting for the country from Crispus Attucks in the American Revolution to the "Double V" campaign during World War II, which sought victories over the Axis powers abroad and racial prejudice at home in the United States.

If Whitman saw the Civil War as the unfortunate but necessary cataclysm that would guarantee a democratic order of citizens, then Ellison thought of World War II as yet another opportunity in an overgrown list to finally add blacks to that order. Central to Ellison's assessment of how the United States would fulfill its democratic potential was the necessity of empowering blacks as political agents, without which the nation would simply slouch toward a recidivist Herrenvolk democracy, as he noted in "The

IVY G. WILSON

Negro and the Second World War" (1943): "And [African American leaders] have the Civil War to teach them that no revolutionary situation in the United States will be carried any farther toward fulfilling the needs of Negroes than Negroes themselves are able, through a strategic application of their own power to make it go. . . . Freedom, after all, cannot be imported or acquired through an act of philanthropy, it must be won."[32]

The American Scene: Viewing Whitman from a Distance

Although Ellison's thoughts on World War II center primarily on the battle between democracy and Fascism, he also used his discussions of the topic to examine the shifting relations between labor and capital, putting him in a conversation about the place of the individual and the masses in the modern world, a concern that had preoccupied Whitman throughout the latter half of the nineteenth century. Among those in these dialogues was C. L. R. James, who wrote the manuscript that would eventually be published as *American Civilization*, in the same postwar period that Ellison published *Invisible Man*, which included a chapter on nineteenth-century intellectuals focusing on the abolitionists, Melville, and Whitman.

James saw in Whitman's engagement with the notion of totality an attempt to reconcile a faith in individualism while maintaining a commitment to the masses, or, at least, what might be called the ideogram of the masses. But he also felt that when blacks or anyone else, for the most part, are listed in *Leaves of Grass* en masse, they are virtually indistinguishable from one another. The catalogs produce a sonic blur that amounts to a kind of white noise that James might, after Fredric Jameson, identify as the "political unconscious" of Whitman's poetry. James reads Melville's representations of individualism in *Moby-Dick* (1852) as authentic and true insofar as they depict the *Pequod*'s crew as characters possessed of body and soul; by contrast, James finds that Whitman's engagement with individualism falls flat insofar as the poet relies too much upon vapid catalogs that principally list types too often bereft of any interiority. James is able to see that individualism exponentially centralized will teleologically lead to the kind of dictatorship and totalitarianism embodied by Ahab. But for James, Whitman's multiplicity of individualism might only yield the simulacrum of democracy and a feigned equality, especially because James felt that Whitman had "mastered the art of substituting the individual for anything that was too difficult for him to overcome in reality."[33] Extending James, it might be said that blacks persisted as the object/subject "too difficult for him to overcome in reality," for while Whitman may have sympathized with the rebel slave before the Civil War (as we see in "A Boston Ballad" and the shadow "Lucifer" passage of "The Sleepers"), he never found a way to imagine free blacks in the new republic after it.

To conclude a reading of Whitman by framing him between Ellison and James also entails considering the relation of race and class at the advent of the American Century. Ellison underscores an interracial genealogy of the United States, one where the black presence is genetic to the nation's cultural pluralism. James underscores the "relation of individualism to democracy as a whole" as a predicament not only for the United States but for the modern world.[34] Ellison and James alike could hear in Whitman's language his position on black Americans. Ellison put currency in Whitman's speculation that a "grand American opera" might come from the voices of blacks, even though these voices remain eerily silent in Whitman's own poetry.

NOTES

1. Ed Folsom, "So Long, So Long! Walt Whitman, Langston Hughes, and the Art of Longing," in *Walt Whitman, Where the Future Becomes Present*, ed. David Haven Blake and Michael Robertson (Iowa City: University of Iowa Press, 2008), 127.

2. Ralph Ellison, "Haverford Statement," in *The Collected Essays of Ralph Ellison*, ed. John F. Callahan (New York: Modern Library, 1995), 430.

3. Walt Whitman, "Slang in America," in *Prose Works 1892*, ed. Floyd Stovall, 2 vols. (New York: New York University Press, 1963–64), 2:572 (emphasis mine).

4. Ibid., 2:572. Among these botanical words are "fermentation," "germinal," "organic," and "crystallize." For more, see Ivy G. Wilson, "Organic Compacts and the Logic of Social Cohesion," *ESQ: A Journal of the American Renaissance* 54, nos. 1–4 (2008): 210.

5. Whitman, "Slang in America," 2:573.

6. Ralph Ellison, "Brave Words for a Startling Occasion," in Callahan, *Collected Essays*, 152.

7. Ibid.

8. Ralph Ellison, "What America Would Be Like without Blacks," in Callahan, *Collected Essays*, 581.

9. Walt Whitman, preface to *Leaves of Grass* (Brooklyn, NY, 1855), reproduced in *The Walt Whitman Archive*, ed. Ed Folsom and Kenneth M. Price, xi–xii, http://www.whitmanarchive.org/works.

10. Ellison, "Haverford Statement," 430.

11. Ralph Ellison, "Hidden Name and Complex Fate," in Callahan, *Collected Essays*, 207.

12. Ellison, "Haverford Statement," 430.

13. Ibid.

14. Ibid.

15. Ellison, "What America Would Be Like," 581.

16. On the "acculturative process," see Ralph Ellison and James Alan McPherson, "Indivisible Man," in Callahan, *Collected Essays*, 369. On the "vernacular" style, see "Indivisible Man," 369; and Ralph Ellison, "Going to the Territory," in Callahan, *Collected Essays*, 608.

17. Mary Louise Pratt, "Arts of the Contact Zone," in *Ways of Reading: An Anthology for Writers*, ed. David Bartholomae and Anthony Petrosky (Boston: Bedford Books, 1993), 444.

18. Whitman, "Slang in America," 572.

19. Ralph Ellison, "The Novel as a Function of American Democracy," in Callahan, *Collected Essays*, 758.

20. Ralph Ellison, "On Initiation Rites and Power," in Callahan, *Collected Essays*, 528. Ellison reiterated this idea during a symposium on the philosopher Alain Locke held on 1 December 1973 (and published later in the Spring 1974 issue of the *Harvard Advocate*): "I think it was sometime in the 1830s that Lowelessa Hoy and Walt Whitman suggested that there would be an American grand opera and that the language of that opera would be found in Afro-American speech, 'the speech of the slaves,' as Whitman put it. Thus it seems amazing to me that we have moved away from that complex, mysterious, perplexing sense of our role in this country to something which is much too simplistic" ("Alain Locke," in Callahan, *Collected Essays*, 442).

21. Justin Kaplan, *Walt Whitman: A Life* (New York: Simon and Schuster, 1980), 178.

22. If Ellison read the version of *An American Primer* edited by Horace Traubel, he would have encountered this passage:

> The nigger dialect furnishes hundreds of outré words, many of them adopted into the common speech of the mass of the people. — Curiously, these words show the old English instinct for wide open pronunciations, as *yallah* for yellow — *massah* for master — and for rounding off all the

corners of words. The nigger dialect has hints of the future theory of the modification of all words of the English language, for musical purposes, for a native grand opera in America, leaving the words just as they are for writing and speaking, but the same words so modified as to answer perfectly for musical purposes, on grand and simple principles. (Walt Whitman, *An American Primer*, ed. Horace Traubel [Boston: Small, Maynard and Company, 1904], 24–25)

23. Ralph Ellison, "Beating That Boy," in Callahan, *Collected Essays*, 147.

24. Ralph Ellison, *Invisible Man* (New York: Vintage, 1952), 185.

25. For more on queer Harlem and crossing the color line, see Shane Vogel, *The Scene of Harlem: Race, Sexuality, Performance* (Chicago: University of Chicago Press, 2009); and A. B. Christa Schwarz, *Gay Voices of the Harlem Renaissance* (Bloomington: Indiana University Press, 2003).

26. Walt Whitman, *Leaves of Grass* (Boston: Thayer and Eldridge, 1860–61), reproduced in Folsom and Price, *The Walt Whitman Archive*, 353, 369.

27. Ellison, *Invisible Man*, 187–88.

28. Ibid., 188.

29. Ralph Ellison, "The Way It Is," in Callahan, *Collected Essays*, 319.

30. When Whitman does write about the black soldier and the Civil War in *November Boughs*, he both admires and is confused by them. His muted admiration never seems unable to grasp the larger symbolism of their participating in the war, and he certainly forgoes endowing the image of these men with the same amount of heroic tragedy that he does for white soldiers whom he believes were fighting as much for preserving the nation as for its democratic ideals:

> Here comes the first Company (B), some 82 men, all blacks. Certes we cannot find fault with the crowd—Negroes though they be. They are manly enough, bright enough, look as if they had the soldier-stuff in them, look hardy, patient, many of them real handsome young fellows. The paying, I say, has begun. The men are march'd up in close proximity. The clerk calls off name after name, and each walks up, receives his money, and passes along out of the way. It is a real study, both to see them come close, and to see them pass away, stand counting their cash— (nearly all of this company get ten dollars and three cents each). The clerk calls George Washington. That distinguish'd personage steps from the ranks, in the shape of a very black man, good sized and shaped, and aged about 30, with a military mustache; he takes his "ten three," and goes off evidently well pleas'd. (There are about a dozen Washingtons in the company. Let us hope they will do honor to the name.) (*Prose Works 1892*, 2:588)

31. For more on "Ethiopia Saluting the Colors," see Ed Folsom, "Ethiopia and Lucifer: Whitman, Race, and Poetics before the Civil War and After," in *A Historical Guide to Walt Whitman*, ed. David S. Reynolds (New York: Oxford University Press, 2000), 45–95; Luke Mancuso, *The Strange Sad War Revolving: Walt Whitman, Reconstruction, and the Emergence of Black Citizenship, 1865–1876* (Columbia, SC: Camden House, 1997), 85–86; and Ivy G. Wilson, *Specters of Democracy: Blackness and the Aesthetics of Politics in the Antebellum U.S.* (New York: Oxford University Press, 2011), 94–96.

32. Ralph Ellison, "The Negro and the Second World War," in *Cultural Contexts for Ralph Ellison's "Invisible Man,"* ed. Eric J. Sundquist (Boston: Bedford/St. Martin's, 1995), 238.

33. C. L. R. James, *American Civilization* (Cambridge, MA: Blackwell, 1993), 61–62.

34. Ibid., 50.

Transforming the Kosmos

Yusef Komunyakaa Musing on Walt Whitman

JACOB WILKENFELD

When the Public Broadcasting Service aired its *American Experience* documentary on Walt Whitman in 2008, three noted contemporary poets—Martín Espada, Billy Collins, and Yusef Komunyakaa—appeared on the program as interviewees and reciters of Whitman's verse.[1] The presence of each writer suggests an affinity with the nineteenth-century poet's work—an observation that is confirmed when one examines the ways in which each poet has engaged with Whitman. Espada, for example, has stated that he views himself "as a branch on the tree of Whitman."[2] A former tenant lawyer, Espada considers his own work as part of a Whitmanian tradition that emphasizes "the concept of the poet-advocate," the writer who speaks on behalf of society's voiceless.[3] Collins, whose wide following in recent years has led *CBS News* to dub him "America's Poet," has been compared to Whitman in terms of his affectionate absorption by a broad audience, in contrast to the niche readership usually associated with contemporary verse.[4] (It is Whitman, after all, who wrote that "the proof of a poet is that his country absorbs him as affectionately as he has absorbed it.")[5] Collins has also published a foreword to a sesquicentennial edition of *Leaves of Grass* that highlights Whitman's demotic idiom and his avoidance of stale poeticisms—two aspects of Whitman's verse that are also notable qualities of Collins's own style.[6]

Of the three poets appearing in the PBS documentary, Komunyakaa's (more subtle) connection with Whitman may appear the least obvious, the most counterintuitive. Yet his engagement with Whitman has been similarly far-reaching through poems that reference him and statements made during interviews. This essay explores Komunyakaa's connection to the good gray poet, arguing that Whitman's work is a key reference in Komunyakaa's oeuvre. My aim is not to hunt for influences or to find a measure of Komunyakaa's "indebtedness" to Whitman. Indeed, Komunyakaa's aesthetic, with its characteristically short lines, is a far cry from Whitman's verse style. Yet throughout his career, Komunyakaa has attested to an interest in Whitman's work—an interest whose contours I hope to sketch in the pages that follow. Rather than underscore the burden of Whitman's specter in Komunyakaa's work, my focus is the artistic antecedent not as a father but as an interlocutor.

In this sense, I explore Komunyakaa's position within a tradition of sorts. In Ed Folsom's words, "The temptation to talk back to Walt Whitman has always been great, and poets over the years have made something of a tradition of it. There's nothing quite like it anywhere else in English or American poetry—a sustained tradition, a century old, of directly invoking or addressing another poet."[7] As poets from Ezra Pound to Komunyakaa have demonstrated, writers have manifested a desire to engage Whitman in dialogue—to praise him, to argue with his writings, and to offer new ways to look at his art. Kenneth Price argues that artists of color have often had additional reasons to feel hesitant in their embrace of Whitman: "When [black artists] acknowledged their troubled kinship with Whitman they demanded something akin to what the mulatto historically lacked: a nameable white father." For Price, part of what is troubling for black artists who embrace Whitman as a poetic ancestor is that "however broad-minded Whitman has sometimes seemed and however liberating he has sometimes been, his primary allegiance was to a particular segment of the population, white working men. Whitman was hardly free of the racism of his culture, yet he has had an extraordinary impact on writers from disadvantaged groups. . . . For various reasons, then, including the open-endedness of *Leaves of Grass* and the sharply different ways that cultural project could be understood, Whitman left plenty of room for his literary progeny to reimagine America." As Price has asserted, writers of color have embraced Whitman, and their embrace of him has also had to confront the shortcomings of Whitman's racial thinking, which "was hardly free of the racism of his culture."[8]

The complexity of Whitman's relationship with later poets is encapsulated by two aspects of Price's argument. On the one hand, Whitman is imagined in the traditional role of an author/father engendering "literary progeny." On the other hand, Whitman's "progeny" stray far enough from the father's poetic vision to "reimagine America." Perhaps Whitman himself states the problem best in "Song of Myself" when he writes, "I teach straying from me, yet who can stray from me?"[9] As Price and Folsom have argued, "Some poets mimic [Whitman's] cadences or style, but many poets have understood . . . that the only way to write like Whitman is to write unlike Whitman, to forge a new kind of poetry instead of to imitate a poetry that already exists."[10] This view of later writers' interaction with Whitman is closer to the one advanced in this essay.

Komunyakaa's published dialogue with Whitman has taken the form of critical assessments expressed in interviews and poems that speak directly to Whitman's oeuvre. The remainder of this essay examines each of these forms of engagement in turn. To this end, I first explore Komunyakaa's references to Whitman in published interviews, in the aforementioned *American Experience* documentary, and in the poet's prose writings. The conversations from which I draw cover a period spanning 1996 to 2008. Allusions to Whitman are often incidental in these texts. For example, he is briefly mentioned in a 1996 essay, "Langston Hughes + Poetry = The Blues," collected in the 2000 volume *Blue Notes: Essays, Interviews, and Commentaries*. I also refer to Michael Collins's 2005 interview with Komunyakaa, published in *Callaloo*, and to a 2006 interview with Jeffrey Dodd and Jessica Moll, published in *Willow Springs* and then collected in Shirley Hanshaw's 2010 *Conversations with Yusef Komunyakaa*. Although the interviews I refer to were conducted during the more recent phases of the poet's career, his interest in Whitman extends back to his childhood in Bogalusa, Louisiana, where—he tells the reader in the 1992 poem "Kosmos"—Whitman's books "were locked / in a glass case behind the check-out desk."[11] The second portion of this essay explores Komunyakaa's engagement with Whitman in poetry, from the direct allusions to him in "Kosmos"

JACOB WILKENFELD

and "The Poetics of Paperwood" (1992) to the subtle revision of Whitman's poetic project in 2011's "Blackbirding on the Hudson." In all of these poems, Komunyakaa's dialogue with his precursor takes the form of both a celebration and a confrontation—which is also how he has defined the art of poetry itself.[12]

Komunyakaa as Critic

In interviews, Komunyakaa has offered probing criticism of Whitman's work. In doing so, he has joined a long line of African American poet-critics who have both celebrated Whitman's groundbreaking verse and confronted their precursor for the blind spots in his poetic vision. From Langston Hughes, who described Whitman as the "Negroes' First Great Poetic Friend," to June Jordan, who cautiously praised Whitman as the progenitor of a democratic "people's poetry," African American poets have frequently cited the author of *Leaves of Grass* as a particularly important voice in American letters and for African American writers.[13] As Price observes in *To Walt Whitman, America*, "The general tendency among African American writers is to applaud and at times even revere Whitman. Still, the response has been anything but simple and uniform."[14]

Komunyakaa, too, has attested to an admiration for Whitman, specifically for his avoidance of abstraction, his inclusiveness, and his treatment of themes considered taboo in his day. As Komunyakaa states in a 2006 interview with Jeffrey Dodd and Jessica Moll:

> I've written about the erasure that takes place in some contemporary poetry through over-experimentation. That's a kind of selling out—to remain in that landscape of the abstract, when there's so much happening to us and around us. Not that the politics of observation should be on the surface of the poem. But we want human voices that are believable, and that's why Walt Whitman is interesting to me. Whitman addresses everything, and is clearly influenced by Italian opera, so everything reaches for a crescendo—but he didn't dodge anything. He really confronts the essence of being an American. Even though there's fetishism, or, I should say, there are certain characters on his poetic canvas that become eroticized.[15]

The contrast Komunyakaa makes between Whitman's work and contemporary poetry that privileges abstraction recalls the Emersonian dictum that poets should "chaunt our own times and social circumstance."[16] The term "over-experimentation" suggests a privileging of form over content—of meters over a meter-making argument. Komunyakaa's poems have displayed an acute attention to form, but not to form for form's sake. Instead, like Whitman's verse, Komunyakaa's work strives toward the apprehension of concrete, multiplicitous realities belonging to particular historical and cultural constellations. Poetry that displays an exaggerated preoccupation with form risks becoming a superficial evasion of real human experiences—both lived and imagined. Whitman displays a similar preoccupation in the preface to the first edition of *Leaves of Grass*. Writing of the role of the poet, Whitman says that "to him enter the essences of the real things and past and present events."[17] Both writers suggest that the poet should address the world around him. Yet for neither poet is the "politics of observation . . . on the surface of the poem," a phrase suggesting a crudely conceived realism. Instead, both Whitman's and Komunyakaa's poetics attempt an intersubjective rendering of perspective; their work aims to contain multitudes. As the latter has said (in a 1999 interview with Angela Salas), "The world is so large, and we are so small. How dare an artist *not* imagine the world from the perspective of someone other than himself? It's all part of the ongoing dialogue we must have between ourselves and the world."[18]

Whitman's multiperspectival chants are appealing to Komunyakaa because of their believability. In the PBS *American Experience* documentary on Whitman, Komunyakaa links this believability to Whitman's empathetic imagination, capable of crossing cultural and racial boundaries: "For some reason I feel like he has the capacity to imagine himself on the auction block as well. . . . It really enters his psyche. I think he's wrestling with himself."[19] Paired with his empathy, however, Whitman also "addresses everything," and this is an important part of his aesthetic. For as Komunyakaa writes in his essay "Langston Hughes + Poetry = The Blues," Whitman's "vision is driven by an acute sense of beauty and tragedy in America's history."[20] Rather than only sing the most picturesque aspects of the American landscape, Whitman strives to include everything in his verses.

JACOB WILKENFELD

As he writes in the 1855 preface to *Leaves of Grass*, the new bard will encompass "the large amativeness—the fluid movement of the population—the factories and mercantile life and labor-saving machinery—the Yankee swap—the New York firemen and the target excursion—the southern plantation life—the character of the northeast and of the northwest and southwest—slavery and the tremulous spreading of hands to protect it, and the stern opposition to it which shall never cease till it ceases or the speaking of tongues and the moving of lips cease."[21] Whitman's conviction that the poet should not evade the more unsightly aspects of modern life was likely inspired by Emerson's lecture "The Poet," which famously muses: "Our logrolling, our stumps and their politics, our fisheries, our Negroes, and Indians, our boasts, and our repudiations, the wrath of rogues, and the pusillanimity of honest men, the northern trade, the southern planting, the western clearing, Oregon, and Texas, are yet unsung."[22] An unflinching treatment of both the beauty and meanness of America endows Whitman's poetry with a vision that doesn't "dodge anything," and in Komunyakaa's view this complexity of representation "confronts the essence of being an American," with all the contradictory traits that designation contains.

Yet Komunyakaa qualifies his praise for Whitman's seeming inclusiveness, noting that "there's fetishism, or, I should say, there are certain characters on his poetic canvas that become eroticized."[23] Komunyakaa suggests that, on some level, Whitman fails in his quest for imaginative, empathetic intersubjectivity. Rather than represent a truly multiperspectival American experience, Whitman sometimes falls back on simplistic, stereotypical images—particularly of nonwhite peoples. The reader need not search far to find exoticized and eroticized stereotypes in Whitman's verse. For example, one could cite the following lines from "Salut au Monde":

> You Hottentot with clicking palate! you woolly-hair'd hordes!
> You own'd persons dropping sweat-drops or blood-drops!
> You human forms with the fathomless ever-impressive
>   countenances of brutes!
> You poor koboo whom the meanest of the rest look down
>   upon for all your glimmering language and spirituality!

You dwarf'd Kamtschatkan, Greenlander, Lapp!
You Austral negro, naked, red, sooty, with protrusive lip,
    groveling, seeking your food!
You Caffre, Berber, Soudanese![24]

Here, Whitman greets the world's various cultures, supposedly on equal terms but with a patronizing air, denoting his inability to transcend the hackneyed racial images of his era despite the otherwise vast reach of his sympathetic imagination. Thus, Whitman's attempt to "address everything" at times relies on stock images rather than on believable empathetic identification. If, as Komunyakaa asserts, Whitman has the "capacity to imagine himself on the auction block" in "I Sing the Body Electric," some of his other poems give short shrift to intercultural understanding. One might also cite the passage involving the marriage of the trapper and the "red girl" in "Song of Myself," particularly as an example of an image that is both "exoticized" and "eroticized":

> I saw the marriage of the trapper in the open air in the far-
>   west . . . . the bride was a red girl,
> Her father and his friends sat near by crosslegged and
>   dumbly smoking . . . . they had moccasins to their feet and
>   large thick blankets hanging from their shoulders;
> On a bank lounged the trapper . . . . he was dressed mostly in
>   skins . . . . his luxuriant beard and curls protected his neck,
> One hand rested on his rifle . . . . the other hand held firmly
>   the wrist of the red girl,
> She had long eyelashes . . . . her head was bare . . . . her coarse
>   straight locks descended upon her voluptuous limbs and
>   reached to her feet.[25]

As Kenneth Price notes, Whitman "underscores the erotic appeal of the Indian bride."[26] The imagery also depicts the indigenous woman and her family and friends as passive and silent while portraying the trapper as possessing a rugged authority, reinforced by his self-assured display of control over both his weapon and his bride. The scene figures the marriage as a representation of the conquest—sexual and territorial—of the North American continent by men of European descent.

Komunyakaa is careful to note that Whitman's attempt to be

JACOB WILKENFELD

inclusive at times descends into stereotypes that threaten his effort to embody other subjectivities in his verse. Whitman claims to let multitudinous voices—particularly those of the disenfranchised—speak through his poems, as in the famous lines from section 24 of "Song of Myself" that begin:

Through me many long dumb voices,
Voices of the interminable generations of slaves,
Voices of prostitutes and of deformed persons,
Voices of the diseased and despairing, and of thieves and
    dwarfs.[27]

The kind of poetic ventriloquism that Whitman imagines in these lines epitomizes what Martín Espada has described as "Whitman the advocate." In Espada's words, "He takes it upon himself to become a voice for the voiceless."[28] Komunyakaa, however, asserts that Whitman is at times capable of silencing the diverse subjectivities he presumes to voice; yet he admires the *attempt* both to embody multitudes in his verse and to imaginatively cross culturally constructed boundaries between peoples, between languages, and between modes of thought and of being. As Komunyakaa told Michael Collins in a 2005 interview for *Callaloo*:

If there's a lingua franca of the soul, of the human spirit, an existential lingua franca, then poetry and music provide the alphabet. Bridges are erected and crossed in the flesh. Is that why Othello damns himself through the agency and language of poetry? There are so many moments in poetry where feelings and insights cross borders, creating an understanding beyond words. Not denying or forgetting Walt Whitman's lapses into exoticism, I think that he creates a terrain in *Leaves of Grass* where people coexist side by side with grace. He says in the first stanza of "Song of Myself": "I celebrate myself, and sing myself, / And what I assume you shall assume, / For every atom belonging to me as good belongs to you." Whitman's concept of language seems cosmic and carnal. I hope to achieve a voice just as inclusive as his, or Pablo Neruda's, and maybe this is possible if I continue to search.[29]

The notion of poetry as a lingua franca suggests that verse is capable of bringing together people of widely divergent linguistic and cultural backgrounds. Everyone uses languages—personal, local, national—yet poetry is linguistic expression at its most universally applicable, at its most intersubjective, and at its most mixed (since lingua franca was originally, in Dryden's words, "a certain compound Language, made up of all Tongues").[30] Intersubjective understanding, then, is poetry's claim to the universal, since it brings together essences of human experience, varied as they are. At the same time, Whitman's poetry aims for universality not solely by essentializing experience but also by underscoring the startling diversity of experience. Thus, Whitman's poetry celebrates the varied nature of the world, and it includes a multiplicity of perspectives and languages. Whitman strives for a poetics without hierarchy in which "people coexist side by side with grace," which is why he denominates himself "Walt Whitman, an American, one of the roughs [. . .] . . . . no stander above men and women or apart from them."[31] Yet, as Komunyakaa notes, Whitman does not always achieve the ideal he sets out for himself. But Komunyakaa praises the effort and "hope[s] to achieve a voice just as inclusive as his."

Komunyakaa as Poet

One of the most intricate ways in which Komunyakaa has engaged with Whitman's work is in the verses of "Kosmos" (1992/1998), "The Poetics of Paperwood" (1992), "Praise Be" (2005), and "Blackbirding on the Hudson" (2011), poems that speak—sometimes directly, sometimes indirectly—to Whitman's oeuvre. As I explore these poems in the pages that follow, I put forth interpretations not intended as conclusive readings (Komunyakaa's open, multivalent aesthetic annuls such an approach); rather, I offer notes toward possible meanings, suggestions of ways in which we might approach Komunyakaa's invocations and evocations of the good gray poet. The order in which I discuss the poems is based on the degree to which each one makes Whitman's verse, his poetic project, and his legacy a central topos.

Komunyakaa's most sustained verse dialogue with Whitman is "Kosmos," a long, four-part poem first published as part of the *Massachusetts Review*'s 1992 "Celebration of Walt Whitman," a collection of verse "appreciations" assembled for the centenary of the poet's death. A revised version was published in the 1998

JACOB WILKENFELD

volume *Thieves of Paradise*. (This essay considers, with a few exceptions noted below, the second published version of the poem.) The title of Komunyakaa's contribution to this gathering of tributes alludes to a central concept in Whitman's work. As David S. Reynolds notes: "To communicate his sense of embodying all time and nature, Whitman fastened on the word 'kosmos.' The word was so important to him that it was the only one he retained in the different versions of his famous self-identification in 'Song of Myself,' which first read 'Walt Whitman, an American, one of the roughs, a kosmos' and ended up as 'Walt Whitman, a kosmos, of Manhattan the son.'" Reynolds observes that Whitman derived the term *kosmos* from Alexander von Humboldt, whose *Kosmos* (English title *Cosmos: A Sketch of a Physical Description of the Universe*), was conceived as a depiction "in a single work of the entire material universe."[32] This encyclopedic undertaking aimed to describe the known universe as "a harmony, or blending together of all created things, however dissimilar in form and attributes, one great whole animated by the breath of life."[33] The Humboldtian concept of the cosmos, then, provided Whitman with a model for his vision of a fundamental, organic unity that transcends differences. Whitman's own notebook definition of *kosmos* extends the term to signify "a person who[se] scope of mind, or whose range in a particular science, includes all, the whole known universe."[34] Whitman's 1867 poem "Kosmos" presents a vision of such a person: "Who includes diversity and is Nature, / Who is the amplitude of the earth, and the coarseness and sexuality of the earth, and the great charity of the earth, and the equilibrium also."[35]

Kosmos is the bardic persona Whitman adopts in much of *Leaves of Grass*, and it is to that persona that Komunyakaa's poem "Kosmos" is addressed. For a celebration, the poem begins on a startling note of accusation that is at once familiar (addressed to "Walt") and suggestive of an essential separateness. The first section images Whitman within a tradition of poetic renderings of the South, a tradition concerned with the significance of southern landscapes—particularly of southern trees—and a tradition of which Komunyakaa himself is an important contemporary exponent. (An allusion to Whitman's "I Saw in Louisiana a Live-Oak Growing" also appears in Komunyakaa's poem "The Poetics of Paperwood," discussed below.) "Kosmos" opens with a startling apostrophe:

> Walt, you shanghaied me to this
> oak, as every blood-tipped leaf
> soliloquized Billie's "Strange Fruit"
> like the octoroon in New Orleans. (1–4)

The speaker images Whitman as an aggressor (as a lyncher?) and emphasizes the speaker's powerlessness. What is the meaning of the accusatory opening? Is Komunyakaa excoriating Whitman for his often conciliatory attitude toward the proslavery South? Is the accusation an expression of the anxiety of influence? Are the lines an acknowledgment that Whitman, in assuming the multitudinous "I's" of America, also assumed the masks of slaveholders and slave auctioneers — of people who likely would have perpetrated a lynching? Whatever the meaning(s) of the accusation, the first section of "Kosmos" clearly figures Whitman as intricately linked to the culture of the South.

For example, the first and second stanzas allude to an "octoroon in New Orleans," thus broaching the traditionally southern topos of miscegenation. The reference here is clearly to Whitman's three-month sojourn in New Orleans in 1848 and to the myth that he had an affair with a woman there. This story was first propagated by Whitman himself, who, in a letter defending himself against charges of homosexuality, invented a story that he had engaged in an affair with a high-born New Orleans lady whose parents had frowned on the match. However, the narrative and its variants were disseminated in some early twentieth-century biographies of Whitman, most notably Emory Holloway's 1926 *Whitman: An Interpretation in Narrative*. On the *American Experience* documentary, Komunyakaa says that "there is, you know, the myth of him actually having a relationship with a black woman or a black man."

While the racial origins of Whitman's supposed paramour do not figure into the poet's own recounting of the story, there is some evidence of Whitman's fascination with southern women of mixed ancestry. One could cite, for example, the infatuation his protagonist displays toward the Creole slave Margaret in Whitman's 1842 temperance novel *Franklin Evans, or The Inebriate*.

JACOB WILKENFELD

There is also his 1888 comment to Horace Traubel on the subject of southern miscegenation:

> I have been in New Orleans—known, seen, all its peculiar phases of life. Of course my report would be forty years old or so. The Octoroon was not a whore, a prostitute, as we call a certain class of women here—and yet *was*, too: a hard class to comprehend: women with splendid bodies—no bustles, no corsets, no enormities of any sort: large, luminous, rich eyes: face a rich olive: habits indolent, yet not lazy as we define laziness North [*sic*]: fascinating, magnetic, sexual, ignorant, illiterate: always more than pretty—"pretty" is too weak a word to apply to them.[36]

The New Orleans poem "Once I Pass'd through a Populous City" also suggests Whitman's infatuation with someone he met in the city—although there is conclusive evidence that the poem was originally about a man rather than a woman.[37] Such an infatuation could substantiate the idea of an octoroon "Who showed you how passion / Ignited dogwoods, how it came / From inside the singing sap" (5–7). Moreover, the octoroon is suggestive of Whitman's passion for southern (and, more broadly, American) identity—for identities that cross artificial yet culturally reinforced barriers.[38] The section also implies a southern inspiration for Whitman's poetry: "You heard primordial notes / murmur up from the Mississippi" (8–9). The initial version of Komunyakaa's "Kosmos" specifies "primordial notes of jazz," suggesting that Whitman's southern experience fomented both the modernity of his poetics and its free-flowing, eclectic style, which still retains a sense of form—another instantiation of the central idea of Whitman's term "kosmos."[39] Thus, the poem plays with notions of literary inheritance, intimating not only Whitman's influence on Komunyakaa but also a black southern influence on Whitman.

More properly speaking, the "primordial notes" Whitman may have heard along the banks of the Mississippi would have been spirituals and other folksongs that helped shape the patterns of the blues and, later, jazz. Whitman would have heard those notes, then, fundamentally as expressions of human suffering, "a clank of chains among the green / ithyphallic totems" (10–11)— the calamus plants that provided Whitman with his most moving symbol of homoerotic affection. The lines suggest that a musical form shaped by the bonds between slaves might have inspired Whitman's trope of adhesiveness—his idea that "the nation is an entity not of institutions and abstract strictures but of relation," as Peter Coviello has noted.[40] The slaves' collective suffering produces haunting sounds within the otherwise bucolic setting. The image of the slaves' chains clanking, juxtaposed to the calumus "totems," evokes the inextricable beauty and tragedy of American history. Whitman sought to embody as much of America's human landscape as he could:

> betting your heart
> could run vistas with Crazy Horse
>
> & runaway slaves. Sunset dock
> to whorehouse, temple to hovel,
> Your lines traversed America's
>   white space, driven by a train whistle. (11–16)

His attempt to traverse "America's / white space" not only via his real travels throughout the country but through his poetic imagination and the lines of his verse suggests that America had not been written yet, as Emerson intimated in "The Poet." The adjective "white" also implies that Whitman's imagination and poetry crossed over from his (presumably comfortable) space of racial whiteness into the identities of racial others. His was a modern song "driven by a train whistle" that tried to capture the rhythms of modernity. Like the octoroon who captured Whitman's fancy, then, Whitman's poems traverse borders—physical, conceptual, political, temporal, and racial.

The opening lines of the second section also suggest Whitman's crossing over of various sexualities and historical epochs:

> Believing you could be three places
> at once, you held the gatekeeper's daughter,
> lured by the hard eyes of his son,
> on a voyage in your head
>
> to a face cut into Mount Rushmore. (17–21)

Whitman's imagination transcends boundaries and deals with subjects, like bisexual desire and the scent of the author's armpits,

JACOB WILKENFELD

considered literary taboos in nineteenth-century genteel poetry. The image of Whitman's imagined voyage to Mount Rushmore suggests his teleological view of America's destined greatness. Yet Komunyakaa does not imply that Whitman was entirely naive in his optimism about America's future prospects. Whitman is as cynical as any regarding the fall of humanity from a state of grace; as Komunyakaa writes, Whitman "knew the curse was in the sperm / & egg" (22–23). Yet Whitman believed that America's imagined community could overcome the iniquities of history— hence his "faith in the soil, / That it'd work itself out in generations" (23–24). Those generations would manifest an eradication of arbitrary boundaries via the force of America's union:

> springs piercing bedrock.
> Love pushed through jailhouses, into bedrooms
> of presidents & horse thieves,
> oil sucked into machines in sweatshops
>
> & factories. (25–29)

These lines are immersed in love's power in much the same way Whitman's poetic persona pushes through borders to connect the nation's most far-flung phenomena. In his own poetic practice, Komunyakaa has looked to Whitman as a model of democratic poetics and of a writerly practice unafraid of confronting the realities of modern America. Even in Komunyakaa's boyhood in the 1940s and 1950s, Whitman's democratic vision was considered dangerous and erotic reading:

> I followed from my hometown
> where bedding an oak is bread on the table;
> where your books, as if flesh, were locked
> in a glass case behind the check-out desk. (29–32)[41]

Section 3 of "Kosmos" presents a series of extraordinary metaphors to describe Whitman's verse:

> Wind-jostled foliage—a scherzo
> Like a bellydancer adorned in bells.
> A mulatto moon halved into yesterday
> & tomorrow, some balustrade
>
> full-bloomed. (33–37)

Komunyakaa has spoken of the musical quality that Whitman achieves in his verse, which "is clearly influenced by Italian opera, so everything reaches for a crescendo." The "mulatto moon" (his striking image of a half-moon) again suggests Whitman's attempt to embody the diverse origins and identities that make up America, past and future, "yesterday / & tomorrow." (These lines may also be a direct reference to Whitman's poem "Kosmos": "The past, the future, dwelling there, like space, inseparable to- / gether" [11].) And Whitman is a "balustrade / full-bloomed"—an artifice, but one that follows an organic pattern (from *balaustra, "wild pomegranate flower"*) rather than a rigidly artificial, invented form.

> But you taught home
> was wherever my feet took me,
> birdsong over stockyards or Orient,
> fused by handshake & blood. (37–40)

The lesson that Whitman teaches is one of curiosity about the world's diversity, for "you taught me home / was wherever my feet took me, / birdsong over stockyards or Orient." Whitman teaches that poetry is all-inclusive in its rendering of the world, that it doesn't "dodge anything." It was a lesson Whitman appears to have learned from Emerson, who in "The Poet" writes: "We have yet had no genius in America, with tyrannous eye, which knew the value of our incomparable materials, and saw, in the barbarism and materialism of the times, another carnival of the same gods whose picture he so much admires in Homer."[42] Toward the end of "Kosmos," Komunyakaa seems to acknowledge Whitman as a literary forebear, only to complicate this idea of influence in the stanzas that conclude the poem:

> Seed & testament, naked
> among fire-nudged thistle,
> from the Rockies to below
> sea level, to steamy bayous,
>
> I traipsed your footpath.
> Falsehoods big as stumbling blocks,
> in the mind, lay across the road,
> beside a watery swoon. (41–48)

Here, Whitman's verse is conceived of both as a germ of Komunyakaa's poetic practice and as a record of the geographical and historical landscape of Whitman's time—Whitman's America is territory contemporary poets like Komunyakaa retread. Yet the fourth, final section of the poem leaves off from the dynamics of fatherly influence. Komunyakaa suggests that Whitman is not the only ancestral guide who has helped him find his voice: "I'm back with the old folk / who speak your glossolalia of pure / sense unfolding a hundred years" (49–51). Komunyakaa, too, seems to foreground not only Whitman's influence but the collective, extraliterary cultural patterns (the glossolalia of the "old folk"— perhaps a reference to African American spiritual practice) that bear on his verse. Whitman's poetry of "pure sense" was radical in both form and sexually explicit subject matter—too much so for some of the poet's contemporaries to comprehend, so that the poet's meaning has been "unfolding one hundred years." Within the repressive culture of mid-nineteenth-century America, *Leaves of Grass* defiantly and steadfastly celebrated the naturalness of sexual union:

> Unlocked chemistry, we're tied to sex,
> spectral flower twisted out of
> filigreed language & taboo
> stubborn as crabgrass. You slept
> nude under god-hewn eyes and ears. (52–56)

It was Whitman who audaciously proclaimed in the poem that would become "Song of Myself," "I will go to the bank by the wood and become undisguised and naked."[43]

Denominating Whitman an "Old hippie / before Selma & People's Park" (58–59) and praising his "democratic nights" as "a vortex / of waterlilies" (60–61), Komunyakaa concludes the poem on a note of hesitation:

> The skin's cage
> opened, but you were locked inside
> your exotic Ethiopia. Everything
> sprung back like birds after a shot. (61–64)

"Kosmos" ends with an image of Whitman as a visionary whose verse attempts to erase the boundary between concepts of self and other. Yet his poetic project was not entirely successful, since he was "locked inside" the objectifying stereotypes that disallowed an uncontaminated empathetic understanding to manifest itself. "Your exotic Ethiopia" likely alludes to Whitman's 1867 poem, "Ethiopia Saluting the Colors"—the postbellum evocation of a formerly enslaved woman's awe at abolition known for its uninspired, stereotype-laden descriptive language ("Who are you dusky woman, so ancient hardly human").[44] Interestingly, the last stanza of the first version of "Kosmos" elides any reference to Whitman's confinement within a stereotypical vision. That version ends as follows:

> Your democratic nights were a vortex
> Of waterlilies. The skin's cage
> Opened by the mind. Everything
> Flew apart, but came back like birds
> To a tree after the blast of a shotgun.[45]

The first published version more explicitly suggests Whitman's notion of *kosmos* as a unity transcending difference ("Everything / Flew apart, but came back"). Yet the second version, which Komunyakaa included in *Thieves of Paradise* and later in *Pleasure Dome*, a volume of new and collected poems, is ambiguous in its praise of Whitman's cosmic vision. Komunyakaa's preference for the second version denotes a continuing preoccupation with the sometimes troubling cultural politics of Whitman's project. Such ambiguity implicitly critiques the very idea of *kosmos* as a system. The poem questions whether even a totality as democratic as Whitman's is truly capable of representing the world's countless differences. Like the other instances of Komunyakaa's engagement with Whitman, "Kosmos" celebrates Whitman's democratic verse but also illuminates blind spots in his poetic vision.

"Praise Be" (2005), another poem that references Whitman, is an homage to Galway Kinnell for his 1960s civil rights activism in Louisiana. Specifically, Kinnell worked for the Congress of Racial Equality's voter registration campaign, an undertaking that eventually consigned him to a week in jail. Komunyakaa's poem places Kinnell within a lineage of northern poets who have directed their gazes southward, beginning with Whitman, who spent three months in New Orleans in 1848, in his words, "im-

JACOB WILKENFELD

printing my brain for future use with its shows, architecture, customs, traditions" and writing articles for the *New Orleans Crescent*:

> When the trees were guilty, hugged up
> to history & locked in a cross-brace
> with Whitman's Louisiana live oak,
> you went into that mossy weather.[46]

The poem alludes to a recent, twentieth-century past when lynching was a common practice. But that past is inextricable from the more distant past of the slaveholding South—a past remote enough to be classified as history. The allusion to "Whitman's Louisiana live oak" is semantically charged. On the one hand, the phrase suggests that the trees Kinnell saw in the early 1960s South were already alive in Whitman's era. The average life span of a live-oak is about 350 years, so it is quite possible to imagine Kinnell could have glimpsed trees Whitman himself encountered in 1848—trees around which Komunyakaa experienced his own Louisiana childhood.[47] Thus, one possible reading of the Whitman allusion would conclude that it intimates the Faulknerian idea that "the past isn't dead; it isn't even past." The poem also alludes specifically to Whitman's "I Saw in Louisiana a Live-Oak Growing" and possibly to his sequence "Live Oak, with Moss," a set of poems that, in their published version, were reorganized as part of the larger "Calamus" cluster. Both the poem and the "Live Oak, with Moss" sequence are explorations of the adhesive love between men that Whitman viewed as essential in the construction of a national union. In particular, "I Saw in Louisiana a Live-Oak Growing" celebrates the tree's capacity to utter "joyous leaves all its life without a friend, a lover, near," though Whitman's speaker concludes that "I know very well I could not."[48] (The poem, then, is indicative of isolation and lack of communication rather than interaction. Perhaps this is the meaning of the live-oak reference in "Praise Be": an image of the South Kinnell protested in as a region ever increasingly isolating itself from the racial mores of the larger American society, much as the antebellum secessionists had posited the South as a self-contained territory.

The second stanza figures Kinnell as a Whitman-like figure:

Did you witness the shotguns at Angola
riding on horseback through the tall sway
of sugarcane, the glint of blue steel
in the blood-red strawberry fields? (5–8)

The question "Did you witness" asks about the place of testimony
among poets. In "Song of Myself," Whitman famously writes: "I am
the man . . . . I suffered . . . . I was there."[49] And Kinnell's "The Last
River," one of his best-known poems, is about witnessing; it describes his 1963 experience of being jailed for his civil rights activism. Yet the poem intimates that it doesn't matter whether Kinnell
actually "witness[ed] the shotguns" at Louisiana's notorious Angola prison. Like Whitman, Kinnell has the empathic capacity to
imagine others' experiences, harrowing though they may be. Thus,
although "Silence was backed-up in the cypress" (9), Kinnell

could hear the birds of woe
singing praise where the almost broken-
through sorrow rose from the deep woods
& walked out into the moonshine as women
& men. (10–12)

Komunyakaa praises Kinnell's power of empathy, for going

among those who had half
a voice
whose ancestors mastered quicksand
by disappearing. (14–16)

Like Whitman, Kinnell identifies with society's marginalized—
in this case, black Louisianans who had to fight for their voting rights in the early 1960s. Within the community of "those
who had half / a voice" was the young Komunyakaa himself, who
was sixteen when Kinnell worked for CORE: "Maybe our paths
crossed / ghosts hogtied in the wounded night," "but it is only
now I say this: Galway, / thank you for going down to our fierce
hush / at the crossroads to look fear in the eye" (18–20). Like Kinnell and Whitman, Komunyakaa has manifested a willingness to
broach explosive, politically charged themes in his verses (as he
does in the poems of *Taboo*, to cite just one prominent example)
and to ventriloquize voices long suppressed by a "fierce hush."

Komunyakaa's brief invocation of Whitman in "Praise Be" is characteristic of his overall engagement with the author of *Leaves of Grass*. Like "Kosmos," "Praise Be" is not a "Whitmanian" poem; it engages with Whitman's verse but does not emulate it. Instead, Komunyakaa's densely allusive poems treat Whitman as one point of reference among myriad others. Two further examples that illustrate this form of engagement are the nostalgic "Poetics of Paperwood," from the 1992 collection *Magic City*, and, perhaps, the historically mindful "Blackbirding on the Hudson," from 2011's *The Chameleon Couch*. In the former, the poet describes felling trees in his Louisiana hometown of Bogalusa, where the paper and lumber industries are the base of the local economy:

> I saw where locusts
> Sang themselves out of
> Translucent shells
> Still clinging to
> Whitman's Live-Oak.[50]

Here, the allusion does not dominate the poem's thrust; instead, the reference serves to echo the verses' thematic focus on musicality—in verse and in life. While the poem's characters—presumably the young Komunyakaa and his father—come to understand that "work / Was rhythm, / & so was love," the allusion to Whitman amplifies the meanings of "work" and "love."[51] In poems like "I Hear America Singing," Whitman displayed an understanding, as Komunyakaa does here, that the poet's rhythms derive from and reflect the rhythms of life: the rhythms of work, of familial and sexual love, and of nature.

In "Blackbirding on the Hudson," there is no explicit allusion to Whitman at all, yet the long prosody is uncharacteristic of Komunyakaa's oeuvre and stylistically recalls Whitman's verse. In an interview in which he discusses his engagement with both Whitman and Dickinson, Komunyakaa describes the latter's poetry as "entirely different from Whitman, although as a poet I embrace Whitman more, with his long lines. And again, the length of the lines, the long lines, seems to beg meditation as opposed to the vertical trajectory of short lines. For the most part, I embrace the short line, and maybe that has something to do with contemporary time, the way everything seems sped up. There's a kind of vertical plunge of the poem."[52] "Blackbirding on the Hudson" is written in long lines that meditate on birds, rivers, and slavery. The title plays on the verb form of "blackbird," a late nineteenth-century term signifying "to engage in the slave trade especially in the South Pacific."[53] Like "Poetics of Paperwood," this is not a "Whitmanian" poem per se, yet it seems to enter into a dialogue—perhaps more subtly than the other poems discussed in this essay—with Whitman, author of what is arguably the most celebrated river poem in American literature, "Crossing Brooklyn Ferry." The meandering flow of Whitman's lines in that poem exalts the ever-constant flux of the present moment as typified by the river's current. (Whitman writes, "Just as you are refresh'd by the gladness of the river, and the bright flow, I was refresh'd.")[54] By contrast, Komunyakaa interrogates the disturbing human history reflected in the passage of time and water—particularly the history of the slave trade, which depended so thoroughly on the use of sea and river ways. Tempted to aestheticize his remembrances of the Hudson River, the poem's speaker instead reluctantly probes the menacing history of bondage evoked by the river's continuity with times past: "But there's another phrase—I think it is 'blackbirding'—pecking fiercely / at my gut. Body of resolve, body of water, do you know anything about this?"[55] Like Whitman's East River in "Crossing Brooklyn Ferry," then, Komunyakaa's Hudson annihilates the trite and simplistic temporal schemes of past, present, and future. Like "Crossing," "Blackbirding" speaks movingly of the presence of the past within the present. But Komunyakaa's river carries haunting, unsolicited memories his speaker would rather not remember:

> I'd love to forget those years when a black boy and girl sent to the grocery store
> at dusk to buy a loaf of bread, or three red apples, or a quart of kerosene,
> or a half pound of salt meat could disappear between a laugh and a cry
> as you pretended to be River Styx. Where are we going, mister?
> Hogtied down in boats, gagged or conked over the head, boys and girls

JACOB WILKENFELD

cried out for mothers & fathers, to God. At what hour of the
  night
the blood remembers that first voyage in the hold across the
  Atlantic?[56]

In "Crossing Brooklyn Ferry" Whitman optimistically embraces
of both time and timelessness—the particularity of the present
moment and the unbroken bonds stretching over the ages.
"Blackbirding on the Hudson" solemnly acknowledges the power
of such bonds, but Komunyakaa's poem insists on the irresolvable tragedy of a past that is never dead, that is never even past.
Thus Komunyakaa revisits one of Whitman's most important
topoi—that of the river—and, as is true of his engagement with
Whitman more generally, he offers the reader an alternative, dis-
orienting, and transformational perspective.

Conclusion

As I have tried to show, it is more instructive to look at what Komunyakaa does with Whitman than at Whitmanian traces in Komunyakaa's work. In a 2011 interview, Komunyakaa himself has
spoken disparagingly of critics who compare his work to Whitman's through the lens of traditional influence-oriented perspectives: "I think the comparison is an easy—less than critical—
gesture."[57] An example of such a comparison is a 2004 *Buffalo
News* review of Komunyakaa's *Thieves of Paradise* entitled "Komunyakaa's Aesthetic Owes Much to Whitman's Democratic
Spirit." The reviewer muses that Komunyakaa "is now the figure
in contemporary American poetry whose body of work most
identifiably qualifies as 'Whitmanesque.'"[58] While there is no
question that the reviewer means to praise Komunyakaa as an
important voice in contemporary American literature, his language also employs the traditional language of influence and indebtedness, thereby downplaying both Komunyakaa's originality
and the inventiveness contained within his reconceptualization
of Whitman's oeuvre. However, rather than assimilate Whitman's
work uncritically, Komunyakaa both celebrates and critiques it.
In doing so, he honors Whitman's own instructions to his readers
as elucidated in "Song of Myself": "He most honors my style who
learns under it to destroy the teacher."[59] Komunyakaa does pre-

cisely that, offering new ways to look at the Whitmanian *kosmos* from the alternate poetic universe of his own imagination.

NOTES

1. *American Experience: Walt Whitman*, directed by Mark Zwonitzer, PBS, WGBH, Boston, 2008.

2. Edward Carvalho, "A Branch on the Tree of Whitman: Martín Espada Talks about *Leaves of Grass*," *Walt Whitman Quarterly Review* 26 (Summer 2008): 25.

3. Luís Alberto Urrea, "On Standing at Neruda's Tomb: An Interview with Martín Espada," *Poetry Foundation*, 5 March 2007, accessed 22 July 2012, http://www.poetryfoundation.org/article/179395.

4. Rebecca Leung, "Billy Collins: America's Poet," *CBS News*, 2 July 2003, accessed 22 July 2012, http://www.cbsnews.com/2100-500164_162-561047.html. As Charlie Rose observes in the CBS segment on Collins, "Becoming a poet in America virtually condemns one to a life of anonymity and, even worse, to a life of poverty. There are exceptions. Walt Whitman was well known during his lifetime. And, of course, Robert Frost was one of the most popular poets ever to grace the language. But they were the exceptions. And now, you're about to meet that truly rare creature—a poet who's not only becoming famous, he's also getting rich, just by writing poetry."

5. Walt Whitman, preface to the 1855 edition of *Leaves of Grass*, in *Poetry and Prose*, ed. Justin Kaplan (New York: Library of America, 1982), 26.

6. See Billy Collins, foreword to *Leaves of Grass: 150th Anniversary Edition* (New York: Signet Classics, 2005).

7. Ed Folsom, *Walt Whitman: The Measure of His Song*, 2nd ed. (Duluth: Holy Cow! Press, 1998), 23.

8. Kenneth M. Price, *To Walt Whitman, America* (Chapel Hill: University of North Carolina Press, 2004), 4, 5.

9. Walt Whitman, "Song of Myself," in *Poetry and Prose*, 26.

10. Ed Folsom and Kenneth M. Price, *Re-scripting Walt Whitman: An Introduction to His Life and Work* (Malden, MA: Blackwell, 2005), 128.

11. Komunyakaa, "Kosmos," lines 31–32, in *Thieves of Paradise* (Hanover, NH: Wesleyan University Press, published by University Press of New England, 1998), 12. Hereafter cited in the text by line number.

12. See Ernest Suarez, ed., *Southbound: Interviews with Southern Poets* (Columbia: University of Missouri Press, 1999), 135.

13. See Langston Hughes, "Calls Whitman Negroes' First Great Poetic Friend, Lincoln of Letters," *Chicago Defender*, 4 July 1953, 11. Also see June Jordan, "For the Sake of People's Poetry," in *Some of Us Did Not Die: New and Selected Essays* (New York: Basic/Civitas, 2002), 242–53.

JACOB WILKENFELD

14. Price, *To Walt Whitman*, 5.

15. Jeffrey Dodd and Jessica Moll with Yusef Komunyakaa, "A Conversation with Yusef Komunyakaa" (1987), in *Conversations with Yusef Komunyakaa*, ed. Shirley A. Hanshaw (Jackson: University Press of Mississippi, 2010), 181.

16. Ralph Waldo Emerson, *Essays and Lectures*, ed. Joel Porte (New York: Library of America, 1983), 465.

17. Whitman, preface to the 1855 edition of *Leaves of Grass*, 7.

18. Angela M. Salas, *Flashback through the Heart: The Poetry of Yusef Komunyakaa* (Selinsgrove, PA: Susquehanna University Press, 2004), 49.

19. The reference is to "I Sing the Body Electric":

A slave at auction!
I help the auctioneer . . . . the sloven does not half know his business.

Gentlemen look on this curious creature,
Whatever the bids of the bidders they cannot be high enough for him."
    (in *Poetry and Prose*, 123)

20. Yusef Komunyakaa, *Blue Notes: Essays, Interviews, and Commentaries*, ed. Radiclani Clytus (Ann Arbor: University of Michigan Press, 2000), 31.

21. Whitman, preface to the 1855 edition of *Leaves of Grass*, 8.

22. Emerson, *Essays and Lectures*, 465.

23. Komunyakaa, "A Conversation with Yusef Komunyakaa," 181.

24. Whitman, "Salut au Monde," in *Poetry and Prose*, 296.

25. Whitman, "Song of Myself," in *Poetry and Prose*, 35.

26. Price, *To Walt Whitman*, 24.

27. Whitman, "Song of Myself," in *Poetry and Prose*, 50.

28. Carvalho, "A Branch on the Tree of Whitman," 24, 25.

29. Michael Collins, "Komunyakaa, Collaboration, and the Wishbone: An Interview," *Callaloo* 28, no. 3 (2005): 634.

30. John Dryden, *The Kind Keeper*, in *The Works of John Dryden*, ed. Vinton A. Dearing and Alan Roper (Berkeley: University of California Press, 1992), 14:24.

31. Whitman, "Leaves of Grass," in *Poetry and Prose*, 50.

32. David S. Reynolds, *Walt Whitman's America: A Cultural Biography* (New York: Alfred A. Knopf, 1995), 244.

33. Whitman quoted in ibid., 244.

34. Whitman quoted in ibid., 246.

35. Whitman, "Kosmos," in *Poetry and Prose*, 516.

36. Horace Traubel, *With Walt Whitman in Camden* (New York: D. Appleton and Company, 1908), 2:283.

37. Justin Kaplan, *Walt Whitman: A Life* (New York: Harper, 2003), 143.

38. For an example of Whitman's passion for southern identity, see his 1860 poem "Longings for Home" (later retitled "O Magnet South"), in *Poetry and Prose*, 584–85.

39. Version 1 of Yusef Komunyakaa, "Kosmos," *Massachusetts Review* 33 (Spring 1992): 87–89.

40. Peter Coviello, *Intimacy in America: Dreams of Affiliation in Antebellum Literature* (Minneapolis: University of Minnesota Press, 2005), 129.

41. "Bedding an oak" is a reference to the lumber trade, an important economic sector in Komunyakaa's hometown of Bogalusa, Louisiana.

42. Emerson, "The Poet," in *Essays and Lectures*, 465.

43. Whitman, "Song of Myself," in *Poetry and Prose*, 27.

44. Whitman, "Ethiopia Saluting the Colors," in *Poetry and Prose*, 451.

45. Komunyakaa, "Kosmos," 89.

46. Whitman, "Once I Pass'd Through a Populous City," in *Poetry and Prose*, 266; Yusef Komunyakaa, "Praise Be," *Callaloo* 28, no. 3 (2005): 474, lines 1–4. Subsequent references to this poem will be cited parenthetically in the text by line number.

47. Richard D. Porcher and Douglas A. Rayner, *A Guide to the Wildflowers of South Carolina* (Columbia: University of South Carolina Press, 2001), 356.

48. Whitman, "I Saw in Louisiana a Live-Oak Growing," in *Poetry and Prose*, 280.

49. Whitman, "Song of Myself," in *Poetry and Prose*, 64.

50. Yusef Komunyakaa, "Poetics of Paperwood," in *Magic City* (Hanover, NH: University Press of New England [for Wesleyan University Press], 1992), lines 23–27.

51. Ibid., lines 51–53.

52. Komunyakaa, "A Conversation with Yusef Komunyakaa," 184.

53. *Merriam-Webster.com*, accessed 22 July 2012.

54. Whitman, "Crossing Brooklyn Ferry," in *Poetry and Prose*, 309.

55. Yusef Komunyakaa, "Blackbirding on the Hudson," in *The Chameleon Couch: Poems* (New York: Farrar, Straus and Giroux, 2011), 58.

56. Ibid.

57. Yusef Komunyakaa, "An Interview with Yusef Komunyakaa, Author of *The Chameleon Couch*," *The Farrar, Straus and Giroux Poetry Blog*, 19 April 2011, accessed 2 December 2011.

58. R. D. Pohl, "Komunyakaa's Aesthetic Owes Much to Whitman's Democratic Spirit," *New Buffalo News*, 4 April 2004.

59. Whitman, "Song of Myself," in *Poetry and Prose*, 83.

{ 148 }   JACOB WILKENFELD

Part Two

7

For the Sake of People's Poetry
Walt Whitman and the Rest of Us

JUNE JORDAN

In America, the father is white; it is he who inaugurated the experiment of this republic. It is he who sailed his way into slave ownership and who availed himself of my mother—that African woman whose function was miserable—defined by his desirings, or his rage. It is he who continues to dominate the destiny of the Mississippi River, the Blue Ridge Mountains, and the life of my son. Understandably, then, I am curious about this man.

Most of the time my interest can be characterized as wary at best. Other times it is the interest a pedestrian feels for the fast-traveling truck about to smash into him. Or her. Again. And at other times it is the curiosity of a stranger trying to figure out the system of the language that excludes her name and all of the names of all of her people. It is this last that leads me to the poet Walt Whitman.

Trying to understand the system responsible for every boring, inaccessible, irrelevant, derivative, and pretentious poem that is glued to the marrow of required readings in American classrooms, or trying to understand the system responsible for the exclusion of every hilarious, amazing, visionary, pertinent, and unforgettable poet from National Endowment of the Arts grants and from national publications, I come back to Walt Whitman.

What in the hell happened to him? Wasn't he a white man? Wasn't he some kind of a father to American literature? Didn't he talk about this New World? Didn't he see it? Didn't he sing this New World, this America, on a New World, an American scale of his own visionary invention?

It so happens that Walt Whitman is the one white father who shares the systematic disadvantages of his heterogeneous off-spring trapped inside a closet that is, in reality, as huge as the continental spread of North and South America. What Whitman envisioned, we, the people and the poets of the New World, embody. He has been punished for the moral questions that our very lives arouse.

At home as a child, I learned the poetry of the Bible and the poetry of Paul Laurence Dunbar. As a student, I diligently followed orthodox directions from *The Canterbury Tales* right through *The Waste Land* by that consummate Anglophile whose name I can never remember. And I kept waiting. It was, I thought, all right to deal with daffodils in the seventeenth century of an island as much like Manhattan as I resemble Queen Mary. But what about Dunbar? When was he coming up again? And where were the black poets altogether? And who were the women poets I might reasonably emulate? And wasn't there, ever, a great poet who was crazy about Brooklyn or furious about war? And I kept waiting. And I kept writing my own poetry. And I kept reading apparently underground poetry: poetry kept strictly off campus. I kept reading the poetry of so many gifted students when I became a teacher. I kept listening to the wonderful poetry of the multiplying numbers of my friends who were and who are New World poets until I knew, for a fact, that there was and that there is an American, a New World poetry that is as personal, as public, as irresistible, as quick, as necessary, as unprecedented, as representative, as exalted, as speakably commonplace, and as musical as an emergency phone call.

But I didn't know about Walt Whitman. Yes, I had heard about this bohemian, this homosexual, even, who wrote something about The Captain and The Lilacs in The Hallway, but nobody ever told me to read his work! Not only was Whitman not required reading, he was, on the contrary, presented as a rather hairy buffoon suffering from a childish proclivity for exercise and open air.

Nevertheless, it is through the study of the poems and the ideas of this particular white father that I have reached a tactical, if not strategic, understanding of the racist, sexist, and anti-American

JUNE JORDAN

predicament that condemns most New World writing to peripheral/unpublished manuscript status.

Before these United States came into being, the great poets of the world earned their luster through undeniable forms of spontaneous popularity; generations of a people chose to memorize and then to further elaborate these songs and to impart them to the next generation. I am talking about people; African families and Greek families and the families of the Hebrew tribes and all that multitude to whom the Bhagavad Gita is as daily as the sun! If these poems were not always religious, they were certainly moral in notice, or in accomplishment, or both. None of these great poems would be mistaken for the poetry of another country, another time. You do not find a single helicopter taking off or landing in any of the sonnets of Elizabethan England, nor do you run across rice and peas in any of the Psalms! Evidently, one criterion for great poetry used to be the requirements of cultural nationalism.

But by the advent of the thirty-six-year-old poet Walt Whitman, the phenomenon of a people's poetry, or great poetry and its spontaneous popularity, could no longer be assumed. The physical immensity and the far-flung population of this New World decisively separated poets from suitable means to produce and distribute their poetry. Now there would have to be intermediaries—critics and publishers—whose marketplace principles of scarcity would, logically, oppose them to populist traditions of art.

Old World concepts would replace the democratic, and these elitist notions would prevail; in the context of such considerations, an American literary establishment antithetical to the New World meanings of America took root. And this is one reason why the preeminently American white father of American poetry exists primarily in the realm of caricature and rumor in his own country.

As a matter of fact, if you hope to hear about Whitman, your best bet is to leave home. Ignore prevailing American criticism and, instead, ask anybody anywhere else in the world this question: As Shakespeare is to England, Dante to Italy, Tolstoy to Russia, Goethe to Germany, Aghostino Neto to Angola, Pablo Neruda to Chile, Mao Tse-tung to China, and Ho Chi Minh to Vietnam, who is the great American writer, the distinctively American poet, the giant American "literatus"? Undoubtedly, the answer will be *Walt Whitman.*

He is the poet who wrote:

"A man's body at auction
(For before the war I often go to the slave-mart and watch
   the sale.)
I help the auctioneer, the sloven does not half know his
   business.

.   .   .   .

Gentlemen look on this wonder.
Whatever the bids of the bidders they cannot be high enough
   for it.[1]

I ask you, today: Who in the United States would publish those lines? They are all wrong! In the first place, there is nothing obscure, nothing contrived, nothing an ordinary strap-hanger in the subway would be puzzled by! In the second place, the voice of those lines is intimate and direct at once; it is the voice of the poet who assumes that he speaks to an equal and that he need not fear that equality. On the contrary, the intimate distance between the poet and the reader is a distance that assumes there is everything important between them to be shared. And what is poetic about a line of words that runs as long as a regular, a spoken idea? You could more easily imagine an actual human being speaking such lines than you could imagine an artist composing them in a room carefully separated from the real life of his family. This can't be poetry! Besides, these lines apparently serve an expressly moral purpose! Then is this didactic/political writing? Aha! This cannot be *good* poetry. And, in fact, you will never see, for example, the *New Yorker* magazine publishing a poem marked by such splendid deficiencies.

Consider the inevitable, the irresistible, simplicity of that enormous moral idea:

Gentlemen look on this wonder.
Whatever the bids of the bidders they cannot be high enough
   for it . . .
This is not only one man, this the father of those who shall be
   fathers in their turns

JUNE JORDAN

In him the start of populous states and rich republics,
Of him countless immortal lives with countless embodiments
   and enjoyments.

Crucial and obviously important, and, hence, this is not an idea generally broadcast: the poet is trying to save a human being while even the *poem* cannot be saved from the insolence of marketplace evaluation!

Indeed, Whitman and the traceable descendants of Walt Whitman, those who follow his democratic faith into obviously New World forms of experience and art, they suffer from the same establishment rejection and contempt that forced this archetypal American genius to publish, distribute, and review his own work by himself. The descendants I have in mind include those unmistakably contemporaneous young poets who base themselves upon domesticities such as disco, Las Vegas, McDonald's, and forty-dollar running shoes. Also within the Whitman tradition, black and First World poets traceably transform and further the egalitarian sensibility that isolates that one white father from his more powerful compatriots.[2] I am thinking of the feminist poets evidently intent upon speaking with a maximal number and diversity of other Americans' lives. I am thinking of all the many first-rank heroes of the New World who are overwhelmingly forced to publish their own works using a hand press, or whatever, or else give it up entirely.

That is to say, the only peoples who can test or verify the meaning of the United States as a democratic state, as a pluralistic culture, are the very peoples whose contribution to a national vision and discovery meets with steadfast ridicule and disregard.

A democratic state does not, after all, exist for the few but for the many. A democratic state is not proven by the welfare of the strong but by the welfare of the weak. And unless that many, that manifold constitution of diverse peoples can be seen as integral to the national art/the national consciousness, you might as well mean only Czechoslovakia when you talk about the United States, or only Ireland, or merely France, or exclusively white men.

Pablo Neruda is a New World poet whose fate differs from that of the other Whitman descendants because he was born into a country where the majority of the citizens did not mistake themselves for Englishmen or long to find themselves struggling, at most, with cucumber sandwiches and tea. He was never European. His anguish was not aroused by three-piece suits and rolled umbrellas. When he cries, toward the conclusion of *The Heights of Macchu Picchu*, "Arise and birth with me, my brother," he plainly does not allude to Lord or Colonel Anybody At All.[3] As he writes earlier in that amazing poem:

> I came by another way, river by river, street after street,
> city by city, one bed and another,
> forcing the salt of my mask through a wilderness;
> and there, in the shame of the ultimate hovels, lampless and
>   tireless,
> lacking bread or a stone or a stillness, alone in myself,
>   I whirled at my will, dying the death that was mine.[4]

Of course, Neruda has not escaped all of the untoward consequences common to Whitman descendants. American critics and translators never weary of asserting that Neruda is a quote great unquote poet *despite* the political commitment of his art and despite the artistic consequences of the commitment. Specifically, Neruda's self-conscious decision to write in a manner readily comprehensible to the masses of his countrymen and his self-conscious decision to specify, outright, the United Fruit Company when that was the instigating subject of his poem become unfortunate moments in an otherwise supposedly sublime, not to mention surrealist, deeply Old World and European but nonetheless Chilean case history. To assure the validity of this perspective, the usual American critic and translator presents you with a smattering of the unfortunate, ostensibly political poetry and, on the other hand, buries you under volumes of Neruda's early work that antedates the Spanish Civil War or, in other words, that antedates Neruda's serious conversion to a political worldview.

This kind of artistically indefensible censorship would have you perceive qualitative and even irreconcilable differences between the poet who wrote:

> You, my antagonist, in that splintering dream
> like the bristling glass of gardens, like a menace of ruinous
>   bells, volleys

JUNE JORDAN

of blackening ivy at the perfume's center,
enemy of the great hipbones my skin has touched
with a harrowing dew.[5]

And the poet who wrote, some twenty years later, these lines from the poem entitled "The Dictators":

lament was perpetual and fell, like a plant and its pollen,
forcing a lightless increase in the blinded, big leaves.
And bludgeon by bludgeon, on the terrible waters,
scale over scale in the bog,
the snout filled with silence and slime
and vendetta was born.[6]

According to prevalent American criticism, that later poem of Neruda represents a lesser achievement precisely because it can be understood by more people, more easily, than the first. It is also derogated because this poem attacks a keystone of the Old World, namely, dictatorship or, in other words, power and privilege for the few.

The peculiar North American vendetta against Walt Whitman, against the first son of this democratic union, can be further fathomed if you look at some facts: Neruda's eminence is now acknowledged on international levels; it is known to encompass a profound impact upon North American poets who do not realize the North American/Walt Whitman origins for so much that is singular and worthy in the poetry of Neruda. You will even find American critics who congratulate Neruda for overcoming the "Whitmanesque" content of his art. This perfidious arrogance is as calculated as it is common. You cannot persuade anyone seriously familiar with Neruda's life and art that he could have found cause, at any point, to disagree with the tenets, the analysis, and the authentic New World vision presented by Walt Whitman in his essay *Democratic Vistas*, which remains the most signal and persuasive manifesto of New World thinking and belief in print.

Let me define my terms in brief: New World does not mean New England. New World means non-European; it means new; it means big; it means heterogeneous; it means unknown; it means free; it means an end to feudalism, caste, privilege, and the violence of power. It means *wild* in the sense that a tree growing away from the earth enacts a wild event. It means *democratic* in the sense that, as Whitman wrote: "I believe a leaf of grass is no less than the journey-work of the stars . . . / And a mouse is miracle enough to stagger sextillions of infidels."[7] New World means that, as Whitman wrote, "I keep as delicate around the bowels as around the head and heart." New World means, as Whitman said, "By God! I will accept nothing which all cannot have their counterpart of on the same terms."

In *Democratic Vistas*, Whitman declared: "As the greatest lessons of Nature through the universe are perhaps the lessons of variety and freedom, the same present the greatest lessons also in New World politics and progress. . . . Sole among nationalities, these States have assumed the task to put in forms of history, power and practicality, on areas of amplitude rivaling the operations of the physical kosmos, the moral political speculations of ages, long, long defer'd, the democratic republican principle, and the theory of development and perfection by voluntary standards and self reliance." Listen to this white father; he is so weird! Here he is calling aloud for an American, a democratic spirit. An American, a democratic idea that could morally constrain and coordinate the material body of US affluence and piratical outreach, more than a hundred years ago wrote:

> The great poems, Shakespeare included, are poisonous to the idea of the pride and dignity of the common people, the life-blood of democracy. The models of our literature, as we get it from other lands, ultra marine, have had their birth in courts, and bask'd and grown in castle sunshine; all smells of princes' favors. . . . Do you call those genteel little creatures American poets? Do you term that perpetual, pistareen, paste-pot work, American art, American drama, taste, verse? . . . We see the sons and daughters of The New World, ignorant of its genius, not yet inaugurating the native, the universal, and the near, still importing the distant, the partial, the dead.

Abhorring the "thin sentiment of parlors, parasols, piano-song, tinkling rhymes," Whitman conjured up a poetry of America, a poetry of democracy that would not "mean the smooth walks, trimm'd hedges, poseys and nightingales of the English poets, but the whole orb, with its geologic history, the Kosmos, carrying fire and snow that rolls through the illimitable areas, light as a feather, though weighing billions of tons."

Well, what happened?

Whitman went ahead and wrote the poetry demanded by his vision. He became, by thousands upon thousands of words, a great American poet:

> There was a child went forth every day,
> And the first object he look'd upon, that object he became,
> And that object became part of him for the day
> Or a certain part of the day,
> Or for many years or stretching cycles of years.
> The early lilacs became part of this child,
> And grass and white and red morning-glories,
> and white and red clover, and the song of the phoebe-bird.[8]

And elsewhere he wrote:

> It avails not, time nor place—distance avails not,
> I am with you, you men and women of a generation, or ever some many generations hence,
> Just as you feel when you look on the river and sky, so I felt,
> Just as any of you is one of a living crowd, I was one of a crowd,
> Just as you are refresh'd by the gladness of the river and the bright flow, I was refresh'd,
> Just as you stand and lean on the rail, yet hurry with the swift current, I stood yet was hurried,
> Just as you look on the numberless masts of ships and the thick-stemm'd pipes of steamboats,
> I look'd.[9]

This great American poet of democracy as cosmos, this poet of a continent as consciousness, this poet of the many people as one people, this poet of diction comprehensible to all, of a vision insisting on each, of a rhythm / a rhetorical momentum to transport the reader from the Brooklyn ferry into the hills of Alabama and back again, of line after line of bodily, concrete detail that constitutes the mysterious the cellular tissue of a nation indivisible but dependent upon and astonishing in its diversity, this white father of a great poetry deprived of its spontaneous popularity / a great poetry hidden away from the ordinary people it celebrates so well, he has been, again and again, cast aside as an undisciplined poseur, a merely freak eruption of prolix perversities.

Last year, the *New York Times Book Review* saw fit to import a European self-appointed critic of American literature to address the question: Is there a great American poet? Since this visitor was ignorant of the philosophy and the achievements of Walt Whitman, the visitor, Denis Donoghue, comfortably excluded every possible descendant of Whitman from his erstwhile cerebrations. Only one woman was mentioned (she, needless to add, did not qualify). No poets under fifty, and not one black or First World poet received even cursory assessment. Not one poet of distinctively New World values and their formal embodiment managed to dent the suavity of Donoghue's public display.

This *New York Times* event perpetuated American habits of beggarly, absurd deference to the Old World. And these habits bespeak more than marketplace intrusions into cultural realms. We erase ourselves through self-hatred. We lend our silence to the American anti-American process whereby anything and anyone special to this nation-state becomes liable to condemnation because it is what it is, truly.

Against self-hatred there is Whitman and there are all of the New World poets who insistently devise legitimate varieties of cultural nationalism. There is Whitman and all of the poets whose lives have been baptized by witness to blood, by witness to cataclysmic, political confrontations from the Civil War through the civil rights era, through the women's movement, and on and on through the conflicts between the hungry and the well-fed, the wasteful, the bullies.

In the poetry of the New World, you meet with a reverence for the material world that begins with a reverence for human life. There is an intellectual trust in sensuality as a means of knowledge, an easily deciphered system of reference, aspirations to a believable, collective voice, and, consequently, emphatic preference for broadly accessible, spoken language. Deliberately balancing perception with vision, it seeks to match moral exhortation with sensory report.

All of the traceable descendants of Whitman have met with an establishment, academic reception disgracefully identical; except for the New World poets who live and write beyond the boundaries of the United States, the offspring of this one white father encounter everlasting marketplace disparagement as crude or optional or simplistic or, as Whitman himself wrote, "hankering, gross, mystical, nude."

I too am a descendant of Walt Whitman. And I am not by myself struggling to tell the truth about this history of so much land and so much blood, of so much that should be sacred and so much that has been desecrated and annihilated boastfully.

My brothers and my sisters of this New World, we remember that, as Whitman said, "I do not trouble my spirit to vindicate itself or be understood, / I see that the elementary laws never apologize."[10] We do not apologize that we are not Emily Dickinson, Ezra Pound, T. S. Eliot, Wallace Stevens, Robert Lowell, and Elizabeth Bishop. Or, as Whitman exclaimed, "I exist as I am, that is enough."

New World poetry moves into and beyond the lives of Walt Whitman, Pablo Neruda, Aghostino Neto, Gabriela Mistral, Langston Hughes, and Margaret Walker. I follow this movement with my own life. I am calm and smiling as we go. Is it not written, somewhere very near to me:

A man's body at auction

. . . .

Gentlemen look on this wonder.
Whatever the bids of the bidders they cannot be high enough
    for it.

And didn't that weird white father predict this truth that is always growing:

I swear to you the architects shall appear without fail,
I swear to you they will understand you and justify you,
The greatest among them shall be he who best knows you
    and encloses all and is faithful to all,
He and the rest shall not forget you, they shall perceive that
    you are not an iota less than they,
You shall be fully glorified in them.[11]

Walt Whitman and all of the New World poets coming after him, we, too, go on singing this America.

NOTES

1. Walt Whitman, "I Sing the Body Electric."

2. I will refer to that part of the population usually termed "Third World" as "First World," given that they were first to exist on the planet and currently make up the majority.

3. Pablo Neruda, *The Heights of Macchu Picchu*, trans. Nathaniel Tarn (New York: Farrar, Straus and Giroux, 1966), sec. 12.

4. Pablo Neruda, *The Heights of Macchu Picchu*, trans. Ben Belitt (Evergreen Press).

5. Pablo Neruda, "Woes and the Furies," in *Selected Poems: Pablo Neruda*, ed. and trans. Ben Belitt (New York: Grove Press, 1961), 101.

6. Neruda, "The Dictators," in *Selected Poems*, 161.

7. Walt Whitman, "Song of Myself."

8. Walt Whitman, "There Was a Child Went Forth."

9. Walt Whitman, "Crossing Brooklyn Ferry."

10. Whitman, "Song of Myself."

11. Whitman, "Song of the Rolling Earth."

8

On Whitman, Civil War Memory, and My South

NATASHA TRETHEWEY

> O magnet-South! O glistening perfumed South! my South!
> O quick mettle, rich blood, impulse and love! good and evil!
> O all dear to me!
>
> WALT WHITMAN

I. The New South

A few years ago I was interviewed for the *Atlanta Journal-Constitution*—a newspaper whose slogan used to be "Covering Dixie like the Dew"—and later, when the article appeared, the headline read, "Poet Digs at Secrets in Her South." Not long after that, I received several e-mail and phone messages from a marketing representative who wanted to get a few lines from me about "my South." In the messages, he said it wouldn't take long and that his firm couldn't pay me for my comments. Well, I was busy, and besides that, I figured he didn't want to hear what I really think about the South. Most likely, he probably wanted some sound-bite clichés about how I like my grits, sweet tea, or barbecue, about how we southerners like sitting on porches and after-church visiting.

Some time after that, I started seeing advertisements for Turner South Network on the sides of buses all around Atlanta. Usually the ads featured a photograph of a man or woman next to a quote about his or her South. The text suggested the kinds of things I suspect that marketing representative was looking for when he tried to contact me; and though I don't know whether it had been the network calling me or not, I couldn't help thinking that there might be some connection. Not only were these images of the New South appearing on buses, they were showing up in some clever and entertaining television commercials too.

In one commercial, a long-haired teenager is driving fast down a dusty road—until he gets pulled over by a police officer. The officer appears menacing behind his metallic aviator sunglasses, and he has the kind of belly and demeanor that are reminiscent of some country sheriff straight out of Hazzard County. Approaching the car, the police officer stands—almost threateningly—for a moment, then says, lifting his shades, "Son, don't forget to pick your sister up from ballet." This is the New South—a riff on the stereotypes of the not-so-new South—and the message is certainly one of change. It's a comforting thought—if not completely true. Watching it, I thought of Walt Whitman and his South: how even his love for this place is underscored by something we'll never see in these commercials or on buses rolling through Atlanta.

The South of Whitman's time was not without its stunning beauty or its stunning cruelty. Writing "O Magnet South" in 1860, Whitman praised the landscape—its rivers, lakes, trees, the native flora and fauna:

> O the cotton plant! The growing fields of rice, sugar, hemp!
> The cactus guarded with thorns, the laurel tree with large
>   white flowers.

His love for the South, however, was complex, and in the poem he acknowledges, too, the darker side of it—"the piney odor and the gloom, the awful natural stillness." When he goes further to mention "the fugitive" and his "conceal'd hut," it is hard not to think of fugitive slaves. Whitman's take on the South is much like my own; it is a love/hate relationship. Later, he would write: "I would be the last one to confuse moral values—to imagine the South impeccable. I don't condone the South where it has gone wrong—its Negro slavery, I don't condone that—far from it—I hate it." Because of his open-armed enthusiasm, his inclusiveness and celebration of everyone, even the lowliest prostitute or degraded slave, Whitman's work has come to represent a poetics of democracy, a humane tradition of antiracism. Even now, there is much more to be learned from him, and from his con-

NATASHA TRETHEWEY

flicted relationship to his subject matter—especially as Americans near and far are still fighting, ideologically, the Civil War.

II. The Lost War

E. O. Wilson has written, "Homo Sapiens is the only species to suffer psychological exile." I've been thinking about that a lot lately, particularly in relation to all the panels I have been on at conferences on contemporary southern literature and culture. I began to notice, after several of these panels, that someone in the audience almost always raised a question about the psyches of southern writers—why we write the way that we do. It seemed to me that, just as often, someone on the panel would answer that question by saying something like, "We southerners write the way that we do because, after all, we lost the war." Each time I've heard this I've had to say, "My South didn't lose the war." On each of these occasions, the other panelists—most likely unintentionally—had responded to the question in a manner that seemed to suggest they had forgotten I was there, and that seemed to define the southern psyche and the southern experience as if they were monolithic. In a sense, their responses echo a type of erasure that has affected the documenting of public history and the dedication of public monuments and has continued to affect our public memory. I'm sure my fellow panelists never meant to exclude me when they said "we." I am a southerner too, but these occurrences are evidence of the public memory of the war and its aftermath that still makes outsiders of black Americans—even as nearly 200,000 fought for freedom in the Civil War—and leaves out many narratives that would give us a fuller, richer understanding of our American experience.

A champion of American experience—the diversity of its people and their labors—Whitman feared that the "real war" would not get written. He believed that war existed in the alternative narrative that might be offered by so many anonymous soldiers—most dead and buried, often in unmarked graves—whose stories would never be told. Whitman's *Specimen Days* becomes a kind of monument to the common soldier—the harsh facts of war recorded in his honest language. And yet, there is still little written of black soldiers, though he mentions tending to them as well: "Among the black soldiers, wounded or sick, and in the contraband camps, I also took my way whenever in their neighborhood, and did what I could for them." This is only a slight acknowledgment from the poet who wrote with great inclusiveness of blacks in such poems as "I Sing the Body Electric" and "Song of Myself." Perhaps a more telling poem, however—one that suggests the complexity of Whitman's conflicted relationship to the South and all her citizens—is "Reconciliation."

> Word over all, beautiful as the sky!
> Beautiful that war, and all its deeds of carnage, must in time
>   be utterly lost;
> That the hands of the sisters Death and Night incessantly
> Softly wash again, and ever again, this soil'd world;
>
>   For my enemy is dead, a man divine as myself is dead;
> I look where he lies white-faced and still in the coffin—I
>   draw near;
> Bend down and touch lightly with my lips the white face in
>   the coffin.

Here, Whitman suggests the reunion of the nation, men on opposite sides of the war drawn together beneath the banner of reconciliation. However, in the final image of the dead, "white-faced" in the coffin, Whitman leaves out the reality of so many dead soldiers whose faces were not white. And further, according to historian David Blight, the poem highlights—in the "kinship" of the dead white brothers—"the ultimate betrayal of the dark-faced folk whom the dead had shared in liberating." This kind of erasure would continue to dominate Civil War memory, as monuments to only part of the story inscribed a narrative on the American landscape—particularly in the South. The lost war, then, is the narrative of black Americans whose stories were often subjugated, lost, or left out of public memory and the creation of public monuments.

III. Memory and Forgetting

Just off the coast of my hometown, Gulfport, Mississippi, is a series of barrier islands—Cat, Horn, Deer, and Ship—that separate the dirty waters of the coastal area, with its dead fish and debris, from the clearer waters out in the Gulf. Ship Island is a Civil

War site, and during the warmer months, anyone can buy passage on one of the small cruisers making daily trips out there and take a brief tour offered by the National Park Service.

The island's history is an interesting one. The first regiments of the Louisiana Native Guards were mustered into service in September, October, and November 1862, the First Regiment thus becoming the first officially sanctioned regiment of black soldiers in the Union Army, and the Second and Third made up of men who had been slaves only months before enlisting. During the war, the fort at Ship Island, Mississippi, called Fort Massachusetts, was maintained as a prison for Confederate soldiers — military convicts and prisoners of war — manned by the Second Regiment. In his wartime reminiscences, Whitman pointed out that "few white regiments [made] a better appearance on parade than the 1st and 2nd Louisiana Native Guards." And yet, visitors to the fort today will learn almost none of this history. Instead, they will see first the plaque placed at the entrance by the Daughters of the Confederacy listing the names of the Confederate men once there. Nowhere is there a similar plaque memorializing the names of the Native Guards, and if tourists don't know to ask about the history of these black soldiers, most likely the park ranger will overlook this aspect of the fort's history in his or her tour, mentioning only that this was a fort taken over by Union forces and that Confederate prisoners were kept there. Even the brochures leave out any mention that the troops stationed on the island were black. This omission serves to further the narrative that blacks were passive recipients of the freedom bestowed upon them by white "brothers" who fought and died in the Civil War.

Monuments all around the South serve to inscribe a particular narrative onto the landscape while at the same time subjugating or erasing another. Fortunately, there are several organizations and historians trying to restore the history of the role of black soldiers to the public memory through monuments. Last February, in the Vicksburg National Military Park, the first monument of its kind in a national park was erected, though not without certain omissions. According to the *Jackson Advocate*, during the earlier groundbreaking ceremony, "Park Superintendent Bill Nichols and Park historian Terry Winschel begrudgingly labeled the black regiments as 'supply guards' in the text on display rather than giving the men their full measure of respect as the fully-recognized infantry, artillery and cavalry units that they were."

That a more inclusive history of black soldiers is not given on Ship Island or in the Vicksburg Military Park and that certain facts are often left out of local historical narratives and (perhaps until most recently) were likely to be given only a small part in larger histories is emblematic of ideological contests about how to remember the Civil War, how we construct public memory with its omissions and embellishments. As David Blight asserts in *Race and Reunion: The Civil War in American Memory*, "Deflections and evasions, careful remembering and necessary forgetting, and embittered and irreconcilable versions of experience are all the stuff of historical memory." Though Whitman had acknowledged black soldiers in his letters and reminiscences, ultimately he often left blacks out of his larger concerns: "When the South is spoken of," he wrote, contrasting the roles of the ruling class and the masses, "no one means the people, the mass of freemen." Here Whitman is referring to the free white masses, even as his language reminds us of the invisible "freedmen" all around the South. In fact, according to Daniel Aaron in *The Unwritten War*, "The Negro did not figure significantly in his calculations for America's future, the Grand Plan of History; and it is just as mistaken to confuse Whitman's prose opinion of the Negro and the poetic use he made of him in *Leaves of Grass* as it is to identify his antislavery position with abolitionism."

At the groundbreaking ceremony for the new monument, historian Jim Woodrich's words seemed to echo Whitman's more-than-a-century-old prediction that the real war would not get into the books: "By being here today," Woodrich began, "we acknowledge the valor and honor" of the black Union troops. Their story, he said, "yearns to be known."

IV. "The Real War Will Not Get into the Books"

William Faulkner has said, "The past isn't dead; it isn't even past." All around us debates about the memory of the Civil War and its aftermath continue to shape contemporary concerns. In many states, the battle over the meaning of the Confederate flag is ongoing, with revisionist versions abounding. Here in Georgia, the battle connects us not only to the Civil War but also to

NATASHA TRETHEWEY

public opposition to desegregation. In Mississippi, my home state, the flag still flies on the beach between Gulfport and Biloxi as a monument to only part of our shared history, whereas an equally significant history is overlooked — that of other southerners, black former slaves who were stationed at Ship Island and who fought for their own freedom and citizenship in contests not far away, thus helping the nation come a bit closer to realizing the full democratic potential outlined in the Constitution. These issues are, ultimately, fights about remembrance — how we see ourselves as Americans within the context of history.

When the Daughters of the Confederacy mounted the plaque at Ship Island, they were working to inscribe their exclusive version of history into the public memory, leaving out the other population on the island. C. Vann Woodward, in his preface to *Jumpin' Jim Crow: Southern Politics from Civil War to Civil Rights*, asserts that during the last two decades of the nineteenth century and the first two of the twentieth it was "white ladies . . . who bore primary responsibility for the myths glorifying the old order, the Lost Cause, and white supremacy." Woodward is referring, specifically, to the United Daughters of the Confederacy, Daughters of the American Revolution, Daughters of Pilgrims, and Daughters of Colonial Governors; they were considered "guardians of the past." "Non-daughters," he writes, "were excluded." The efforts of the Daughters of the Confederacy extended beyond the erecting of monuments and the naming of roads; indeed, they commissioned the history textbooks written for southern schools and oversaw the material contained within them in order to control the narrative of the South's role in the war — that is, to tell a story that was rife with omissions and embellishments, that sought to cast the causes of the war only in terms of states' rights and not at all in terms of the matter of slavery.

It would seem that Whitman, in his conflicted attitudes toward the roles of both North and South, toward slavery and black suffrage (he hated slavery but did not believe blacks capable of exercising the vote), could foresee such one-sided narratives and the need for a fuller understanding of the roots of the conflict — a history more inclusive than what would be told and written for several generations: "But what of the main premonitions of the war?" he asked. Decades later, W. E. B. Du Bois would begin to answer him—furthering Whitman's own ideas about the war's origins—and in so doing point out the embellishments and omissions in the history put forth by a generation of scholars. In his essay "The Propaganda of History," Du Bois would take to task American historians, asserting that among the profession "we have too often made a deliberate attempt so to change the facts of history that the story will make pleasant reading for Americans."

Whitman knew all too well that the real war he feared would not get written was not a pleasant one. Referring primarily to the "seething hell and the black infernal background of countless minor scenes," he nonetheless foreshadows another backdrop—the narratives of blacks relegated to the margins of public memory. "Long, long hence," he anticipated, "when the grave has quenched many hot prejudices and vitalities, and an entirely new class of thinkers and writers come to the argument, the complete question, can perhaps be fairly weighed."

V. What Would Whitman Do?

On billboards around the South and on church marquees proclaiming the theme of upcoming sermons, a frequent question stands out: What Would Jesus Do? I ask, instead, what would our earthly father—father of modern American poetry, father of the poetry of a democratic vision—what would our Whitman do? OK, so this question is overly speculative. I can hear the voices out there saying that people are products of their historical moment. The defenders of Thomas Jefferson as well as his detractors are getting their guard up. I'm not interested in arguing the omissions of the past, only the restoration of those omissions in the present. Perhaps not restoration: acknowledgment is a better word. When Robert Penn Warren returned to his South to write *Segregation*, he was a man in the midst of change—he was rethinking his position as a contributor to the anthology *I'll Take My Stand*. The nation was changing, and he was changing along with it.

When Whitman took on the task of setting down on paper some of his thoughts about the Civil War, its causes and its aftermath, he probably did not have the image of the black soldier in the foreground of his thinking. Though his wartime reminiscences would consider regiments of black troops, his poem "Ethiopia Saluting the Colors" focuses on a "dusky woman, so ancient hardly human," and not black soldiers who were participants in the war rather than bystanders. However, the omissions, inherent even in his later writings about the war, underscore the questions of historical memory with which future generations would contend: "Probably no future age can know, but I well know, how the gist of this fiercest and most resolute of the world's warlike contentions resided exclusively in the unnamed, unknown rank and file; and how the brunt of its labor of death was, to all essential purposes, volunteered."

Here, Whitman directs us to the unnamed, unknown rank-and-file white soldier and, inadvertently, to black soldiers as well—the legions of runaway slaves and freedmen who flocked to Union camps, first as contraband and then later as men (and women) eager to enlist—whose story has been left out of public memory of the Civil War and has only begun to be inscribed onto the man-made, monumental American landscape.

VI. Coda

A lot of things have changed since Whitman declared his love for the South and her contradictions. Some have not. Contradictions abound in this landscape of beauty and ugliness, this cauldron of nostalgic remembrances and willed forgetting. In Mississippi and Alabama, lawyers and concerned citizens are continuing to work to bring to trial the perpetrators of heinous crimes—Byron de la Beckwith; the bombers who blew up a church in Birmingham, killing four little girls; the men responsible for the murders of Cheney, Schwerner, and Goodman. An exhibit about the history of lynching is touring the country, even as opponents of this necessary remembering here in Atlanta opine in letters to the editor that some things are best left buried, forgotten. I live with the ghosts of the past every day; when Halloween comes around, I see in the decorative skeletons hanging from my neighbors' trees the specter of lynching. And even worse, I encounter the specter of what put real bodies in trees still lingering in the kind of willed forgetting and intolerance we haven't yet overcome. From where I stand, it's easy to feel the kinds of contradictions evident in Whitman's work, those things he revealed both intentionally and inadvertently.

Like him, I love my South. And I hate it too.

Whitman

Year One

ROWAN RICARDO PHILLIPS

I

As a child growing up in New York City I knew two Walt Whitmans. Each seemed large, impressive, and durable; but neither had much to do with poetry. This was a time in my life before I read poetry. And as brief as that time may have been, why deny it its primacy and its privilege? Why not begin from there? There is always a time before poetry.

The two Whitmans I knew were not the famed dual identities of Whitman himself. Not the worker Walter Whitman and his counterpart, the poet Walt. The Walt Whitman Library and the perfunctory if not beautiful Walt Whitman Bridge: these were my Walt Whitmans. And when I hear Whitman's name it still frequently summons an image of either of these two places in my mind.

To put it another way: in those days Walt Whitman may as well have been a president. His name was just as splendid, just as righteous and officious. Grover Cleveland, James K. Polk, the ubiquitous Washington and Lincoln: their names seemed before us whenever we needed to line up, be quiet, or get a pass. "Walt Whitman," like those other names, was a power. Imagine! The man was born from Quakers. But the imprint of his name was like Braille, for even if you kept a blind eye to poetry, Walt Whitman's residue had acquired a near-imperial normalcy. Just as so many of the names of the children I went to school with—Jefferson, Jackson, Monroe, Grant—neither sung of nor stung like the past.

In retrospect, how fitting those two Whitmans were: the Jeffersonian idea of the American public library on the one hand and on the other a structure that brings land and people together. Whitman was, nevertheless, a name emblazoned on polis-approved architecture.

What follows should be the *volta* of this reflection. Of how next I discovered the real Whitman's work and was moved and instructed and saw my vision changed. But that is not what happened. I did eventually start to read Whitman, and regarding the Whitman that I read, what to say? I admired and then grew skeptical of his ideas—America, democracy, capacious love, instructive death—it was the eighties in New York City after all. Whitman, however, seemed to anticipate this antipathy when he wrote: "Democracy has been so retarded and jeopardized by powerful personalities, that its first instincts are fain to clip, conform, bring in stragglers, and reduce everything to a dead level." Yet he himself had become one of those powerful personalities: I loved his best poems without loving his poetry. His rhythms seemed marooned by the Bible. He often was hard to believe. It was the era of the Great Communicator. And I never, even at that age, wanted to be a straggler. So I turned to other poets and left Walt Whitman behind.

Nevertheless, soon after, I met another Walt Whitman; a Whitman that brought me back to Whitman; Whitman freer and yet less himself, like a horse that has returned home without its rider.

II

"none of them loved the huge leaves"

Lorca's "Ode to Walt Whitman" begins on the other side of the East River from Whitman's Brooklyn. Though this poem is by and large about sexual identity and self-love, I would like to focus here on the inner workings of the poem and how these relate and tie in to thoughts on both Whitman and race. In "Crossing Brooklyn Ferry" Whitman traverses that same East River and sees "the flags of all nations, the falling of them at sunset." Here, at a similar time of day and a little farther up the river, Lorca invokes the slurs of many nations as later in the poem he writes:

Always against you, who give boys
drops of foul death with bitter poison.
Always against you,
Fairies of North America,
Pájaros of Havana,
Jotos of Mexico,
Sarasas of Cádiz,
Apios of Seville,
Cancos of Madrid,
Floras of Alicante,
Adelaidas of Portugal.

Lorca turns from Whitman's idiosyncratic tactic of monologic pluralism (even his "Song of the Answerer" is in his own voice) in favor of a voice that threatens annihilation of that same voice. The famed Adamic power of naming at use by Lorca here is violent and cyclical: a naming of the same thing but again and again and again.

The East River, a *locus classicus* of Whitman's work, is recontextualized in order to circumscribe a world that still calls for Whitman's presence. For despite Whitman's tendency to permeate his presence throughout all available essences — "What I shall assume you shall assume"; "Whoever you are, now I place my hand upon you, that you be my poem"; etc. — his constant insistence that he *is* leads to the suspicion that in fact he is *not*. Yet his Romantic sense of death and our tendency to read anaphora as subject-derived affirmation cloud in Whitman's work what Lorca seemed to grasp: that Whitman's power comes precisely from his absence. Despite the bright catalog of things accompanying Whitman in "Crossing Brooklyn Ferry," Lorca still sees Whitman as "man alone at sea." Though "virile" and "Macho," Whitman emerges from Lorca's imagination yes as poetic inspiration but also as an indeterminate flirtation with emptiness (e.g., Lorca sees Whitman as "a column," but "a column made of ash"). And it is from this recognition of void within Whitman — a void that Lorca's poem attempts to fill ("your beard full of butterflies") — that Lorca's poem offers the balm of negation.

Not for a moment, Walt Whitman, lovely old man,
have I failed to see your beard full of butterflies,

ROWAN RICARDO PHILLIPS

nor your corduroy shoulders frayed by the moon,
nor your thighs pure as Apollo's,
nor your voice like a column of ash,
old man, beautiful as the mist,
you moaned like a bird
with its sex pierced by a needle.
Enemy of the satyr,
enemy of the vine,
and lover of bodies beneath rough cloth . . .

Not for a moment, virile beauty,
who among mountains of coal, billboards, and railroads,
dreamed of becoming a river and sleeping like a river
with that comrade who would place in your breast
the small ache of an ignorant leopard.

Not for a moment, Adam of blood, Macho,
man alone at sea, Walt Whitman, lovely old man,
because on penthouse roofs,
gathered at bars,
emerging in bunches from the sewers,
trembling between the legs of chauffeurs,
or spinning on dance floors wet with absinthe,
the faggots, Walt Whitman, point you out.

"Not for a moment" (Ni un solo momento) means in this case "always." But "Not for a moment" causes the anaphora of the following lines to stress negation prior to each possessive pronoun. And thus, though the sense of the statement would be the same if "Not for a moment" were instead "always," the stress of it would not.

Here Whitman's presence, as well as his sense of self-possession, is postulated against the possibility of its negation: *nor* your, *nor* your, *nor* your. In the second instance of "Not for a moment," in which Whitman becomes "Adam of blood" and "Macho," both anaphora (Whitman's signature style) and negation are gone. As Whitman enters further into the poem he is pointed out:

the faggots, Walt Whitman, point you out.

He's one, too! That's right! And they land
on your luminous chaste beard,

and, as a solution to the poetic (if not to the societal) problem, he is encircled. The enticing emotional architecture of the Whitman line cedes to a reordering of the poetic line.

the faggots, Walt Whitman, the faggots,
[los maricas, Walt Whitman, los maricas]

Summoning Whitman cannot eradicate evil from the world, much less make a poem better. And transposing Whitman over other scenes and social climates is an avoidance of the problems in Whitman's poetic approach (consider Hughes in his most Whitmanic moments such as "Let America Be America Again"). Instead, Whitman must transform with us and in a manner so that his inclusion in our lives, whether in peace or during turbulence, is spoken of with Whitman's power but not necessarily with Whitman's pleasure—Pound's radiograph of "that horrible rectitude with which Whitman rejoices in being Whitman." "He's one, too!" a group of others—a "they"—says, instead of hearing Whitman again say, "I am one, too."

Life comes to Whitman not in the first-person voice we tend to misread as presence but in the voices of others who have the power to animate the second- and third-person Whitman into a being alive and distinct in our world.

Sleep on, nothing remains.
Dancing walls stir the prairies
and America drowns itself in machinery and lament.
I want the powerful air from the deepest night
to blow away flowers and inscriptions from the arch where
    you sleep,
and a black child to inform the gold-craving whites
that the kingdom of grain has arrived.

It would be too easy here to place weighted importance on the black child's appearance at the end of the poem. *Poet in New York* leaves it clear that Lorca wrote of blacks on the sensual level. He reveled in their exteriority in the way a great poet would revel in a skyscape or an oak in that same autumnal sky. And it is essential to reckon with the fact that the black child here appears in the subjunctive mood and thus is presently contrary to fact. In the original Spanish the arrival of the kingdom of grain does not share this mood: the last line of the poem translates literally to "the arrival of the kingdom of the wheat." The black child's power to inform of a kingdom exists here in an undetermined time, one that Lorca leaves for the child and Whitman to settle on at the edge of hope and hypothesis, which is where poetry remakes itself under the guise of no other name. Whether that black child is me, or you, or someone else, let us leave to the poems of the future to decide.

AFTERWORD

At Whitman's Grave

GEORGE B. HUTCHINSON

Eleanor Ray, the caretaker of Whitman's home in Camden, showed me the piece of paper on which Whitman had contracted for the building of his tomb: New England granite from Quincy quarry, where, as a college student, I had learned rock-climbing some fifteen years before. The tomb caught Whitman's disciples by surprise. Believing he was destitute, for years they had been holding subscription birthday dinners and organizing evenings for his lecture on the death of Abraham Lincoln, while he'd been quietly hoarding $1,500 for a mausoleum—which ultimately cost about $4,000, more than twice what his house on Mickle Street had cost.

Dr. Bucke, who thought of Whitman as an improvement on Christ Jesus and the Buddha, was taken aback. But evidently the old man knew what he was about. He chose the spot with a view to posterity. He was one to whom generations mattered— generations and geography, our placement in this world.

I was in Philadelphia in 1987, a week after the celebration of the poet's 168th birthday, to coach a pair-oared crew I'd brought up from Tennessee for the Dad Vail championships on the Schuylkill. There Thomas Eakins, who did the death mask and a famous portrait of the poet, had painted the Biglin brothers racing back in Whitman's day. While I was in the area I was determined to visit Whitman's home and, if I could, his grave. One of my oarsmen, a white Philadelphian, sent me off with a warning about Camden: "It's a rough place," he said. He smiled wryly: "I wouldn't stay past dark if I were you."

I picked my way through the torn-up streets of Philly trying to find the Walt Whitman Bridge over the Delaware River but finally settled for the Ben Franklin Bridge instead. It's more direct for reaching Whitman's house. Caught in the afternoon rush hour, I

{ 179 }

gazed on the river below, bearing who knows what to the polluted bay. Then the weird terrain of Camden suddenly engulfed me—all those row houses block on block, uniformly three stories, the mélange of faded colors, the curious flatness of the city, its repetitiveness, its poverty.

Finding the right street was not so hard, but I missed Whitman's house the first time past. I'd expected to find it in the midst of a block of dilapidated row houses, but it sat quite primly amid a small group of them nicely kept up on Mickle Boulevard—not Mickle Street anymore, but a broad and empty thoroughfare divided by a median in a nearly deserted stretch of the city. Across the street some sort of large civic building in the middle stages of construction was rising. The boulevard itself dead-ended into a half-constructed bridge the city had begun and then, it seemed, changed its mind about.

The whole block where Whitman had lived was a kind of twilight zone, strangely cut off from the rest of the city. It was so deserted that Saturday that I began to wonder if Mickle *Street* had been bodily moved, all in one piece, to another spot. How could it be so barren of people? And the few houses left looked too neat from the outside, like lawyers' or architects' offices on yuppiedom's urban frontier.

I parked, walked up to 328 Mickle Boulevard, and knocked. No answer. Knocked again, harder. Still no answer, and no sign that this was Whitman's home. But I was sure I had the address right. I looked in the windows. "Too modern inside," I concluded. Then I went next door, 330 Mickle Boulevard, the one with the flag flying from the top story. At least I could ask someone here what had happened to Whitman's house. Surely it would not have been torn down. Was there a Mickle *Street* somewhere? As I asked myself this, I saw a brass plaque designating the place as Whitman's. The number had changed since Whitman's day.

There was no answer to my knock. This can't be it, I thought. I looked at the sign again, the hours posted. It should be open, I thought. I knocked again. Nothing. I started to walk away, went back, knocked one more time, harder. Just as I was turning away again, the knob turned from the inside. The door opened. A woman's face appeared, said come on in—and disappeared to the back of the hallway. She was black.

As I waited for her to come back, I looked around in the entryway. It was just an old person's house, the way it felt to me. It smelled like my grandparents' when I was a little boy. Yes, Walt Whitman had lived here. He was an old man. Inside the house, apart from the bizarre silence and emptiness of the boulevard, it was still his world. His big cane-bottomed chair sat quietly by the window in the front parlor, sunlight falling obliquely across it.

Eleanor Ray did not seem at all like the guides one usually meets in places like this. She was an attractive woman, about fifty maybe, with what seemed at first a scholarly air. Her whole manner of speaking of the place seemed aloof. Her speech was precise, her manner elevated, distant. For the first few minutes I took her for a professor from the Camden campus of Rutgers University, which was associated with the home. I was afraid I had interrupted her work.

When we got to talking, my impression changed. She would point to a picture and we'd talk about it, sharing what we knew. She had magnetism. Her hands were long, slender, active as she spoke. When we got to the photo Richard Maurice Bucke had called the "Christ likeness," taken in the early 1850s when Whitman was working on the first edition of *Leaves of Grass*, I mentioned that I'd used it for the cover of my book. She bent half over, saying, "That's my favorite! Look at that expression. You can see the effect of what he wrote about in 'Song of Myself,' where his soul makes love to his body, 'and then arose and spread around me the peace and knowledge that surpass all the art and argument of the earth.'" She was of Whitman's tribe.

She told me of how she'd been raised a devout Baptist, described how she'd sat each Sunday in church next to her sister and mother, how righteous she had felt, secure in the truth of God's word. Later, she'd married a staunch church-going man. Then, by chance, she'd taken the job at Whitman's home.

"You know," she said, "I didn't know anything about him at that time. We had read 'O Captain, My Captain' in high school, I guess, but that was all I knew. When I took this job I started getting books out of the library to learn about him." She read *Leaves of Grass* then for the first time and got caught up in it. Her family worried.

"Oh, I was angry," she said. "I was angry at how I had been

fooled for so long! But you know, he was angry, too. When you read 'Song of Myself' you can feel that anger. Oh yes, he was angry at those ministers after what he learned."

As often as she must have taken people on the tour of the house, Ms. Ray's presence remained electric as she pointed out the relics, as we lingered on them. We compared impressions about people long dead: Dr. Bucke and "Horace," as she called Traubel, Whitman's Boswell—"he was quite a character." She spoke exactly as though she had once known them all. She knew the whole story of Mary Davis, Whitman's last housekeeper, but gave a slant very different from the one provided by biographers. For her, it was all quite personal.

Here, he was Walt, Mr. Whitman, an old man of red flesh. The home still smelled of the man who died, the dust of his skin, the slant of the sunlight through the window by which he sat in his old straw-bottomed chair. The narrow bed they turned him in as he suffered through his last illness. Eleanor told anecdotes about Warry Fritzinger, who interrupted his travels as a sailor to help Mary Davis care for Walt. We laughed about Dr. Bucke showing up with barrels to hold Walt's papers, trying to make sure he got every scrap of the messiah's writings, while the corpse was still in the front room for the wake. Eleanor laughed, "Oh, yes, Dr. Bucke, he was a character! Let me show you this picture of him." She spoke like one passing on stories of old relatives. And she showed me the newspaper photo of brother George's daughter in a hospital bed in the 1950s—the niece of Walt Whitman!

After touring the last rooms, we lingered by the glass case with Whitman's instructions for the building of his tomb, specifying thick slabs of Quincy granite. I asked for directions to Harleigh cemetery, expecting it to be miles away and hard to find. In fact, Eleanor said, it was easy to reach from the house. "Go two or three miles on Haddon Avenue until you see a hospital on the left. The cemetery is right after the hospital."

Bleak blocks of decaying row houses stretched on and on under the sun in a city of concrete. Then I saw the hospital, and then the cemetery. It was like entering another world, pastoral, several shady acres of rolling landscape, tree-shaded, cool green. Suburban and genteel. Three men were loading a lawn mower into a pickup as I entered the gates.

I missed the sign that points toward the grave because the pickup was parked in front of it. But I didn't want to ask where Whitman's grave might be; I wanted to find it on my own. I wandered over the whole place twice, avoiding a funeral entourage that came in close after me. I was sure I would recognize the grave immediately, but as a matter of fact I must have missed it at least once.

Several times I thought I had come upon it, felt disappointment over a too fancy look or a too prominent place, but each time the name was wrong. I took two or three circuits through practically the whole cemetery, coming again and again on the pond in its center, until I began to feel baffled.

Finally, it appeared, tucked up under a slope behind several mountain laurels and two large trees as I coasted around a curve in a secluded part of the cemetery. It was all by itself. "Walt Whitman." There it was. It's really more ordinary than people tend to describe it, not so imposing compared to some of the other tombs around there. I parked in the grass at the side of the lane across from the tomb. The place was deserted, almost disheveled. I walked self-consciously up to it, feeling kind of silly.

There were dead leaves and spider webs in the "vestibule" (as Whitman called it in his instructions to the builders that I'd seen at the house). I looked through the iron grating, which was chained shut and padlocked. It smelled damp. I read the names on the blue marble inside. Walt Whitman. Louisa Van Velsor Whitman. Walter Whitman (Walt's father). George Whitman (his brother). Louisa Whitman (George's wife). Walter Whitman, the poet's nephew who had died as an infant. Hannah Whitman (Walt's sister). Edward Whitman (Walt's epileptic brother, whom he had slept with in youth).

What are you supposed to do when you visit a great poet's grave? How long do you stay? There was a faded plastic blossom attached to the grating. I had not brought anything to leave there. I looked at the tomb from various angles. I walked up on top of it. The roof was covered with bare dirt and dead leaves. A squirrel was scratching away under an oak tree nearby.

I walked back down, looked at the tomb from the side. Nothing special from that angle. I went up to the entry again and looked in. Still nothing special, just the same damp smell and the dead leaves. Then I turned around, sort of half shut in by the mountain laurel.

A stone walk angled off to one side, leading to the paved lane. I followed it. Now what? I was stumped. I went over to my car on the other side of the lane, got in, and smoked a cigarette with the door open, waiting for something to happen. Some people—two black women and a little girl—drove by in a big Chevy and looked at me curiously, slowing down and then moving on. I got back out of the car. The grave was just sitting there. It was framed by two great oak trees that had been carved elaborately with graffiti so long ago they seemed tattooed—J.S. & P.T., Carl & Maria, a huge and shapely penis with balls.

I sat on the ground behind the car, chewing on a piece of grass. It was long, with a spear of seeds. The grass had not been mown for quite a while. That's interesting, I thought. I stood up in it then and looked around behind me, away from the grave. I was sitting on the edge of a low, damp meadow. There were no graves in this little half-acre. And never could be, I slowly realized, because it would turn swampy after any good rain.

The grass was growing up nearly a foot high all around me. In the midst of the well-manicured, genteel cemetery, this place was too low for burials, and the meadow could only be mown intermittently in the driest times. (A week later, from Tennessee, I asked one of the groundskeepers some questions over the phone. He was apologetic about the grass, said they try to get to it when it's not too wet. He also was defensive about there being no graves in that area, saying it would not be a good spot because of the water. "I been thinking we ought to put a mausoleum in there, though. The problem is, that spot where Whitman is is kind of out of the way, and people have trouble finding it. I thought if we put something else up in there it might help.")

At this point I went back across the lane and climbed to the top of the tomb again to get a good look. Yes, it was a peaceful little meadow, surrounded by low slopes, fringed with trees. Probably even swampier in the 1880s and 1890s.

Suddenly it occurred to me that the proper thing was not to look at the tomb at all but to look out from it. So I walked back down to the left corner of the tomb and sat in the leaves. As I sat there next to the entryway, I looked all around, just waiting, letting in the day.

And what came to me, maybe a hundred feet off to the left, was a corner of the pond I had been circling around as I was waiting for the tomb to choose me. *A pond.* I nearly said it out loud.

On a little peninsula jutting out into the pond were two Canada geese, a male and a female, and their brood of several goslings, which were waddling around on the verge of the water and nibbling at the ground. In a corner closer to me, in the shadow of a tree, I eventually made out another pair, a couple of mallards. The male was circling around the female, which appeared to be settled down on her nest. A bird was singing in a tree fringing the meadow. A squirrel dug in the leaves behind me. Everything else was quiet.

I sat there by the entry to Whitman's grave and gazed on this for a long time.

ACKNOWLEDGMENTS

"For the Sake of People's Poetry: Walt Whitman and the Rest of Us,"
copyright © June Jordan. Reprinted by permission of Basic Civitas Books,
a member of the Perseus Books Group.
"On Whitman, Civil War Memory, and My South,"
copyright © Natasha Trethewey, originally appeared in the
Virginia Quarterly Review. Reprinted by permission of
Natasha Trethewey.

SELECTED BIBLIOGRAPHY

American Experience: Walt Whitman. Directed by Mark Zwonitzer.
PBS. WGBH, Boston. 2008. Television.

Contains an extended discussion of Whitman and slavery and includes an appearance by poet Yusef Komunyakaa reading from the slave auction section of "I Sing the Body Electric" and commenting on Whitman's racial attitudes.

Beach, Christopher. *The Politics of Distinction: Whitman and the Discourses of Nineteenth-Century America.* Athens: University of Georgia Press, 1996.

Beach's book underscores Whitman's pursuit to create a radical poetics rather than a radical politics per se. In his chapter on race and slavery, Beach argues that Whitman proved to be "radically innovative" and more aligned with "an ideal of democratic poetry, which demanded that he inhabit the subjectivity of each human being" to read the seeming contradictions of passages like those of the hounded slave in "Song of Myself" and the slave auction in "I Sing the Body Electric"; thus, rather than seeing these passages as contradictions, Beach sees in them the apotheosis of Whitman's democratic poetry. In at least one critical respect, then, chapter 2 of Beach's book contests some of the central premises of Karen Sánchez-Eppler's article on "merger and embodiment."

Collins, Michael. "Komunyakaa, Collaboration, and the Wishbone: An Interview." *Callaloo* 28, no. 3 (2005): 620–34.

In Yusef Komunyakaa's interview with Michael Collins, he concludes their discussion by noting that "Whitman's concept of language seems cosmic and carnal" and that he hopes to "achieve a voice just as inclusive" in his own poetry.

Ellison, Ralph. *Going to the Territory.* New York: Random House, 1986.

Ellison's second collection of essays and addresses covers literature, music, and culture. It includes "The Novel as a Function of American Democracy" (1967), in which he underscores that Whitman's poems were an important contribution to describing the American experience, as well as "On Initiation Rites and Power" (1974) and "Alain Locke" (1974), in which Ellison recalls Whitman's statement that a "native grand opera in America" may one day come from the tongues of African Americans.

———. *Invisible Man.* New York: Vintage, 1952.

At a crucial moment in Ellison's epic novel, the author features an exchange in chapter 9 where the protagonist finds himself in a confusing conversation with a young white professional male who likens their relationship to Jim and Huck and asks the protagonist if he has ever frequented Club Calamus.

———. *Shadow and Act.* New York: Random House, 1964.

Ellison's first collection of essays and addresses covers literature, music, and culture, with particular emphasis on the mutual exchange between blacks and whites in the creation of American identity. Includes an early essay "Beating That Boy" (1945), in which Ellison notes the significance of Whitman in the context of Emerson, Thoreau, Hawthorne, Melville, and Twain and, importantly, their influence for his own writing.

Folsom, Ed. "Lucifer and Ethiopia: Whitman, Race, and Poetics before the Civil War and After." In *A Historical Guide to Walt Whitman*, edited by David S. Reynolds, 45–95. New York: Oxford University Press, 2000.

Turning away from the issue of the figurative black presence in *Leaves of Grass* (as in the "hounded slave" passage in "Song of Myself" or the slave auction scene in "I Sing the Body Electric") or the nonpresence (as in "A Boston Ballad"), Folsom analyzes the relationship of Whitman's poetics and race by examining the question of voice and agency in separate poems on opposite sides of the Civil War. Folsom notes that, while Whitman turns his narration over to a rebellious black slave at the heart of the "Lucifer" passage in "The Sleepers," Lucifer and the voice of black radical dissent vanish from the final 1881 edition of *Leaves*. Folsom then addresses the 1870 poem "Ethiopia Saluting the Colors," in which an old black woman has a voice but is seemingly confused and without a discernible sense of agency. Folsom traces the various placements of "Ethiopia" within *Leaves* as Whitman continually rearranges the volume.

———. "So Long, So Long! Walt Whitman, Langston Hughes, and the Art of Longing." In *Walt Whitman, Where the Future Becomes Present*, edited by David Haven Blake and Michael Robertson, 127–43. Iowa City: University of Iowa Press, 2008.

Noting that Whitman uses the poem "So Long!" to close every edition of *Leaves of Grass* from 1860 on and that Langston Hughes opened his volume *Selected Poems* (1960) with the same words, Folsom explores the recurrence of the idiomatic expression in their poetry as a central trope in their attempts to write an American democracy into being.

Gibson, Donald B. "The Good Black Poet and the Good Gray Poet: The Poetry of Hughes and Whitman." In *Langston Hughes: Black Genius*, edited by Therman B. O'Daniel, 65–80. New York: Morrow, 1971.

While noting a number of similarities between Hughes and Whitman, including formal ones such as the use of personae, thematic ones such as "wanting to break down distinctions of all kinds," and psychological ones such as lacking a "sense of evil," Gibson maintains that Hughes is not a direct descendant of Whitman (any more or less than other influences like Carl Sandburg and Vachel Lindsay) but concedes that "had Whitman not written, Hughes could not have been the same poet."

Glicksberg, Charles I. "Whitman and the Negro." *Phylon* 9, no. 4 (1948): 326–31.

Glicksberg's essay trades in familiar criticisms against Whitman for not being vocal enough (or at all) against "the evil of racial intolerance and racial discrimination," noting that Whitman was not an abolitionist in the vein of John Greenleaf Whittier before the war nor a believer in black political equality through the franchise, as was his then-friend William Douglas O'Connor after the war. The importance of the essay, however, remains in its underlying thesis that, in circuitously evading the "Negro problem" (at least in his publications), Whitman failed to see that it was "precisely the Negro who symbolized . . . the essential promise of democracy." Glicksberg's essay extended some of the thoughts about race that he explored more than ten years earlier in his book *Walt Whitman and the Civil War* (Philadelphia: University of Pennsylvania Press, 1933).

Higgins, Andrew C. "Wage Slavery and the Composition of *Leaves of Grass*: The 'Talbot Wilson' Notebook." *Walt Whitman Quarterly Review* 20 (Fall 2002): 53–77.

Higgins addresses the rediscovery of the "Talbot Wilson" notebook and the subsequent redating of it to 1853–54 rather than 1847–50 (thereby making it one of the later notebooks rather than one of the earliest) to argue that Whitman's preoccupation about class (rather than the issue of the racial slavery of blacks as critics, as David S. Reynolds, Betsy Erkkila, and Martin Klammer have suggested) "propelled [him] towards poetry in the mid-1850s." Higgins's essay is as important for his meticulous textual analysis of the document as it is for illustrating the ongoing debate between scholars about how Whitman's thoughts on class and race informed the creation of, and made their way into, *Leaves of Grass*.

Hughes, Langston. *The Big Sea*. New York: Knopf, 1940.

In the manuscript of Hughes's first autobiography, he describes leaving the United States for Africa and Europe and, after being compelled to discard his books, deciding to safeguard his copy of *Leaves of Grass* for his journey.

———. "Calls Whitman Negroes' First Great Poetic Friend, Lincoln of Letters." *Chicago Defender*, 4 July 1953, 11.

The first editorial in what would become an exchange with Lorenzo D. Turner about the racial politics of Whitman's poetry. In Hughes's estimation, Whitman's poetry denounced slavery and proclaimed equality, underlined by "the amplitude of his democracy," which was able to include blacks, "Asiatics," and "darker peoples" in general. The essay is significant for at least three important reasons. First, the essay extends Hughes's efforts to fashion Whitman as a "black poet" (as he would also include some of Whitman's poems in *The Poetry of the Negro* [1956] anthology he edited with Arna Bontemps). Second, it correlates Whitman to Abraham Lincoln and both of them to the larger political history of black America. Finally, it outlines the lines of critical inquiry that have underlined many of the analyses of Whitman, race, and black America, with one line focusing on Whitman's poetry, the other focusing on Whitman's prose.

———. "The Ceaseless Rings of Walt Whitman." In *I Hear the People Singing: Selected Poems of Walt Whitman*, 7–10. New York: International Publishers, 1946.

Notwithstanding his romantic if not idealized tone, in his brief introduction to an edited volume of Whitman's poetry, Hughes understands Whitman's attempt at creating a poetry of (and for) democracy also as an attempt to create a poetry of (and for) human freedom. Hughes speculates that the half-dozen or so slaves on his family's farm may have been where he acquired his "sympathy for the Negro people and his early belief that all men should be free."

———. "An English Professor Disagrees on Whitman's Racial Attitudes." *Chicago Defender*, 18 July 1953, 11.

In this response to Hughes's initial editorial, Lorenzo D. Turner, a professor of English at Roosevelt College in Chicago, disputed Hughes's claim of Whitman's democratic "amplitude." To gain a fuller, if not more accurate, image of Whitman's views about blacks, Turner insisted that one should turn to Whitman's prose where he attacked abolitionists, advocated a colonization scheme for blacks, praised John C. Calhoun, and conveyed hesitance about federal interventions with the institution of slavery.

———. "Like Whitman, Great Artists Are Not Always Good People." *Chicago Defender*, 1 August 1953, 11.

Noting that it is *Leaves of Grass* through which Whitman is largely known, Hughes argued in his rejoinder to Turner that Whitman, like all other artists, should be praised for attempting to reach "his own highest ideals" rather than for seeming contradictions or failures to reach those ideals.

Hutchinson, George B. "Langston Hughes and the 'Other' Whitman." In *The Continuing Presence of Walt Whitman: The Life after Life*, edited by Robert K. Martin, 16–27. Iowa City: University of Iowa Press, 1992.

Accentuates Hughes's decades-long engagement with Whitman's work, which includes no fewer than three anthologies of Whitman's poetry, editorials about Whitman's work in the *Chicago Defender*, the poem "Old Walt" in 1954, and including several Whitman poems in *The Poetry of the Negro* anthology. Hutchinson intimates that Hughes encounters an international Whitman not simply through poems with an explicit international theme but through his encounters with international poets like Federico García Lorca, Miguel de Unamuno, and Pablo Neruda, who all read Whitman.

———. "Race and the Family Romance: Whitman's Civil War." *Walt Whitman Quarterly Review* 20, no. 3 (2003): 134–50.

Using "household" as an analytic trope for analyzing Whitman's understanding of the Civil War, Hutchinson posits that the relationship of African Americans to the war remains "almost entirely unspoken" by Whitman because he did not see them as part of the national family. Examines Whitman's family and the war, Whitman's time in Washington, DC, the "Lucifer" passage, and the "Vigil Strange I Kept on the Field One Night" poem, among others.

———. "Whitman and the Black Poet: Kelly Miller's Speech to the Walt Whitman Fellowship." *American Literature*, March 1989, 46–59.

Turning to the speech that Kelly Miller, then dean of the College of Arts and Sciences at Howard University, delivered to the first annual meeting of the Walt Whitman Fellowship in 1895, Hutchinson reveals how Miller's praise of Whitman's universalism provides a reason why "Whitman would later provide inspiration for important authors of the Harlem Renaissance." Hutchinson's essay is as important for its exemplary reading of Miller as it is for how it discloses the presence of Whitman in academic periodicals like the *CLA Journal* and *Phylon* dedicated to African American studies (avant la lettre).

———. "The Whitman Legacy and the Harlem Renaissance." In *Walt Whitman: The Centennial Essays*, edited by Ed Folsom, 201–16. Iowa City: University of Iowa Press, 1994.

Invoking such writers as Alain Locke, James Weldon Johnson, Countee Cullen, Jean Toomer, and Langston Hughes, Hutchinson argues for an understanding of Whitman's circulation in the Harlem Renaissance not as a means to exculpate Whitman for his antiblack racist views but to illuminate the "mulatto" aspects of American traditions that yield a multicultural distinctiveness in the United States.

James, C. L. R. *American Civilization*. Cambridge, MA: Blackwell, 1993.

Written in the wake of World War II, James's book discusses the rise of the United States as a hegemon and, in the chapter on nineteenth-century intellectuals, includes an analysis of Whitman's poetry.

Johnson, James Weldon. *Along This Way*. New York: Penguin, 1933.

In his autobiography, Johnson, one of the most important African American artists and political figures from the turn of the century through the Harlem Renaissance, recounts introducing *Leaves of Grass* to the poet Paul Laurence Dunbar. Johnson describes how being under the "sudden influence" of Whitman prompted him to write different forms of poetry.

Jordan, June. "For the Sake of People's Poetry: Walt Whitman and the Rest of Us." In *Some of Us Did Not Die: New and Selected Essays*, 242–56. New York: Basic/Civitas, 2002.

In this essay, originally published in 1980, Jordan characterizes Whitman as someone who shared "the systematic disadvantages of his heterogeneous offspring" and who shared a vision of what the later "people" and "poets" would come to embody. She lauds Whitman's attempts to "figure out the system of language," praising his creation of a voice that is "intimate and direct." As a writer whose poetry was centrally concerned with issues surrounding civil rights, feminism, and LGBT rights, Jordan self-identifies as one of what she calls "the traceable descendants" of Whitman.

Klammer, Martin. *Whitman, Slavery, and the Emergence of "Leaves of Grass."* University Park: Pennsylvania State University Press, 1995.

The first monograph to analyze the centrality of slavery in Whitman's development as a poet and of the first edition of *Leaves of Grass* in the context of antebellum America. Klammer addresses a number of topics—Whitman's only novel, *Franklin Evans, or The Inebriate*; his growing support of the Free Soil Party, especially in the wake of the Wilmot Proviso, while editor of the *Brooklyn Eagle*; his sojourn in New Orleans in 1848 to work for the *Crescent*; and the Compromise of 1850—to evince that "Whitman's thinking about African Americans and slavery . . . [was] essential to the development and poetry of the 1855 *Leaves of Grass*." The central reading of Klammer's monograph appears in condensed form as the essay "Slavery and Race," in *A Companion to Walt Whitman*, edited by Donald D. Kummings (Malden, MA: Blackwell, 2006), 101–21.

Lott, Eric. *Love and Theft: Blackface Minstrelsy and the American Working Class*. New York: Oxford University Press, 1993.

Historicizing Whitman in the context of his admiration for blackface minstrelsy in chapters 3 and 4, Lott notes that Whitman's views of African Americans ultimately divulge the simultaneous contradictory and complementary limits of class egalitarianism as the basis for an antiracist politics.

Major, Clarence. "Discovering Walt Whitman." In *Necessary Distance: Essays and Criticism*, 29–30. Minneapolis: Coffee House Press, 2001.

A brief but important note by Clarence Major, an African American poet of the Black Arts generation (but never a part of the movement), detailing the importance of reading Whitman as a young boy growing up in Chicago's South Side.

Mancuso, Luke. *The Strange Sad War Revolving: Walt Whitman, Reconstruction, and the Emergence of Black Citizenship, 1865–1876*. Columbia, SC: Camden, 1997.

Mancuso examines Whitman's writings—including the three editions of *Leaves* (and the incorporation of *Drum-Taps* and *Sequel to Drum-Taps*) as well as *Democratic Vistas*—in the context of the political history of Reconstruction America, weighing through the Thirteenth, Fourteenth, and Fifteenth Amendments and their effective retraction. The central argument of Mancuso's thesis is that, in becoming a "federalizing" poet during this period, Whitman shifted his rhetorical strategy about nation building from that of the family to that of the anonymous, conceptualizing community not out of kinship per se but by virtue of comradeship. Acknowledging that there "was no explicit mention of blacks in *Drum-Taps*," Mancuso nonetheless argues that Whitman's move away from a discourse about the nation as family would later allow him to "make the riskier move of reaching out to strangers, beyond kinsfolk, in a gesture that became the cornerstone of his constructing a consolidated nation out of diverse ethnic and racial differences."

Miller, Kelly. "What Walt Whitman Means to the Negro." *Conservator* 6 (1895): 70–73.

After delineating the four primary ways blacks are represented in modern literature and underscoring that the growth of this literature was co-extensive with the rise and development of African slavery, Miller offers the slave auction scene from "I Sing the Body Electric" to evince the sensitivity with which Whitman illustrated blacks in his poetry and his breaking with received conventions of how to depict blacks.

Outka, Paul. "Whitman and Race ('He's Queer, He's Unclear, Get Used to It')," *Journal of American Studies* 36 (August 2002): 293–318.

Outlining the two major positions of how scholars understand the place of racialized blackness in Whitman's works, Outka suggests that critics should take Michael Moon's notion of the "fluidity, substitutability, and indeterminacy" of Whitman's position on masculine identity and sexuality and apply it to analyses of race, thereby avoiding deterministic conclusions. Outka reads a number of important passages in Whitman's poetry, including the "Guilty of the body and the blood of Christ" section from "Blood Money," the hounded slave section of "Song of Myself," the "Black Lucifer" passage of "The Sleepers," and the slave auction scene in "I Sing the Body Electric."

Price, Kenneth M. "The Lost Negress of 'Song of Myself' and the Jolly Young Wenches of Civil War Washington." In *"Leaves of Grass": The Sesquicentennial Essays*, ed. Susan Belasco, Ed Folsom, and Kenneth M. Price, 224–43. Lincoln: University of Nebraska Press, 2007.

By returning to the extant Whitman manuscript in which they appeared, Price examines two lines about an African American woman that were intended for but ultimately excised from *Leaves of Grass*. Price also discusses a seemingly related manuscript to the first "negress" passage, noting that at least some phrases, if not lines, from this manuscript made their way into *Leaves of Grass*. Price concludes that had Whitman retained her presence, "she would have reinforced the importance of African Americans to the 1855 edition of *Leaves*."

———. *To Walt Whitman, America*. Chapel Hill: University of North Carolina Press, 2004.

Price traces Whitman's influence in twentieth-century literature and film, with particular attention to forms other than poetry. In the fifth chapter on the multicultural reception of Whitman, with Price discussing William Least Heat-Moon and Ishmael Reed, he also considers a symbolically freighted scene in Gloria Naylor's *Linden Hills* where one of the male characters paraphrases Whitman to express his desire for another man.

———. "Whitman's Solutions to 'The Problem of the Blacks.'" *Resources for American Literary Study* 15 (Autumn 1985): 205–8.

Working through a piece that was not included in *Notebooks and Unpublished Prose Manuscripts*, Price analyzes a manuscript titled "The Problem of the Blacks" in all likelihood written after the Civil War. In it Whitman outlines three possible resolutions to reconcile the black presence in the United States: "filtering," by which Whitman probably meant to intimate a "purging of black characteristics"; "gradually eliminate & disappear" through some terminal evolutionary process; or develop into a "leading and dominant race." The value of this manuscript, in Price's estimation, is that it illustrates "a habit of mind" for Whitman whereby his inability to reach resolution in his prose allowed for an "extraordinary poetic inventiveness."

Sánchez-Eppler, Karen. *Touching Liberty: Abolition, Feminism, and the Politics of the Body.* Berkeley: University of California Press, 1993.

Deploying the critical trope of "embodiment" as a theory for understanding Whitman, in chapter 2 of *Touching Liberty* Sánchez-Eppler examines how the slave auction of "I Sing the Body Electric" simultaneously initiates his poetic project of engendering democratic equality and "poses the major obstacle" to its very achievement.

Selzer, Linda Furgerson. "Walt Whitman, Clarence Major, and Changing Thresholds of American Wonder." *Walt Whitman Quarterly Review* 29 (2012): 159–70.

Explores the place of the West as both a natural landscape and the US frontier for both Whitman and Major and, more specifically, reveals Major's "September Mendocino" as a direct response to Whitman's "Song of the Redwood-Tree" (1873).

Sill, Geoffrey. "Whitman on 'The Black Question': A New Manuscript." *Walt Whitman Quarterly Review* 8, no. 2 (Fall 1990): 69–75.

Sill examines the William Kurry manuscript of an unpublished Whitman memoranda—"Of the black question"—concerning black citizenship and the future of the South. Whereas Kenneth M. Price considers an earlier version of the manuscript that was most likely intended as a private note to himself, the Kurry manuscript Sill examines was "unmistakably addressed to a public readership." Like the Price manuscript and other unpublished works (including drafts of poems), the Kurry manuscript reveals Whitman's more extended engagement with the question of race that is continually being unearthed in ephemera in the shadow archive of his work not published during his lifetime nor included in one of the many subsequent volumes of his work.

Trethewey, Natasha. "On Whitman, Civil War Memory, and My South." *Virginia Quarterly Review* 81 (Spring 2005): 50–57.

This article was commissioned for the sesquicentennial anniversary of *Leaves of Grass*. In it the poet and Mississippi native Trethewey considers Whitman poems such as "O Magnet South" and "Reconciliation" and places her own reflections about the aftermath of the Civil War with Whitman's to illustrate how both poets, more than a century apart, attempt to reconcile the conflicted history of the South in their poetic landscape.

Wilson, Ivy G. *Specters of Democracy: Blackness and the Aesthetics of Politics*. New York: Oxford University Press, 2011.

In addition to examining "A Boston Ballad," Wilson analyzes the significance of sound to Whitman's political aesthetics in "Ethiopia Saluting the Colors" and traces this relationship to the African American classical composer Harry Thacker Burleigh's art song version of "Ethiopia Saluting the Colors."

CONTRIBUTORS

ED FOLSOM is the Roy J. Carver Professor of English at the University of Iowa, editor of the *Walt Whitman Quarterly Review*, codirector of *The Walt Whitman Archive*, and the author or editor of five books on Whitman. His essays on American poetry have appeared in numerous journals and books, including *American Literature* and *The Cambridge Companion to Walt Whitman*. His most recent book, coauthored with Kenneth Price, is *Re-scripting Walt Whitman*.

CHRISTOPHER FREEBURG is an associate professor of English at the University of Illinois, Urbana-Champaign, specializing in American and African American literature and culture. He has recently published *Melville and the Idea of Blackness: Race and Imperialism in Nineteenth-Century America*, and he is currently revising his new book manuscript, "Black Writers and the Unhistoric Life of Race." He is also in the early stages of composing an intellectual biography on James Baldwin and the origins of the New World.

AMINA GAUTIER is an assistant professor at DePaul University in Chicago, Illinois, where she teaches both creative writing and literary criticism. She has published dozens of short stories, and her first collection, *At-Risk*, won the Flannery O'Connor Award.

GEORGE B. HUTCHINSON is the Newton C. Farr Professor of American Culture and professor of English at Cornell University. He is the author of *The Ecstatic Whitman: Literary Shamanism and the Crisis of the Union*, *The Harlem Renaissance in Black and White*, and *In Search of Nella Larsen: A Biography of the Color Line*, which won the Christian Gauss Award. He also edited *The Cambridge Companion to the Harlem Renaissance* and coedited with John K. Young *Publishing Blackness: Textual Constructions of Race since 1850*. He is currently writing a book on American literature and culture in the 1940s, for which he held a Guggenheim Fellowship in 2011–12.

JUNE JORDAN was a poet, activist, journalist, essayist, and teacher who used her platform as a writer to champion the civil rights, feminist, and LGBT movements, among other progressive causes. As a writer, she published more than twenty-five works, including *Who Look at Me, Some*

Changes, Living Room, and *Talking Back to God.* Appointed professor of African American studies at the University of California, Berkeley, in 1988, she founded the Poetry for the People program.

ROWAN RICARDO PHILLIPS is the author of a book of poems, *The Ground;* a book of criticism, *When Blackness Rhymes with Blackness;* and the first translation from Catalan into English of Salvador Espriu's collection of short stories *Adriana in the Grotesque Labyrinth.* Currently he is an associate professor of English at Stony Brook as well as director of the Poetry Center.

MATT SANDLER teaches in the Robert Clark Honors College of the University of Oregon. He is currently completing a manuscript entitled "Self-Help Poetics: Genealogies of an American Vernacular." His work has appeared in the *African American Review, Atlantic Studies,* and *Callaloo.*

NATASHA TRETHEWEY is the Charles Howard Candler Professor of English and Creative Writing at Emory University. She is the author of four volumes of poetry: *Domestic Work, Bellocq's Ophelia, Native Guard* (winner of the 2007 Pulitzer Prize), and *Thrall.* She is currently the United States Poet Laureate.

JACOB WILKENFELD is a doctoral candidate in comparative literature at the University of North Carolina at Chapel Hill. His research focuses on nineteenth- and twentieth-century literatures of the Americas. His dissertation explores inter-American imaginaries in nineteenth-century Brazilian and US American literature, particularly in the work of Walt Whitman and Sousândrade. He has published essays in the *Walt Whitman Quarterly Review* and *The Limits of Literary Translation: Expanding Frontiers in Iberian Languages.*

IVY G. WILSON is associate professor of English and director of the Program in American Studies at Northwestern University, where he teaches courses on the comparative literature of the black diaspora and US literary studies with a particular emphasis on African American culture. In addition to publishing edited volumes on James M. Whitfield and Albery A. Whitman, he has recently published *Specters of Democracy: Blackness and the Aesthetics of Politics.*

INDEX

"Black Lucifer," in Whitman's manuscripts, 11–12

black presence, in Whitman's manuscripts, 3–26

black soldiers in Civil War: erasure of history concerning, 20–21, 165–171; Whitman's visits with, 20–21, 29n.36; in Whitman's writing, 122n.30

Blake, or The Huts of America (Delany), 65–66, 72, 75

Blight, David, 166, 168

Blue Notes (Komunyakaa), 126

body imagery in Whitman's work: black body images, xvi; bleaching of, 20; intemperance and corrosion of, 34–36, 41–42, 48–50; in *Leaves of Grass*, 7, 9; mutilation and disintegration of bodies, 84–87, 93–94; nude aesthetics and, 90–91, 139; racial violence and, 89–94; slavery and, 60, 69–70; soul-body union, 65–66

Bontemps, Arna, xvii

The Book of American Negro Poetry, vii–viii

Borges, Jorge Luis, xvi–xvii

"A Boston Ballad" (Whitman), 120

Boukman, Dutty, 74

Bowen, Sayles Jenks, 25–26

Brooklyn Daily Eagle, 54, 62

Brooks, Van Wyck, 105, 114

Brown, William Wells, 69–70

Bucke, Richard Maurice, 181

Buffalo News, 145

Cable, George Washington, 87

"Calamus" section in *Leaves of Grass*, 104, 114–115, 141

Calhoun, John C., 111–112

Callaloo (journal), 126, 189

The Canterbury Tales (Chaucer), 152

capitalism: Ellison on labor and, 119–120; Whitman's writing in context of, 104

Carlyle, Thomas, 25, 30n.56, 68

catalogs: Ellison's use of, 116–118; Whitman's use of, 109–113

CBS News, 124, 146n.4

"The Ceaseless Rings of Walt Whitman" (Hughes), xi

"Celebration of Walt Whitman," 132–133

The Chameleon Couch (Komunyakaa), 143

Chase, Richard, 114

Chesnutt, Charles, 90

"Christ likeness" (Bucke), 181

citizenship for African Americans: Ellison's views on, 118–119; Whitman's ambivalence concerning, 13, 23–25

civil rights movement, 105–106

Civil War: civil rights movement and, 105–106; Southern attitudes concerning, 165–171; in Whitman's writing, 85–94, 105–106, 118–119, 169–171

class hierarchy and slavery, 68–69

Cleveland, Grover, 172

Code Noir, 72

Cold War, 104–120

Collect (Whitman), 60–61; "Notes Left Over" section, 26

Collins, Billy, 124, 146n.4

Collins, Michael, 126, 131–132, 189

Communism, Whitman's writing in context of, 104–105

Compensated Emancipation Proclamation, 24

Congress of Racial Equality (CORE), 140–141

Conversations with Yusef Komunyakaa (Hanshaw), 126

Cosmos (Humboldt), 133

Coviello, Peter, 86–87, 136

Crane, Stephen, 114

Creole episode in *Franklin Evans*, 32–33, 37–50, 52n.24, 60–61

Creoles in New Orleans: culture of,

55–56; Whitman's poetics and, 58–77

white supremacy: in Johnson's writing, 84, 95–96; Whitman's remarks on, 88–94

Whitman, Edmund B., 20–21

Whitman, Jeff, 78n.22

Whitman, Slavery, and the Emergence of "Leaves of Grass" (Klammer), xiii, 7, 194–195

Whitman, Walt: African-American criticism of, 125–127, 145–146, 151–161; *American Experience* program on, 124; claims of illegitimate children by, 55–58; cultural legacy of, 172–177; dialogue with in Komunyakaa's poetry, 132–146; fascination with capitol dome in Washington D.C., 15, 28n.32; grave of, 179–185; influence on feminist poets, 155–161; influence on First World poets, 155–161; internationalism and, James's view of, 119–120; Johnson and, 82–100; Komunyakaa's criticism of, 127–132; as *New Orleans Daily Crescent* editor, 54–55; and Mardi Gras, 50–71, 80n.50; politics of vernacular style and, 106–113; writings for *New York Times*, 14–18

"Whitman and Race ('He's Queer, He's Unclear, Get Used to It')" (Outka), 196

"Whitman and the Black Poet" (Hutchinson), 193–194

"Whitman and the Negro" (Glicksman), 82, 191

Whitman (Holloway), 134

"Whitman on the 'The Black Question'" (Sill), 197–198

"Whitman's Solutions to 'The Problem of the Blacks'" (Price), 197

"The Whitman Legacy and the Harlem Renaissance" (Hutchinson), 194

Whittier, John Greenleaf, 28n.22

Wilkenfeld, Jacoob, xv, 124–146

Willhite, Keith, 11–12

Willow Springs (journal), 126

Wilmot Proviso, 54

Wilson, E. O., 165

Wilson, Ivy G., 104–120

Windrush Caribbean immigrant generation, xvii

women, 34–35, 52n.13

Wood, Amy Louise, 84

Woodward, C. Vann, 169

Wordsworth, William, 73

World War II, 117–119

"The Wound-Dresser" (Whitman), 86–87

Wright, Richard, 105

Zamir, Shamoon, x

THE IOWA WHITMAN SERIES